AFGHAN WARS

South West Asia

AFGHAN WARS

EDGAR O'BALLANCE

BRASSEY'S

Afghan Wars 1839 to the present

First English edition 1993
This revised paperback 2002

UK editorial offices: Brassey's, 9 Blenheim Court, Brewery Road, London N7 9NT

A member of the Chrysalis Group plc

USA orders: Book International, PO Box 960, Herndon, VA 20172, USA

Library of Congress Cataloging in Publication Data
A catalogue record for this book is available from the British Library

British Library Cataloguing in Publication Data available

ISBN 1 85753 308 9

Edgar O'Ballance has asserted his moral right to be identified as author of this work.

Photoset in North Wales by
Derek Doyle & Associates, Mold, Clwyd
Printed and bound in Great Britain by
Creative Print and Design Wales, Ebbw Vale

Contents

Preface

This is a brief account of the five wars Afghanistan has experienced since 1839, which span the turbulent century and a half of its modern history, prior to which it was more a geographical region than a nation state. This period covers the so-called 19th Century Great Game between the British in India and Czarist Russia for colonial expansion into Afghanistan and Turkistan. The first two Anglo-Afghan Wars were ones of colonial aggression. In the first, British soldiers were uniformed and accoutred much as they had been in the Peninsular Wars and at Waterloo, only their muskets being slightly modernised. In the second the British wore khaki uniforms and had breech-loading rifles, which gave them an advantage over their Afghan adversaries.

In both these wars, British and Indian troops suffered terrible hardships and disasters, some due to incompetent commanders; but they also won glorious victories that appealed to the British public and produced Victorian heroes, such as the popular General 'Bobs' Roberts, famous for his relief march from Kabul to Kandahar, and a man with a flair for personal publicity. A new look is taken at some of the previous, well-aired establishment opinions on aspects of these two wars, from which the British gained little.

The Third Anglo-Afghan War, started by the Afghans, turned out to be a 'near-run thing' as, in an atmosphere of demobilisation after the First World War, for the first time military morale tended to become uncertain amongst those waiting to be shipped home to Britain, or to their homes in India, while civil unrest in India overshadowed events. The war was brought to a quick, expedient end by the fledgling RAF's bombing of Kabul, which frightened the aggressive Amir into accepting negotiation, as he thought his capital was about to be heavily blitzed by aircraft specially designed to bomb Berlin. The British loss, apart from face, was its hold over

Afghanistan's foreign policy.

From being a backward, xenophobic tribal society, plagued with blood-feuds and quarrels, Afghanistan's political development was slow, but a form of constitutional monarchy appeared in 1964. The following year, the Soviet-inspired and assisted People's Democratic Party of Afghanistan (PDPA) was secretly founded; it was to influence and later dominate Afghan politics. Afghanistan remained strictly non-aligned, until Soviet military aid and arms were received in quantity during the 1960s.

In December 1979, when the Afghan President, Hafizullah Amin, was suspected by the Soviets of seeking closer contacts with Western powers, they organised his downfall and, bringing in their own replacement candidate, Babrak Karmal, mounted a military invasion to prop up his government in Kabul, which was beset by a resistance movement swelling up in protest against Soviet-type reforms that were being forced on the people.

The main part of the book deals with the fourth war, the occupation of Afghanistan by the Limited Contingent of Soviet Forces, which lasted for nine years and nine weeks, and its struggle against the Mujahideen (Holy War Warriors), operating across an open border from adjacent Pakistan. Throughout, the most of Afghanistan was off-limits to Western journalists, and although a few adventurous ones trekked over mountain trails to visit certain Mujahideen groups in their valleys, their vision was necessarily restrictive.

The United States began sending arms to the Mujahideen, and Afghanistan became a pawn in the Cold War. Consequently, the Western media, somewhat naturally sympathetic towards anyone fighting against the Soviet Union, tended to view the scenario as having 'goodies' and 'baddies'. Relying all too often on favourable 'bazaar' gossip and refugee tales, few of which could be verified, the Western media tended to over-emphasise the Mujahideen's good points and successes, while playing down those of the Soviet and puppet Afghan armed forces. With the benefit of hindsight, some misleading impressions are rectified.

Under Presidents Andropov and Chernenko, the Brezhnev doctrine on Afghanistan stultified, but as each side settled down to a long haul, all factions were convinced that time was on their side. In 1985, Gorbachev came to power in the USSR, bringing new radical policies, which eventually led to the withdrawal of the Limited Contingent of Soviet Forces. The last Soviet soldier to leave, General

Gromov, crossed Friendship Bridge over the Amu Darya (Oxus) with panache and before waiting world TV cameras on 15 February 1989 declaring that the Soviet Union had completed its sacred duty to Afghanistan.

Once the Soviets had left, the fifth war erupted – a stark civil war, with Afghan fighting Afghan, which is still in progress. Pundits almost without exception, having absorbed slanted media reports and Western assessments of the respective qualities and capabilities of the Afghan armed forces and the Mujahideen, predicted that President Najibullah would be lucky to survive in power for more than a few weeks.

The test came in early 1989, when the besieged Afghan army garrison at Jalalabad successfully held out for 10 weeks before the Mujahideen backed away. By this time the conduct of some of the Mujahideen operations was being manipulated by the Pakistan Inter-Services Intelligence Branch (ISI), which selectively distributed US munitions. A few small and remote Afghan army garrisons were overrun by the Mujahideen, and many were withdrawn by the Kabul government due to their vulnerability, and so that its military strength could be concentrated in strategically important cities and air bases; these withdrawals were often claimed as Mujahideen victories.

Mujahideen military elements moved sluggishly as, lacking sophisticated weaponry and with a deeply-rent leadership, they seemed incapable of forming a united strategic master plan, and so gained few victories, even though Afghan armed forces themselves were factionalised by a vicious feud between the Khalk and Parcham factions of the PDPA. Meanwhile, Kabul and other main cities and garrisons suffered periodic rocket bombardments, some quite heavy, while government forces replied with aerial bombing, helicopter-gunships and Soviet SCUD-B ballistic missiles. The USSR continued to supply the Kabul government with munitions, and the USA sent arms to the Mujahideen through Pakistan.

The ending of the Cold War and the demise of the USSR, brought a decline in international interest in the Afghan problem and, in an effort to break the log-jam, the UN stepped in with a Peace Plan, in May 1991, which called for an interim coalition government preparatory to a general election. This has been stalled because of disagreement on its composition, and by Islamic Fundamentalists insisting that first President Najibullah must step down, which he is reluctant to do. Today, Afghanistan is more bitterly factionalised than it has ever been.

Opinions, commentary and analysis in this book are my own, (unless otherwise duly acknowledged) and may at times be contrary to the perceived wisdom expounded by some defence experts and historians.

Lastly, as seems inevitable when writing a book on wars in Asia, there have been problems in the spelling of place and proper names, so I have had to select those most generally used in Western circles: and give my sincere apologies to any purists I may have unwittingly offended.

Edgar O'Ballance
31 March 1992

Acknowledgements

A major part of my research for this book consisted of visits to Afghanistan, Iran and Pakistan where I had a series of briefings, interviews and discussions with VIPs, combatants and others interested or involved in the Afghan problem.

Where material has been gained from other sources, due credit is given within the text.

I would particularly like to thank the staffs at the India Office Library, the National Army Museum, and the RAF Historical Records Branch.

Maps

Chronology

BC: 329 Alexander the Great reaches the Oxus river
BC: 327 Alexander crosses the Hindu Kush into India

AD: 8th Century   Islam penetrated the Afghan region

1219: Genghis Khan and his Mongol armies sweep into the Afghan region
1398: Timur led a Mongol invasion of the Afghan region
1525: Babur the Tiger, an Afghan warlord, descends on India
1600: (British) Honourable East India Company formed
1747: Amir Ahmad Shah became dominant in the Afghan region
1773: Amir Timur Shah succeeded his father
1793: Amir Zaman Shah (blinded and deposed in 1801)
1801: Amir Mahmoud Shah (deposed in 1803)
1803: Amir Shah Shuja (deposed in 1809)
1809: Amir Mahmoud Shah (returns – retains title until 1818)
1818: Sikh army seized Peshawar
1825: Unsuccessful Russian attempt to take Khiva (Turkistan)
1826: Dost Mohammed gained suzerainty over Ghazni
1828: Russians defeat Persians
1829: Amir Kamran Shah (driven from Kabul to Herat, murdered in 1842)
1837: Afghan and Sikh armies clash in the Khyber Pass
1838: Tripartite Treaty, and Simla Manifesto
1839: 23 July: Battle for Ghazni
       7 August: Kabul occupied by the Army of the Indus
       18 September: Major part of the Army of the Indus marched out of Kabul
1840: 1 January: Army of the Indus disbanded
       2 November: Amir Dost Mohammed surrendered to the British
1842: 6-13 January: British retreat from Kabul
       13 January: British last stand at Jagdalak
       6 March: British surrender at Ghazni
       5 April: General Pollock forced the Khyber Pass
       7 April: Battle of Jalalabad
       25 April   Amir Shah Shuja assassinated at Kabul
       June: Fateh Jang became Amir (abdicated in October)

	30 August:	Battle of Karabagh
	4 September:	Ghazni re-entered by the British
	12 September:	General Pollock at Tezmin Pass
	15 September:	General Pollock in Kabul
	12 October:	British-Indian forces marched out of Kabul
	December:	Dost Mohammed returned to Kabul as Amir
		First Anglo-Afghan War ended
1855:		Anglo-Afghan Treaty
1863:		Amir Dost Mohammed died
1868:		Amir Sher Ali (regained power)
1873:		Anglo-Russian Understanding
1878:		Treaty of Berlin
	August:	Russian mission arrived at Kabul
	21 November:	Second Anglo-Afghan War began
	22 November:	Battle for the Khyber Pass
	1 December:	Battle of Peiwar Kotal
1879:	21 February:	Death of Amir Sher Ali
1879:	26 May:	Treaty of Gandamak
	3 September:	British Political Officer assassinated in Kabul
	6 October:	Battle of Charasia
	8 October:	General Roberts reaches Kabul
	11 October:	Amir Yakub Khan abdicates
	December:	General Roberts besieged in Kabul
	24 December:	Siege of Kabul lifted
1880:	19 April:	Battle of Ahmad Khel
	27 July:	Battle of Maiwand
	31 July:	Abdur Rahman became Amir
	8-31 August:	Roberts's March from Kabul to Kandahar
	11 August:	British march out from Kabul
1881:	23 May:	End of the Second Anglo-Afghan War
1885:	March:	Pendjdeh crisis
	September:	Anglo-Russo Agreement
1893:		Anglo-Afghan Convention
1901:		Death of Amir Abdur Rahman (succeeded by Amir Habibullah)
1905:		Anglo-Afghan Treaty
1907:		Tri-National Convention
1919:	19 February:	Amir Habidullah assassinated (succeeded by Amanullah)
	3 May:	Third Anglo-Afghan War began
	7 May:	Peshawar Uprising aborted
	9 May:	First Battle of Bagh
	11 May:	Second Battle of Bagh
	18 May:	Battle of Dakka
	24 May:	Kabul bombed by RAF
	27 May:	Battle of Spin Baldak
	28 May–1 June:	Siege and Battle of Thal
	3 June:	Armistice

	8 August:	Treaty of Rawalpindi
		End of the Third Anglo-Afghan War
1926:		Amir Amanullah assumes title of King
	August:	Soviet-Afghan Treaty of Neutrality and Non-Aggression
1929:	14 January:	King Amanullah abdicated
	October:	Nadir Shah becomes King
1933:	November:	King Nadir Shah assassinated (succeeded by Zahir Shah)
1937:		Turkish Military Mission arrived at Kabul
1955:	December:	Bulganin and Khrushchev visited Afghanistan
1957:		Soviet Military Mission arrived in Afghanistan
		First Soviet arms arrived in Afghanistan
1963:	November:	Soviet-Afghan Treaty
1964:		Soviets complete the Salang Tunnel
1965:	1 January:	Formation of the PDPA
1973:	17 July:	King Zahir Shah deposed – Republic declared
		Mohammed Daoud became President
1975:	January:	Land Reforms announced
1978:	27 April:	Saur Revolution – Mohammed Taraki became President
	July:	Fighting between factions of the PDPA
	December:	Soviet-Afghan Friendship Treaty
1979:	14 February:	Death of US Ambassador at Kabul
	12 March:	Mujahideen declared a *Jihad* against the Kabul regime
	14–16 September:	President Taraki killed in coup
		Hafizullah Amin became President
1979:	September:	Ghazni Uprising
	8–9 December:	Soviet Special forces flown into Afghanistan
	24 December:	President Amin taken to the Darulam Palace (last seen alive)
	28 December:	Babrak Karmal declared President of Afghanistan
1980:	January:	UN Resolution condemning Soviet invasion
	April:	Soviet Status of Forces Agreement
	June:	Soviet troops enter Wakhan Strip
1981:	June:	Formation of the NFF
		Soviet-Afghan agreement over Wakhan Strip
	July:	Fighting in Paghman area
	December:	US allegations Soviets using CW
1982:	June:	Proximity Talks began in Geneva
	September:	Friendship Bridge opened
	October:	First 'all-Afghan' operation
1983:	January:	Truce in Panjshir Valley
	August:	Afghan conscription measures tightened up
1984:	January:	Mujahideen attack on Khost failed
		Siege of Urgun lifted
	April:	Battle for Kandahar

		Government troops move into the Panjshir Valley
	May:	Battle for Herat
		Siege of Baricot lifted
	June:	Mujahideen attack on Bagram air base
	July:	US authorises military aid to the Mujahideen
	September:	Kabul government authorises local militias
1985:	January:	Afghan army reorganised
	May:	Islamic Unity of Afghanistan coalition formed
	July:	US approved delivery of Stingers to Mujahideen
	December:	Proximity Talks produce a Four-Point Agenda
1986:	March:	Afghan conscription regulations tightened up
	April-May:	Fighting around Zhawar
	May:	Najibullah appointed Secretary General of the PDPA
	June:	Mujahideen driven from the Panjshir Valley
	June-August:	Fighting at Herat
	July:	Mujahideen attacks in Logar province
	September:	Kabul government began a displacement programme
	October:	Token withdrawal of Soviet troops
		First Stinger and Blowpipe missiles arrived for the Mujahideen
1987:	March-May:	Mujahideen attacks on Soviet territory
	May:	Babrak Karmal arrested
	May-June:	Fighting at Kandahar
	June:	Battle for Ali Khal
	July:	Supreme *Jihad* Council formed
	September:	Najibullah appointed Chairman of the Revolutionary Council
	November:	Najibullah appointed President of the Afghan Republic
	November-December:	Battle for the Gardez-Khost road
1988:	January:	Khost relieved
	February:	Afghan Interim Government formed
	March:	Mujahideen seize Sumankat
	April:	Geneva Accords signed
		General election in Afghanistan
1988:	May:	Soviet withdrawal begins
		Soviets evacuate Jalalabad
	June:	Government of Reconciliation formed at Kabul
	July:	Battle of Kalat-i-Ghilzai
	August:	Soviets evacuate Kandahar
		Battle of Kunduz
	November:	Soviets halt their withdrawal
1989:	January:	Soviets resume their withdrawal
	February:	Last Soviet troops withdrawn from Afghanistan

		Supreme Council for the Defence of the Homeland formed
	March–May:	Battle for Jalalabad
	July:	More fighting at Jalalabad
1990:	March:	Tanai coup attempt
	April–May:	Fighting in the Laghman and Paghman areas
	May:	State of Emergency in Afghanistan lifted
	June:	The PDPA became the Homeland Party (*Hizb-i-Watan*)
	October:	Karin Kot fell to the Mujahideen
		Mujahideen attack on Kabul
1991:	March:	Khost taken by the Mujahideen
	May:	UN Peace Plan
	September–October:	Battle for Gardez
1992:	January:	US and Soviets end arms supplies
	March:	Tribal militia revolt at Mazar-i-Sharif
		Najibullah's pledge to stand down
1992:	16 April:	President Najibullah resigns
	17 April:	Gardez falls to the Mujahideen
	19 April:	Jalalabad falls to the Mujahideen
	20 April:	Mazar-i-Sharif falls to the tribal militias
	25–27 April:	Battle for Kabul
	27 April:	Islamic Republic of Afghanistan proclaimed
	29 April:	Ahmad Shah Masoud appointed Defence Minister
	5 May:	President Mujadidi announced his provisional government

1

The First Anglo-Afghan War: 1839-42

In ancient times the wild mountainous and desert region that lies between the Punjab, in India, and what today is Iran, bounded on the south by the Indian Ocean, and on the north by the arid expanses of two great deserts, the Kara Kum (Black Sands) and the Kizil Kum (Red Sands), divided by the Oxus river, was known as Ariana or Bactria, and later as Koristan. A great mountain barrier, the Hindu Kush, a western extension of the Himalayan mountain massifs, runs diagonally (north-east to south-west) across the northern Afghan region, forming a natural barrier between India and Turkistan.

Conquering armies have periodically marched across the Afghan region, sparse pickings giving them no cause to linger longer than necessary. Alexander the Great passed this way, reaching the Oxus river, which rises in the Pamirs and flows into the inland Aral Sea, in 329 BC, where he defeated a 'nomad army'. He then rested his military force of some 27,000 warriors by that river until 327 BC, when he crossed the Hindu Kush and made his descent into India. A commonly-accepted explanation for the name 'Hindu Kush' is that 'kush' in Hindustani means 'killer', and arose because so many Indians captured for sale in the slave markets of Turkistan, perished while crossing it. Eventually, in the 8th Century, Islam penetrated into this remote region.

The inhabitants of this wild region came to be known as 'Afghans', although they are of diverse origins. The major ethnic group was, and still is, the Pathans, whose distant origins are debatable: it seems they have always been there. Today, the Pathans live in two large areas, separated from each other by other ethnic peoples, and are loosely known as the 'Eastern Pathans' and the 'Duranis', the latter living in western and south-western Afghanistan. Other ethnic groups seem to have arrived with, or because of, successive migrations, or conquering armies.

In 1219, Genghis Khan, with his Mongol hordes, embarked upon what is considered to be the greatest cavalry campaign of conquest in military history against the Kwariznian Empire, which then encompassed parts of the Caucasus region, Persia, Turkistan and the Afghan region up to the Indus River. The Kwariznian leader, Ala-Addin Mohammed, who had himself brought this vast empire under his rule by conquest, was out-manoeuvred and defeated.

Genghis Khan advanced, slaughtering populations wholesale, sparing only some individuals with skills that could be of use to him, such as artisans and technicians. Inhabitants of the mountainous areas in the Afghan region came out of this holocaust, and other succeeding ones, better than most other races, mainly because the Mongol cavalry advances tended to avoid mountainous terrain and areas where there was insufficient fodder and grazing for their horses. So, while populations in the main cities did not escape massacre, tribes in the valleys were often able to escape into the mountains, to hide out until the tides of death and destruction had rolled past them.

Another similar five-month swathe of butchery and carnage, led by Timur the Mongol, occurred in 1398, after which Mongol power declined sharply, and Mongol armies returned home to north-east Asia. The Hazaras, who mainly inhabit the area between Kabul and Herat, in central Afghanistan, are said to be descendants of the Mongol invaders.

The Afghan region spawned a number of military leaders and conquerors. One, who virtually carved out what became the Moghul Empire that dominated northern India for some six centuries, was Sultan Mohammed, an Afghan warlord from Ghazni, who is said to have mounted 17 military compaigns into India. One of the Afghan warlords to rule Moghul India was Babur the Tiger, who was brought up in Kabul and descended on the northern Indian plains in 1525. Before his death, his domain spread from the Oxus river to Bengal. Babur's early conquests were largely due to his army's possessing the early match-lock musket, used in battle for the first time in this part of the world. He was also the proud possessor of a crude mortar which allegedly could project a heavy stone up to a mile.

At times Moghul Emperors in India campaigned against unruly

peoples and tribes in the Afghan region, one being Shah Jahan, who built the Taj Mahal in honour of his favourite wife, Mumtaz Mahal. For three years (1645-47) he fought against the Uzbeks of Balkh, in northern Afghanistan, and had previously launched an unsuccesful attempt to wrest Kandahar from the Persians in 1637; further unsuccessful efforts to seize that city were made in the period 1647-53. The Persian Safavid Empire had already expanded into the northern Afghan region in the 16th Century, to neutralise the Uzbeks, who were trying to move southwards.

More often than not, the Persians managed to retain possession of both Herat and Kandahar. It is generally said that the Qizzilbash, who now inhabit an area around Kabul and certain western parts of Afghanistan, are descendants of Persian armies and garrisons. They are Shia Muslims (the predominant Islamic sect in Iran today), while most of the remainder of the population of Afghanistan are of the Sunni persuasion. Some authorities say the Ghilzais, another minority, who inhabit an area in central Afghanistan wedged between the Hazaras and the Eastern Pathans, are of mixed Turkic and Pathan stock, but all do not agree.

The Pathans have a tribal social structure, with clans and families interlinked, shackled together by age-old customs, such as extracting vengeance for wrongs against them, which can quickly escalate into blood-feuds between families and tribes. Other ethnic groups, including those which arrived through migration, such as the Tadjiks and Uzbeks, are generally less tribally orientated.

A National Identity

For centuries the Afghan region was a grey area within which petty warlords rose and fell, quarrelled with each other, and sometimes allied themselves with Persian or other invaders, switching loyalties whenever it was expedient. There was no recognisable national unity. Prizes of war were the main fortified cities and trading centres of Kabul, Ghazni, Kalat, Kalat-i-Ghilzai, Kandahar, and others, there being little real wealth or resources of any significant value to attract predatory armies.

The Persian, Nadir Shah who (in 1737) had marched his army into India, sacked Delhi and slaughtered its inhabitants, and had also reduced the Turkistan Khanates of Khiva and Bokhara, was murdered by his military commanders while campaigning in the northern Kurdish mountains in 1747. Ahmad Shah, an Afghan commanding Nadir Shah's mercenary bodyguard of a reputed 3,000 Pathan horsemen, made a fighting withdrawal with his men through hostile territory, eventually reaching Kandahar. On this hazardous march he encountered the huge elephant and camel train, carrying loot from Nadir Shah's sack of Delhi a few years previously (which included the famous Peacock Throne), making its slow laborious way westwards, and this he seized.

Ahmad Shah was now in a very strong position, having both a veteran, battle-hardened mercenary corps, and money to pay them. This enabled him to defeat, or otherwise bring under his suzerainty, most of the petty warlords and major tribal and ethnic leaders in the Afghan region. He assumed the title of Amir Ahmad Shah Abdali (now Durani), and brought the first concept of nationalism to the Afghan region. During his lifetime he continued to extend his authority and expand his territory. He, and his descendants, the 'Sadozai Dynasty', ruled the Afghan region, or parts of it, until 1826.

The Sadozai Dynasty

Amir Ahmad Shah died in 1773, to be succeeded by his son, Timur, who died in 1793, after which Timur's several sons fought and intrigued against each other for the succession. One of them, Zaman Shah, became Amir. Much of the first part of the 19th Century in the Afghan region was taken up with struggles between rival claimants for the Amir's throne, in which armed force, assassination, intrigue and treachery all played a part. For example, in 1801, Amir Zaman Shah, was captured and blinded by his brother, Mahmoud Shah. Zaman Shah escaped to India, to become a pensioner of the Honourable East India Company (HEIC). In 1803, Amir Mahmoud Shah was in turn driven from Kabul by his brother, Shah Shuja, who held the Amirship until 1809, during which period Sind (India) declared its 'independence' from the 'Kingdom of Kabul', while the Persians reconquered other parts of the Afghan region. Shah Shuja was defeated in battle by his brother, Mahmoud Shah, who regained the Amirship, which he held until 1818.

Warfare in the Afghan Region

Warfare in the Afghan region in the early 19th Century was much the same as it had been for centuries previously. Amirs and warlords had regular bodyguards and, since they did not trust their own kinsmen overmuch, they were invariably mercenary soldiers, armed with lances, swords and knives, often carrying a small, round Turkish-style shield, and sometimes wearing bits of old body-armour, such as breast-plates and even knightly metal helmets; some were mounted and others were foot-soldiers.

By this time the old match-lock muskets had generally been replaced by flint-locks. These household troops were often known as 'Jezailchis', the regional name of the long-barrelled muskets with slender curved butts which they carried. The 'jezail' was muzzle-loaded, taking two minutes or more to make ready, and was of doubtful accuracy, accordingly having to be fired in volleys to have any real effect. Horsemen would carry three or more Jezailchis when riding into action, fire them off rapidly, and then quickly retire to reload.

A few Amirs and warlords had accumulated vintage cannon, serviced by foreign mercenaries, usually Persian or Turkish, often deserters from their own national armies, some of whom had expertise in siege warfare. Many foreign builders and artisans found employment in constructing fortresses, some reminiscent of Crusader castles of the Middle Ages, which were established near cities, trade centres and strategic cross-roads, and often in need of repair, or even extension.

In time of wars and alarms, the small number of regular household troops were reinforced by hordes of armed tribesmen, ever eager to turn out for a short fight, especially if there were good prospects of loot. Tribal or group affiliations with local warlords were precarious and changeable. A weapon of some sort, be it a Jezail, lance, sword or simple knife, no matter how antiquated, was a symbol of manhood to all Afghan males. Some notables were given land on the semi-feudal condition of providing a quota of armed warriors when required.

Normally, when called upon, tribal or group warriors would turn out with their own arms and sufficient food for a few days, after which, if the warlord wanted to keep them in the field, and especially if there was no sign of ready loot, he would have to feed and pay them. These levies and volunteers were unreliable on campaign, often reluctant to rush into battle and risk losing their own valuable horses and weapons, unless they saw rich pickings.

Each Afghan fighting man regarded himself as a free person, to come and go as he pleased, and moreover, to switch allegiances as might be convenient. The main tactic was to make a massive, all-out wild charge at an enemy group to overwhelm it quickly; if successful, thereafter all discipline and military cohesion were lost as it became every man for himself in a gigantic looting spree. Only regular mercenary elements retained some discipline, and were expected to make a counter-charge. If the first charge failed, local warriors would fade away to the safety of the hills. While they could be fairly good at laying ambushes on their home ground, they were usually hopeless in protracted defence.

There were no roads in the modern sense in the Afghan region but there were age-old, well-worn routes between cities along which merchants, government officials, troops and others slowly travelled either on horse-back or foot, goods being carried by elephant, camel, pack-horse or donkey, as well as by human porters. Artillery was either towed by yokes of oxen, or carried on elephants.

In practice, slow-moving military supply columns limited the size of armies, and consequently few large battles took place, most clashes being in the skirmish category. The mobility and size of armies was further restricted by the terrain's inability to sustain more than a limited number of men or animals for more than a few days. Intrigue and treachery were more prevalent than military operations and battles but, of course, military force, shrewdly applied, was always the ultimate sanction.

The Great Game

By the beginning of the 19th Century two great European Powers, Britain and Russia, had begun to expand their Empires into central and southern Asia. By 1820, Britain had become the prominent military power in the sub-continent of India, and although still vying with certain strong princely states and confederations, the British were feeling confident and aggressive. The Honourable East India Company, which had been founded in 1600, had grown into a gigantic trading organisation, acquiring both political and military power in pursuit of trade and wealth, and had accordingly played a predominant role in the development of British India; but by this time its former freedom of political action had been curbed by the British government. Military force in British India was deployed in the armies of the three Presidencies, of Bengal, Bombay and Madras, and consisted of both British and Indian units of cavalry, artillery and infantry.

Communications between the three British Indian Presidencies and

Britain, and the outside world, were by sea and caused no anxiety as by this period the British navy was openly ruling the international waves. British expansionist eyes were turning towards the Afghan region, and were particularly interested in the Indus river route, erroneously believing that a 'land route' by way of the Afghan region was possible from India to Europe. Such a route could open up new trading areas in the Afghan region and Turkistan, and perhaps even as far as the Caucasus.

The British did not seek direct colonisation, but to persuade local rulers to accept British 'advice', which in practical terms meant accepting a resident British political officer, and British control over their foreign relations, so that rival, acquisitive nations, especially Russia, could be excluded. The British thought, less erroneously, that the Russians saw the Afghan region as their land-route into India.

In 1801, Russia had annexed the Kingdom of Georgia, and then went on to acquire other territory in the Caucasus region; its victory in 1828, after a long war with Persia, reduced Persian territory and influence, and enhanced that of the Russians, who now replaced the Persians as the 'bogeyman' to the British in India. It seemed that all Turkistan, with its legendary oasis cities of Tashkent, Samarkand, Bokhara, Khiva and others, along the age-old Silk Road, as well as the Afghan region, were now open to the Russians, who seemed to be forever wanting to push their land frontiers eastwards.

This confrontation became known as the 'Great Game'. There are various claims as to who first coined this expression, but it certainly caught on, and was repeated so often that it almost developed into a dogma. Much later, the expression was institutionalised by Lord Curzon, twice Viceroy of India, who wrote 'Turkistan, Afghanistan, Transcaucasia and Persia—to many these words breathe only a sense of utter remoteness ... but to me they are as pieces on a chess-board upon which is being played out a game for the domination of the world'. That was how generations of British consuls, administrators and senior military commanders were conditioned to view the situation beyond the north-west frontier of India.

It is doubtful whether the Russians saw their expansion towards India in quite the same light, being somewhat deterred by the vast empty Kara Kum and Kizil Kum deserts, shielding the Silk Road oasis cities from them. The Russians regarded the city of Khiva as being the gateway into Turkistan, and one they had great difficulty in forcing open. By 1825, they had already made four expeditions (the first in 1609) against Khiva, which lay some 200 miles south of the inland Aral Sea, all of which foundered in disaster, the main enemies being the desert and harassment by hostile mounted tribesmen.

For logistic reasons alone, the Russian military was well content with the fruits of its Persian victory, and was reluctant to embark upon any more long-distance desert campaigns, especially in view of commissariat limitations in those days. Eventually, the Russian military was prodded into moving into Turkistan by the Czar, who complained that slave-raiders were 'stealing men' from his Empire, and of the indignity in Christian European eyes of Christian slaves being offered for sale in the slave-markets of Khiva and other Turkistan cities.

The Afghan Region

Back in the Afghan region in 1818, Amir Mahmoud Shah (a Sadozai), captured, blinded and then killed Wazir Fatah Khan (a Barakzai), which roused the wrath of the Barakzai clan, who drove him from Kabul to Herat, which he governed independently until his death in 1829. Previously, in 1826, Dost Mohammed (a Barakzai) gained suzerainty over the city of Ghazni. Then, in 1833, from his exile in India, Shah Shuja (a Sadozai), with some help from the Maharajah Ranjit Singh, the Sikh leader in the Punjab, marched on Kandahar, seized that city, and briefly held it. The following year, Dost Mohammed raised an army, marched to Kandahar, and defeated Shah Shuja in battle. Shah Shuja again retired to India, and Dost Mohammed became Amir. Even so, Dost Mohammed had limited power as Kandahar was held by a hostile brother, and Herat by this time was held by Kamran Shah (a Sadozai), a son of the former Amir Mahmoud Shah. Dost Mohammed's fief was once again really only a Kingdom of Kabul.

Another hostile brother, and indeed rival claimant for the Amirship, Sultan Mohammed, had been sheltering in Peshawar, just to the east of the Khyber Pass, a city held by Maharajah Ranjit Singh, since 1818. In 1837, Amir Dost Mohammed mustered an army which, commanded by his eldest son, Mohammed Akbar Khan, was dispatched to recover Peshawar. The Sikh defenders were defeated in battle, but a group of Sikhs held out in Jamrud Fort, situated in the eastern end of the Khyber Pass. After a few days happy looting, the Afghan army withdrew to Jalalabad, and so Peshawar remained in the hands of the Sikh leader.

Maharajah Ranjit Singh was dissatisfied, claiming that when he had helped Shah Shuja regain Kandahar (in 1833), he had been promised in return the city of Shikarpur, near the Indus river, some 300 miles north of Karachi. To complicate this claim, Shikarpur was held by the Amirs of Sind, a loose alliance controlling an area somewhat similar to that of present day Sind Province in Pakistan, who had snatched it from the Durani Pathans in 1824, and had no intention of relinquishing it. The complainants sought British support, Amir Dost Mohammed wanting to regain Peshawar, and Maharajah Ranjit Singh wanting Shikarpur. The British were in a quandary as they could not please both and, moreover, if they supported the Sikh leader, they would make enemies of the Amirs of Sind.

The British chose an unusual course, which was to sweep aside Amir Dost Mohammed and replace him with ex-Amir Shah Shuja. Shah Shuja had promised the British that if they installed him in Kabul, he would open up routes through his territory to enable them to take their trade into the city state markets of Turkistan. This must have been one of the worst decisions made by the British around this period, as Shah Shuja was completely without popular support in his own country.

Meanwhile, a Persian army was carrying out a siege of Herat, still held by Kamran Shah. In 1834, the Shah of Persia was persuaded by British diplomatic guile to lift the siege, although the Russians were urging him to continue it. This was the heyday of British 'gunboat diplomacy', and a British naval contingent landed at Kharak, in the Persian Gulf, which persuaded the Shah to see things the British way. This was a prestige one-upmanship move against the Russians.

Amir Dost Mohammed sent envoys to the Shah of Persia, offering to support him if he would try to repossess Herat. Encouraged, the Shah raised an army, and marched to Herat. A siege ensued in which the Shah was subjected to conflicting pressure from both the British and Russians. In June 1838, the Persians launched a major assault on the city, which failed disastrously, even though the British had consistently refused to give arms to Kamran Shah, the resident Afghan defender. This was regarded as another British prestige triumph, and a corresponding loss of face for the Russians.

Treaty of Simla

The year of 1838 was one in which India was swept with rumour and counter-rumour of insurrection against British rule, but even so Lord Auckland, the Governor-General, decided to support Shah Shuja with military force. A Tripartite Treaty, often referred to as the 'Treaty of Simla', was signed on 25 June 1838, which briefly authorised Maharajah Ranjit Singh to remain in possession of Peshawar, and also to station there 1,000 troops, under a Muslim General, to assist Shah Shuja as necessary. Shah Shuja agreed to accept British control over his foreign policy, and to relinquish certain territory in Sind, in return for a large financial consideration.

The Simla Manifesto of October 1838 explained the British reasons for the decision to launch a military campaign into the Afghan region to depose Amir Dost Mohammed, and to replace him with Shah Shuja, stating that British forces would be withdrawn as soon as this had been accomplished. Both the Treaty and the Manifesto were based on faulty intelligence, it being believed by the British that a majority of the inhabitants of both Kabul and Kandahar would welcome Shah Shuja—which was far from the truth.

The Army of the Indus

The British, together with their allies, Maharajah Ranjit Singh and Shah Shuja, mustered a military force of some 39,000 troops, mainly Indian units although including some British ones, which became known as the 'Army of the Indus'. Mostly both British soldiers and Indian sepoys were armed with the India Pattern Flintlock musket, first introduced into the British army in 1797 (which had a 39-inch barrel, an overall length of 55 inches, and a calibre of 0.75 inches). British infantry, engineers and heavy cavalry all wore red coats during this campaign; the light cavalry and artillery wore blue coats, Indian sepoys in the infantry wore red uniforms, and the cavalry grey, while irregular troops had no common colour for their uniforms. (*National Army Museum*).

This expeditionary force was basically in two parts, one from the Bengal Army, and the other from the Bombay Army. The Commander-in-Chief of the Bombay Army was nominated Commander of the Army of the Indus. Shah Shuja raised about 4,000 troops.

The Bengal Army contingent was the first to move across the Sind desert, through the Bolan Pass to reach Quetta. Over 30,000 camels had been requisitioned to carry supplies, a large proportion of which was fodder for the camels while crossing desert terrain. The troops suffered considerable hardship on this approach march, being on

10

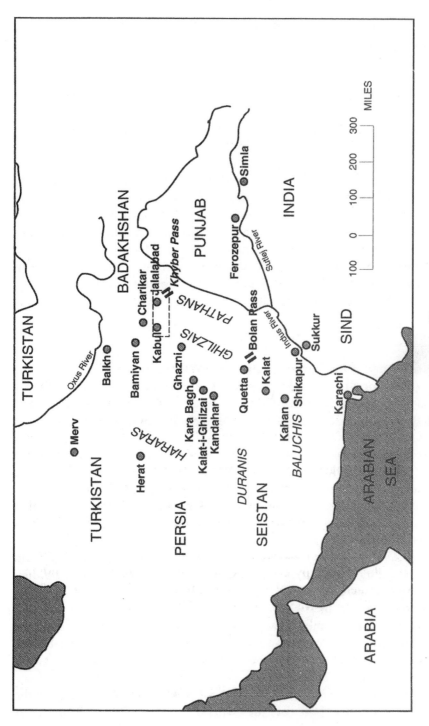

First Anglo-Afghan War
(1839-42)

half-rations for part of the time. They were also harassed by unfriendly tribesmen. Quetta was reached on 26 March 1839, and the Bombay Army contingent arrived a week later.

The Khan of Kalat, unhappy at the scavenging of his terrain for supplies by the Army of the Indus, was now asked to accept the suzerainty of Shah Shuja. Also, about 10,000 troops assembled at Peshawar, comprising some 6,000 of Maharajah Ranjit Singh's Sikh soldiers, and Shah Shuja's contingent, many of the latter being Gurkhas (with a Hindu culture); all were under the nominal command of Timur Khan, the son and nominated heir of Shah Shuja.

On the Afghan side the number of 'troops' and armed tribesmen opposing the Army of the Indus was much harder to assess. They consisted of Amir Dost Mohammed's household contingent, perhaps some 5,000 or so, supplemented by levies of cavalry with Jezails, lances and swords, and less well-armed infantry which, because of their mercurial nature and tendency to change loyalties abruptly, were almost impossible to number with any accuracy.

The Storming of Ghazni

The Army of the Indus marched out of Quetta on 7 April 1839, and by 14 April had reached the open Kandahar plain, where supply shortages were eased and morale began to improve. The Army had suffered many casualties due to exhaustion and sickness, and lost many camels for the same reasons. The first Afghan strongpoint encountered was the fortress city of Ghazni, said then to be the largest and strongest in Central Asia, and once the base of Sultan Mohammed, who had imposed Muslim rule on northern India. A reconnaissance revealed that all the side-gates of the walled city had been blocked with masonry, only the massive timber main 'Kabul Gate' being operative.

The Army began its assault in the early hours of 23 July: the main gate was blown open by British gunners, and both British and Indian troops swarmed through the opening into the walled city. By dawn the British flag flew above the citadel. The Afghan commander of Ghazni, Mohammed Afzal Khan, and part of his army, had abandoned the fortress and withdrawn westwards towards Kabul. There had been no moon that night, and a howling gale raged throughout the battle.

The Battle of Ghazni was one of the most successful fought by the British in that part of the world. In one action Amir Dost

Mohammed had lost his strongest outlying city fortress; over 600 of Amir Mohammed Afzal Khan's army had been killed, and another 1,000 captured, while the cost to the Army of the Indus was 18 dead and 173 wounded (*Army in India*). Amir Dost Mohammed sent emissaries to the British commander offering terms, which were rejected.

Kabul Occupied

On 30 July, the Army of the Indus marched out of Ghazni towards Kabul, where Amir Dost Mohammed, owing to the reputation the Army had gained in battle, was having difficulty in rallying support. The Amir, his household troops and supporters, pulled out of Kabul, withdrawing northwards. Unhindered on its march, the Army of the Indus entered Kabul unopposed on 7 August 1839: it had marched over 700 miles across wide deserts, crossed rivers and mountain ranges, losing over 20,000 camels.

After a six-week period of rest, recuperation and ceremonial, the major part of the Army of the Indus marched out from Kabul on 18 September, retracing its steps, but pausing to detach a force to deal with the dissatisfied Khan of Kalat. This arrived at his fortified city on 11 November. The first attempt to blow open the main gate of Kalat failed, and casualties were incurred. The Khan had five guns and a large number of Jezailchis, mainly local Baluchis. The next attempt, by Indian gunners, was successful, and infantry rushed through the open gate into the city. The Khan was killed in the fighting, after which the defence crumbled.

The British installed a rival claimant, Shah Nawaz Khan, then aged about 14 years, as Khan of Kalat and he was persuaded to transfer certain territory, including Quetta, to Amir Shah Shuja. Considering that they had satisfactorily settled the matter, the British-led contingent marched away. Some five years previously the unfortunate Khan of Kalat had extended sanctuary and help to Shah Shuja, then making his unsuccessful attempt to reclaim his Amirship, and had rallied local Baluchi tribes to his support—an example of the changing alliances and treachery so common in the Afghan region.

The Army of the Indus was formally disbanded on 1 January 1840, at Ferozepur, in the Punjab, although elements remained in the Afghan region to help Amir Shah Shuja establish himself securely. But this was not the end of the First Anglo-Afghan War.

Kahan and Kalat

In retrospect it was soon clear that the British had made a great mistake in withdrawing the major part of the Army of the Indus back into India so abruptly, leaving only token detachments behind. For example, Kamran Shah, who still ruled in Herat, and remained hostile to Amir Shah Shuja, was causing the British some anxiety with his slave-raiding and slave market activities, and they also feared the Shah of Persia might be tempted to mount another campaign to recover Herat.

Slow recovery from the shock of a foreign invasion was followed by a reactive wave of anti-British feeling which swept through the Afghan region. The first to suffer from its effects was the small British garrison left at Kahan, principal centre of the Marri tribe, in the Baluchistan area, which came under attack in April 1840, when its camel supply train was seized. A siege followed. All attempts to relieve Kahan failed, but eventually terms of surrender were arranged, and on 3 October, the garrison was allowed to march out with all honours of war, taking its guns, wounded and camp followers with it. This was one of the few agreements made with the British that the Afghans kept.

Britain's young puppet ruler at Kalat, Shah Nawaz Khan, was unpopular with the local Brahui tribe, which favoured another claimant to the Khanate, one Nasir Khan who, in August 1840, marched to take that city by force. The British Political Officer was seized and held captive in chains, the small, mainly Indian, garrison was either murdered or subverted, officers were held for ransom, and Shah Nawaz Khan abdicated. Then followed what has been described as a 'war of outpost skirmishing' (*Norris*). As a British relief column neared Kalat, the British Political Officer was murdered. A compromise agreement was reached on 6 October under which, in vague terms, Nasir Khan retained the Khanate, but accepted the suzerainty of Amir Shah Shuja.

Dost Mohammed Again

After hastily evacuating Kabul just before British troops marched in, Dost Mohammed had fled northwards to take refuge first with the Khan of Balkh, with whom the British had tried unsuccessfully to negotiate, and then with the Khan of Bokhara. At Bokhara (in Turkistan), two British envoys were still imprisoned in squalid circumstances. Not trusting the Khan of Bokhara, Dost Mohammed had taken the precaution of leaving his family in the care of the Khan of Bamiyan, who arranged their safe conduct to India. Dost Mohammed's negotiations with the Khan of Bokhara were sterile, and the situation became such that Dost Mohammed, with his companions, decamped by night in disguise, to return to the Afghan region—a wise decision, as later (June 1842) the two unfortunate British envoys were publicly beheaded.

Raising a force of about 6,000 Uzbek 'lancers', Dost Mohammed marched southwards towards Kabul and, on 2 November 1840, ran into a small contingent of Indian cavalry at Parwandara, a few miles north of Kabul; this force, overawed by the strength of the Uzbek lancers, refused orders to charge and, when attacked, broke and fled in disorder. Dost Mohammed then moved alone to the outskirts of Kabul, surrendered to the senior British Political Officer (Sir William Macnaghten, technically the British Representative at the Court of the Amir), and was escorted off into comfortable exile in India.

This may seem to be a somewhat surprising action on the face of it, but Dost Mohammed was no fool; he saw trouble ahead, and wanted to sit back in security and let others fight to retrieve his throne for him. After a British military contingent had crushed a revolt by elements of the Durani Pathans, a false sense of security seemed to settle on the Afghan region under the rule of Amir Shah Shuja.

Change of British Policy

This deceptive calm caused the British to decide to help Amir Shah Shuja regularise and up-grade his 'armed forces', so that all British and Indian detachments left to support him could be withdrawn from the Afghan region. Meanwhile, British authorities in India embarked upon a cost-cutting exercise. Subsidies paid to various Afghan tribes for their quiescence, and for keeping certain routes open for British forces, were reduced, which caused discontent, especially among the Jezailchis holding vital passes between Kabul and Jalalabad. This was probably the most short-sighted decision the British could have made at this particular juncture.

For example, a brigade at Peshawar was due to relieve the brigade in Kabul but, instead of it marching out to Kabul to accomplish the change-over in the normal way, it was ordered to remain at Peshawar to await the arrival of the brigade from Kabul, before setting off; which meant a much depleted garrison remaining at Kabul. How much in rupees this rather odd military arrangement could have actually saved can only be surmised. Had it not been proposed, the relief British brigade would have been seen to be marching towards Kabul, which perhaps might have altered the course of history and averted a British disaster.

The Charikar Massacre

The first real sign of trouble occurred in October 1841, at Charikar, some 50 miles north of Kabul, which was garrisoned by Amir Shah Shuja's Gurkha battalion. This contingent was attacked unsuccessfully, and a siege ensued, during which sickness struck the Gurkhas, and subsequently the water supply failed. On 2 November, the only Gurkha troops fit to bear arms, about 200 in all, leaving their wounded and sick, and their families behind, decided to fight their way out. Only two British officers and one sepoy made it to the safety of the British cantonment at Kabul. History does not tell us who made this degrading decision.

Kabul Besieged

The British garrison at Kabul consisted of about 4,500 military personnel, both British and Indian (*Army in India*), with about 12,000 camp followers, and included some wives and children. Commissariat trains accompanying armies in those days were large, cumbersome and slow-moving, being over-laden with officers' and troops' baggage, there being little restriction in such matters. Kabul was an ancient walled and fortified city, encompassing a mass of humanity. The Amir's fortress palace, the Bala Hissar, was on a small hillock outside, and just apart, from the walled city, while the British contingent, basically of seven major units, was encamped in the open about two miles from the city, and had the disadvantage of being overlooked by low hills.

The military commander at Kabul was Major General William Elphinstone, generally regarded as 'elderly' (although only 55), who had fought at the Battle of Waterloo in 1815, whose health was poor, and who was due to return to India with the next military column to march out. Elphinstone was clearly not up to the task before him, lacking aggressive energy and, unlike most of his fellow officers, he regarded Afghans as allies and not as the enemy. A few other officers in the Army of the Indus had also fought under Wellington at

Waterloo and in the earlier Peninsular Campaigns. Fortunately, not all were in this category, one being Major General William Nott, commanding the British contingent at Kandahar, who had been nominated to take over command from Elphinstone. Nott was said to be short-tempered, but also competent and energetic.

On 2 November 1841 a senior British Political Officer, Sir Alexander Burnes, and two colleagues were attacked at their Residency in Kabul, and killed as they attempted to escape from the mob in disguise. The inhabitants of Kabul held their breath nervously as normally heavy retribution would have automatically followed but, due to Elphinstone's conciliatory attitude, nothing was done, which the Afghans took as a sign of weakness, and which encouraged insurrection.

Soon the British cantonment outside Kabul was besieged, and at once began to experience problems of supply and communication. The encampment came under artillery fire from the surrounding hills and, on 23 November, a raiding party from the garrison, attempting to destroy Afghan guns, met with disaster, being trapped and suffering casualties. Indian troops refused to advance, and the only gun the raiding party had taken with it became over-heated (*Heathcote*). The raiding party withdrew leaving its gun and wounded behind, scrambling back to camp in ignominy.

Even before news of the Charikar massacre reached Kabul, Elphinstone had ordered Nott, at Kandahar, to send a brigade to reinforce his contingent, but winter had set in, snow blocked the route, and the brigade had to return to Kandahar; they arrived back on 8 December, having left a small garrison to hold Kalat-i-Ghilzai, mid-way between Kandahar and Ghazni.

Also, Elphinstone ordered the brigade (commanded by Major General Sir Robert Sale, a 60-year-old veteran, but made of sterner stuff), due to be relieved by one from Peshawar, which had marched out from Kabul a few days earlier, to return to Kabul. Sale did not think it feasible to force his way back through mountain passes, some choked with snow, and now held by hostile Jezailchis, so he pushed on to Jalalabad, where he constructed a fortified encampment.

In Kabul, Macnaghten opened negotiations with leaders of the Afghans besieging the British cantonment, but made little progress. They were joined by Mohammed Akbar Khan (son of Dost Mohammed), who brought with him the 6,000 Uzbek lancers his father had raised, pretending to be a neutral. Amir Shah Shuja remained inactive in his Bala Hissar fortress.

Retreat from Kabul

A Council of War was held by the indecisive Elphinstone, where conflicting suggestions were put forward; some wanted to fight their way out, but others protested that with 700 sick and wounded personnel, women and children, and a host of camp followers, this was not feasible; others suggested they fight their way across the Kabul River to join Amir Shah Shuja in his Bala Hissar fortress. In fact, on 5 December 1841, Jezailchis blew the bridge across that river.

Meanwhile, winter was rapidly closing in and supplies were becoming a problem. Eventually, it was agreed that the whole contingent and its dependants would march out together towards India, but there were delays as local Afghan leaders demanded further concessions for allowing unrestricted passage. Afghan emissaries tricked Macnaghten, (who was eventually murdered) into signing a false agreement indicating collusion with Dost Mohammed's supporters against Amir Shah Shuja, in an attempt to discredit the British.

Then British retreat from Kabul began on 6 January 1842, the column consisting of '4,330 soldiers, nine guns and 12,000 camp followers' (*Norris*). The sick and wounded were left behind as local Afghan leaders had promised to look after them, but most were subsequently massacred. Almost at once the retreat became a rout as a panic traffic jam built up at the bridge over the Logar river, when drivers and camp followers fought each other to get across. Much of the baggage was abandoned at this point. Only five miles were covered on the first day's march.

The column straggled on, being harassed by mounted Jezailchis, and discipline seemed to waver. Soldiers and sepoys alike seemed willing to take offensive action, but officer leadership seemed to be wanting. On occasions when sorties were made, Jezailchis kept their distance for a while, but the British rearguard was frequently attacked. By the end of the second day the column had only reached the Khurd Kabul Pass, a further five miles on.

Frequently, in critical situations, indomitable British women seem to have come to the fore to inspire and shame their menfolk. On this occasion it was Lady Sale, whose husband had reached Jalalabad, and her daughter, whose husband had just died of his wounds. Both ladies wanted to lead cavalry charges against harassing tribesmen. At this point Mohammed Akbar Khan appeared, and offered sanctuary

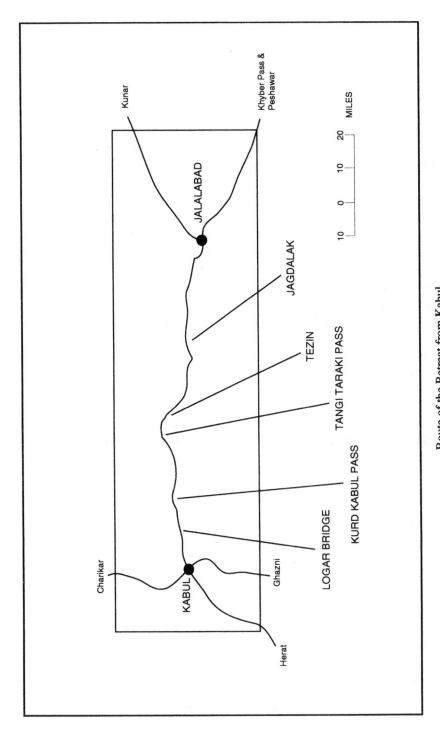

Route of the Retreat from Kabul
January 1842

to the women, their husbands and children, in his own camp. He said the passes ahead were held by Ghilzais, over whom he had no influence, and who were determined to block the column's progress. This offer was accepted.

The next major misfortune was on 9 January, when the column entered the Tangi Taraki Pass, and was trapped by Ghilzais. Sepoys of the rearguard were annihilated, rocks rained down on the main body in the defiles, and the casualty rate was exceptionally high. Only General Elphinstone, 'his staff, 100 cavalrymen, and 16 gunners with one gun', reached Tezin, on the eastern side of the Pass (*Norris*). Mohammed Akbar Khan invited Elphinstone and his senior Brigadier General to his camp for a conference, where he gave them hospitality, but would not let them return to the column.

Brigadier General Anquetil, the senior surviving officer in the column, gathered together soldiers and sepoys able to fight and, abandoning the wounded and sick, tried to slip through the Pass during the hours of darkness, but secrecy was given away by noisy camp followers, who tried to accompany him. A last stand was made at Jagdalak, on 13 January, where the route ahead was barricaded. A few last charges were made by small groups of British soldiers and Indian sepoys, arousing admiration among the Ghilzais.

A few individuals did manage to escape and make their way towards Jalalabad, but most, though not all, were followed and killed, some within sight of that city. One officer wrapped his Regimental Colour round his body under his coat to save it, but was wounded and taken prisoner, his life being spared for ransom as the richly embroidered Colour gave his captors the impression that he was an extremely wealthy individual whose family could afford to pay a large sum of money for his safe return.

One survivor, Assistant Surgeon Brydon, himself wounded and riding a wounded horse, made it to the Jalalabad encampment, and gained fame as 'The Only Survivor', from a Victorian painting depicting the scene of his arrival. The 'Brydon incident' gave rise to an Afghan legend, it being said later that Mohammed Akbar Khan had boasted that he would destroy the whole British contingent at Kabul, but leave just one man alive to tell the tale. The British retreat from Kabul in January 1842, was one of the worst disasters in the history of British arms, in which 'over 16,000 men were massacred due to Afghan treachery' (*Army of India*).

Surrender at Ghazni

The British suffered yet another serious defeat at Ghazni, where a small Indian garrison was besieged in the citadel, in the course of the general anti-British uprising sweeping through the Afghan region. The garrison held out for a while, but eventually agreed to surrender in return for being allowed to march out with full honours of war and a safe conduct. On 6 March 1842, as these troops left the citadel, the Indians were mostly massacred, and the handful of British officers taken prisoner for ransom.

Siege of Jalalabad

Meanwhile, the Afghans approached Jalalabad but hesitated to attack what had developed into a well-fortified encampment. After some negotiation, Mohammed Akbar Khan offered the garrison a safe conduct to Peshawar, which was refused as the British no longer trusted Afghan leaders. On 19 February (1842), an earthquake flattened the fortifications of the Jalalabad camp, the earth tremor throwing up dust and snow, which was seen by the British hostages still held by Mohammed Akbar Khan in his camp some 10 miles distant. The defenders worked hard to repair the damage, and had almost completed the task by the end of the month when Mohammed Akbar Khan decided to close the siege.

Soon the defenders were on half-rations, and received the bad news that the British relief column from Peshawar had not been able to enter the Khyber Pass to reach them. Sale decided to risk all in a last desperate attack in strength, which began on 7 April. Some 1,500 British and Indian troops were pitched against the 6,000 Uzbek lancers, who had joined in the massacres on the retreat from Kabul. Infantry 'formed square' against the charging Uzbek cavalry, but firm discipline carried the day, forcing the Afghans to quit the field of battle.

Seizing the opportunity, Sale's troops rushed forward to capture Mohammed Akbar Khan's base camp, recovering four guns previously lost, and confiscating 500 sheep, which gave the half-starved men a good meal. Wounded in the fighting, Mohammed Akbar Khan disappeared into the hills, taking the British hostages with him. This was an impressive British victory which did much to deter Afghan harassment and further attacks.

21

Kandahar

The small garrison of two Indian units and some British gunners left at Kalat-i-Ghilzai, had also been besieged, but managed to hold out during the winter period, even though on half-rations much of the time. The Ghilzais made a determined attack on 21 May (1842), but were driven back, and a week later the garrison was reinforced by a strong column arriving from Kandahar.

Meanwhile, at Kandahar, Nott had been conducting an extremely aggressive defence against besieging tribesmen, sending out strong raiding parties against them. On 11 March, there was a near disaster when, while a major part of the garrison was out on a 'search and destroy' operation, a large group of Durani tribesmen mounted an attack on the walled city. The main gate was set on fire and there was fighting throughout the night, with artillery fire decimating the attackers. The depleted garrison held out successfully, the tribesmen fading away into the hills as the main body of troops returned.

In the struggle for Kandahar, Timur Khan (one of Amir Shah Shuja's sons) remained in alliance with the British, while another son, Saftar Jang, was hostile to them; this being somewhat typical of the struggle for the Afghan succession. In mid-May, British reinforcements, arriving by way of Sind and the Bolan Pass, reached Kandahar.

Amir Shah Shuja's Fate

While the momentous events surrounding the British retreat from Kabul were unfolding, Amir Shah Shuja still remained behind the walls of the Bala Hissar fortress, seeming to stand aside from the opportunity-seeking local leaders and their followers, who were swirling around the capital and who even put up an alternative Amir at one stage. Eventually, on 25 April (1842), Amir Shah Shuja was persuaded to leave the Bala Hissar to review Afghan military reinforcements before they marched off to attack Jalalabad. As he was about to do so he was assassinated by a member of the Barakzai family. Fighting then broke out amongst the several factions, and it was not until the middle of June that they agreed to support a compromise candidate, Fateh Jang (another of Shah Shuja's sons) and to accept Mohammed Akbar Khan as Wazir (Governor) of Kabul.

Ellenborough Arrives

Meanwhile, in February 1842, a new Governor General, Lord Ellenborough, had arrived in India, intent on withdrawing all 'red-coat' garrisons from the Afghan region. This expression was a reference to the fact that British Infantry of the Line units still wore their traditional red uniform jackets, as they had done for so many years on so many foreign battlefields. Realising the British had been backing the wrong man in Kabul, Ellenborough authorised what he thought would be a limited expedition to restore the prestige of British arms, before withdrawing completely from the Afghan region.

Arriving at Peshawar he found a garrison of demoralised soldiers, of whom almost 2,000 were casualties due to sickness and frostbite. He appointed a new military commander, Major General George Pollock, who immediately set about raising morale and organising an Expeditionary Force. Pollock drastically reduced the baggage train which, with civilian drivers, had been such a handicap during the retreat from Kabul. In March, more reinforcements arrived in Peshawar, and soon the Expeditionary Force had four cavalry and seven major infantry units, field and siege guns, and a corps of mounted Jezailchis.

Forcing the Khyber Pass

Pollock's first task was to force open the 35-mile-long Khyber Pass, blocked by local Pathan tribesmen, which he began to do on 5 April 1842. Before dawn he sent out large flanking contingents to gain the summit of the heights on either side of the Pass, and when daylight came the Afghans below were taken completely by surprise by being fired on from above, probably for the first time ever, and they soon gave way under volleys of British musket fire.

This was really the first time this tactic of picketing was used in action in this area, which was rather surprising, and perhaps accounts for several previous unfortunate British setbacks in ambushes. It was then known as 'crowning the heights' (*Heathcote*), an expression that was soon changed to the now more familiar 'picketing the heights', which became standard drill in mountain warfare to afford flank protection to bodies of troops moving through defiles.

Pollock took the whole length of the Khyber Pass for the loss of 14 killed and 104 wounded (*Heathcote*, and moved on to arrive at Jalalabad on 15 April, where a few days earlier Sale had scattered Mohammed Akbar Khan's Uzbek lancers. These two victories were a significant boost to British and Indian military morale, and correspondingly dampened the ardour of hostile Afghan Jezailchis and tribesmen.

Blind Eyes to the Telescope

These two British victories seemed to satisfy Ellenborough's plan for a limited expedition into the Afghan region to restore the prestige of British arms, his main concern being that Peshawar was physically separated from British India by the huge Sikh Kingdom in the Punjab, and the fact that the Sikhs were doubtful allies. Not knowing of Sale's victory, Ellenborough ordered Pollock to withdraw the garrison from Jalalabad. The heliograph was the main means of instant communication, having a maximum limit of some 40 miles on a clear sunlit day, but a direct line of sight was essential, and the Khyber Heights nullified contact with Jalalabad. Ellenborough also sent orders to Nott to withdraw from Kandahar, fall back on Quetta, and then retire through the Bolan Pass to Sukkur, on the Indus river.

Disliking these orders, both commanders played for time, and both 'regretted' they were unable to move until adequate camel transport arrived. These two 'fighting Sepoy Generals', determined and competent, were deeply ashamed of the way the retreat from Kabul had been handled. Nott in particular had been outspoken in criticism of the Commander-in-Chief, India, (General Sir Jasper Nicolls), Elphinstone and other senior officers in the Army of the Indus.

As whispers of this criticism came to the ears of Ellenborough, he complained that 'Nott and Pollock have not a grain of military talent' (*Heathcote*): a much mistaken evaluation. The British handicap was no longer lack of competent Generals in the field. It is tempting to speculate on how, if Nott had relieved Elphinstone as scheduled, he would have handled the situation, and whether events might have taken a different course.

The Duke of Wellington, himself a former successful 'Sepoy General' wrote critically to Ellenborough, urging swift retribution for the disaster of the retreat from Kabul, as did other prominent Empire-builders. This prodded Ellenborough into formulating a more aggressive plan. Another point that rankled with the Generals, and others, was that in adversity, in the mad scramble of 'every man for himself', wounded, sick, women and children had sometimes been abandoned.

The C-in-C, India, and his military staff, were all for a quick withdrawal, being ever conscious of wasteful expenditure. This led Ellenborough to bypass the C-in-C and issue orders direct to Generals in the field, which caused friction and backbiting between senior military officers and senior civilian officials. Eventually, Ellenborough said that Pollock could march on to Kabul if he thought he had sufficient resources, but should return before winter set in; and that Nott could also march to Kabul 'if he wished'. This was just what these two Generals wanted, and both set off towards Kabul with vengeance in mind. These orders from Ellenborough were 'confidential' to Pollock and Nott only, and the C-in-C was not informed.

Nott's Victories

At Kandahar in mid-May (1842), Nott, with only 2,000 troops, routed a Durani tribal force of over 8,000, for the loss of one soldier killed and 52 wounded (*Army in India*). Then some 3,000 camels, his return transport, arrived, some of which he used to send Shah Shuja's contingent, and certain other unreliable units back to India, as he prepared to march on Kabul. Nott's opinion of Shah Shuja was that he 'was as great a scoundrel as ever lived' (*Heathcote*).

Nott's next battle was at Karabagh where, on 30 August, he defeated an army of some 10,000 Ghilzais, and then advanced to Ghazni, which he attacked on 4 September. Fighting went on all day inside the city walls, and throughout the night, but by the following dawn, once again the British flag fluttered above the citadel, as the Afghan defenders decamped. British and Indian prisoners were released, the citadel was blown up, and the city walls were flattened. Nott was now only 50 miles from Kabul.

Pollock Advances

Meanwhile, Pollock too was hurrying towards Kabul, his force leaving Jalalabad on 20 August. Using his flank-shielding tactic of picketing the heights as he advanced, he encountered comparatively little opposition. There was just one action of note, at Mamu Khel, on 24 August, when the Afghan opposition was scattered without difficulty. On 8 September, Pollock arrived at Jagdalak, the scene of the massacre, where resistance was again quickly pushed aside. Nott's troops were now marching along the route of the British retreat, which was littered with skeletons in tattered uniforms, some piled in heaps, and others lying in the roadway where they fell. Any feelings of compassion were erased. 'As we marched our gun wheels crushed the bones of our dead comrades' (*Norris*).

On 12 September, Pollock arrived at the Tezin Pass to find it blocked by Mohammed Akbar Khan, now Wazir of Kabul, who had mustered some 16,000 Afghan Jezailchis and tribesmen. As usual, Pollock sent out flanking units to picket the heights and fire down on the Afghans in the Pass below. He also left a strong cavalry force in the rear to guard the baggage train, anticipating that the Afghans would try to repeat their old looting tactics. This was a wise move, and his cavalry drove off bands of scavenging Afghans. Pollock forced the Tezin Pass for the loss of 32 killed and 130 wounded (*Army in India*), the Afghans leaving over 1,000 dead and three guns on the field when they retreated.

The following day Pollock was approached by Amir Fateh Jang and some of his supporters who were 'peddling promises' and urging him not to march on Kabul. Pollock brushed them aside, and on 15 September, his troops entered the Bala Hissar fortress and the walled city of Kabul. British and Indian troops formed their encampment outside the city.

The Bala Hissar fortifications were blown up, as was the Great Gate to the Bazaar, reputedly one of the wonders of southern Asia, on which the remains of the assassinated Macnaghten had been publicly displayed. Many hundreds of Afghans were killed or executed. There is no doubt that British retribution in Kabul was very heavy indeed. A brigade was detached to march northwards to avenge the massacre of the Gurkhas at Charikar, and it behaved in a similar merciless manner. A few days later, the forward elements of Nott's column reached Kabul.

The British Hostages

British military prestige had been restored and military honour redeemed, albeit with bloody hands, but there still remained the slur of the British hostages who had been consigned to the care of Wazir Mohammed Akbar Khan. For some time they were held in Kabul in reasonable conditions, inspired by the indomitable Lady Sale, as the 'senior wife'; and had been able to send and receive letters and parcels, through the good offices of the astute Wazir who, knowing how unstable and unpredictable the situation could become in Afghan ruling circles, was hedging his bets.

Lady Sale wrote long letters to her husband at Jalalabad, which he forwarded on to the Press in London, and which were published, bringing her widespread fame. The prize hostage, General Elphinstone, had died on 24 April 1842, and the Wazir sent his body to Jalalabad for burial. The shrewd Wazir looked on this act, and other small courtesies and help he gave the British hostages, as something of an insurance for a comfortable exile in India, should his fortunes ever change for the worse.

As the British columns neared Kabul, the hostages were packed off to Bamiyan, some 70 miles north-west of the city, where they were held in more squalid circumstances. A small British column marched to Bamiyan, and by a combination of a show of military force, bribery and intrigue, all 82 remaining British hostages were rescued safely.

The British Evacuate

Ellenborough now firmly ordered the British columns at Kabul back to India, and they began their return march on 12 October 1842, leaving chaos behind, and experiencing only minor harassment during their withdrawal. Lord Ellenborough was waiting for them at Ferozepur, in the Punjab, where he held a review of 40,000 troops and 100 guns, before the men dispersed to their peacetime cantonments.

Officially, the military casualties for the whole of the First Anglo-Afghan War were 15,000 all ranks, killed or died of wounds or sickness (*Army in India*). Civilian camp follower casualties do not seem to have been collated, being considered perhaps of less importance than camels, whose deaths were meticulously logged. British authorities in India bemoaned the cost of the war, which had not in any way furthered trade expansion, calculated as the equivalent (it was reckoned in rupees) of about £20 million, a considerable sum in those days. Others bemoaned the loss of over 50,000 camels, and the effect this had on the economies of the areas from which they had been requisitioned.

The Afghan region was left in a state of shock, confusion and uncertainty. Fateh Jang refused to continue as Amir and, in fact, withdrew with the British columns to a comfortable exile in India. In his stead, the Wazir appointed Shahpur Khan (another son of Shah Shuja). Taking advantage of the power vacuum in Kabul, and tired of being the power behind the Governor of Herat, Yar Mohammed murdered his master, (Kamran Shah), and took control of the city himself, correctly calculating that neither Persia nor Russia would want to become entangled in war to snatch this prize from him.

Concluding Comments

Historically, the First Anglo-Afghan War will always be primarily remembered for the disastrous British Retreat from Kabul, the fault of an ageing, incompetent General, rather than for the more virile and effective actions of Nott, Pollock and Sale. The parsimonious government of India, ever conscious of the profit motive, cut subsidies paid to Afghan tribes controlling Passes along the route from Kabul to Peshawar. One wonders just what other reaction could have followed.

The main British political mistake was to prefer the Sikh Maharajah Ranjit Singh to Dost Mohammed, and to back Shah Shuja, continuing to do so until his assassination. If it had been left to the Governor General and the C-in-C, India, the British disaster would have been unavenged, and only criticism from the prestigious Duke of Wellington, and others, forced a change in attitude. One has to remind oneself that the political aim of the First Anglo-Afghan War was to depose Dost Mohammed and replace him with Shah Shuja. This was accomplished, but nullified by the withdrawal of the main part of the Army of the Indus, and the assassination of Shah Shuja, who had little, if any, popular support. The main underlying aim had been to open up trade routes westwards towards Turkistan, and this had failed. However, British aggressive use of the military option in the Afghan region alarmed the Russians, confirming their suspicions of British expansionist tendencies, and so fuelled the illusion of the Great Game.

2

The Second Anglo-Afghan War: 1878-81

The shrewd ex-Amir Dost Mohammed remained in comfortable exile in India until the end of 1842 when, by arrangement with the British, he returned to Kabul to resume his interrupted reign. Wazir Mohammed Akbar Khan, who had done so much to restore his father to the throne, died in 1847, for ever remembered as the Afghan hero, in suitably embellished song and story of his defeat of a Sikh army at Jamrud, and for carrying out his promise to eliminate the British-Indian garrison at Kabul, sparing only one man to return to tell the tale.

British Conquests in India

The First Anglo-Afghan War initiated a period of further British conquest and expansion in the sub-continent, particularly in terrain adjacent to the Afghan region. In 1843, the Sind was brought under direct British control by a brilliant campaign by General Sir Charles Napier, who with an army of about 3,000 troops, defeated a force of over 20,000 Baluchis at Meanee, on the lower reaches of the Indus river.

The British then turned their attention to their last and most powerful antagonist, the Sikh State of the Punjab, encompassing territory between the Indus and Sutlej rivers, and headed for many years by the previously mentioned Maharajah Ranjit Singh, who had died in 1839. After a period of anarchy, a large Sikh army crossed the Sutlej river into British Indian territory in December 1845, and so began the first Anglo-Sikh War. This was terminated in February the following year by the Battle of Sabraon, when some 15,000 British and Indian troops successfully stormed entrenchments held by over 20,000 Sikh soldiers.

The Second Anglo-Sikh War began in the Spring of 1848, when much of the Punjab rose in insurrection against British authority, under Chattar Singh. The indecisive Battle of Chillianwala was fought in January 1849, when both armies quit the field of battle with heavy losses. The Second Anglo-Sikh War ended the following month after the Battle of Gujerat, when a British-Indian force of about 20,000 men dispersed a Sikh army about 60,000-strong. The boundary of British India now marched uncertainly with the eastern boundary of the Afghan region and some British eyes were being cast enviously at fringe Afghan territory.

The Anglo-Persian War: 1856-57

Fearing attacks by the Persians, Amir Dost Mohammed, who had previously veered towards the Russians, now turned towards the British, and the Anglo-Afghan Treaty was signed in 1855. Involved in the Crimean War, the Russians were hoping to entangle Britain in a diversionary war with Persia, and were urging the Shah of Persia to repossess Herat, which he managed to do. The British reacted, and the Anglo-Persian War began in December 1856, when an Expeditionary Force from the Bombay Army, under General Sir James Outram, landed in Persia, and defeated the Shah's army.

In April 1857, the British compelled the Persians to withdraw from Herat which, however, still remained independent of Kabul, and it was not until 1863, that Amir Dost Mohammed took that city by storm. He had already driven his hostile brother from Kandahar, and by 1859, had established his authority northwards to the Oxus river. During the Anglo-Persian War the British sent arms to the Khan of Kalat, to enable him to defend his Makran border against Persian incursions.

Russian Reaction

Russian reaction to the British invasion of the Afghan region in 1839 had been to mount yet another campaign against Khiva, this time in mid-winter, in January 1842. Previous attempts had been made in the Summer campaigning season, when heat and drought, which even Cossack horsemen could not tolerate, had been the major causes of failures. This time 'General Winter' was the main enemy faced by the '5,000-strong Russian force' (*Hopkirk*). Soon snow became so deep the Cossacks could not force a way forward for the infantry, artillery or camels. After three months, and not half way to Khiva, the Russians abandoned the expedition without a shot being fired or a slave freed, having lost over 1,000 men and 9,000 camels.

This Russian failure gave some satisfaction to the British in the Great Game stakes, as it tended to counter-balance the disastrous British retreat from Kabul. However, the Russians seemed to step ahead again when, in 1844, by arrangement with the Khan of Khiva, they established a military base at Muinak, on the Aral Sea, near the mouth of the Oxus river—a valuable stepping stone to Khiva.

That year relations between Russia and Britain seemed to thaw a little when they became joint-mediators in a dispute between the Ottoman Empire and Persia; there was also a State Visit by Czar Nicholas II to Queen Victoria in Britain, which was heralded by the Press as being the start of Anglo-Russian détente. After a decade, this illusion was shattered when the Crimean War (1854-56) began, with Britain, France and Turkey lined up against the Russians.

The Indian Mutiny: 1857-58

The next major event on the sub-continent was the Indian Mutiny, known colloquially at the time as the 'Great Sepoy Mutiny', and which today in India is referred to as the 'First Indian War of Independence'. It began in May 1857 at Meerut, involving mainly the Bengal Army, and quickly spread across northern and central India, to be quelled with a very heavy retributive hand. During the Indian Mutiny, Amir Dost Mohammed retained a seemingly friendly stance towards the British, firmly resisting the urging of his Muslim Mullahs to take advantage of this British misfortune, and declare a *Jihad* (Holy War) against them.

The major political change caused by the Indian Mutiny was that the Honourable East India Company, which had done so much to foster British supremacy in India, was formally phased out in December 1858, all its authority passing directly to the British Crown, the Governor General later assuming the additional title of Viceroy. Responsibility for both political and military matters on the sub-continent was exercised in London by the Secretary of State for India, through the India Office, which became fully effective when the telegraph reached India.

The Indian military establishment was reduced to 150,000 (from over 200,000), while the British military establishment was increased to 75,000 (from about 38,000) (*Army in India*). The Indian element was deprived of most of its artillery, and the number of British officers in each unit was increased. The military remained in the separate armies of the Bengal, Bombay and Madras Presidencies.

Amir Sher Ali

In Afghanistan, Amir Dost Mohammed died in 1863, and was succeeded by one of his sons, Sher Ali Khan, who was soon ousted from power by his brothers, first by Mohammed Afzal Khan, and then Mohammed Azam Khan, each of whom ruled briefly in Kabul, until Sher Ali regained his throne in 1868.

Looking enviously at the standing armies in British India, the Ottoman Empire, Russia and Persia, and realising what a military void existed in his own country, Amir Sher Ali concentrated upon raising, organising and arming an 'Afghan Army', which was to be uniformed and disciplined. Admiring the Russian system, in which a required number of men were conscripted, and retained in military service for the whole of their active life, the Amir sought to put a similar system into operation.

Conscription proved to be unpopular, especially among the independently-minded Pathans, and initially conscripts were obtained from the Hazaras, Ghilzais, Qizilbashias. Tadjiks and Uzbeks. But the material was poor as cities, towns and groups of villages did not send their best men. However, although not an unqualified success, the Afghan army took shape, and soon reached a strength of about 50,000 men (albeit with a fairly large mercenary content), which was armed, given some training and pressed into units.

Considerable Turkish assistance was given in training this new model Afghan army, but it had one main drawback: it lacked a dedicated professional officer corps, having, for quite some time, to rely upon mercenaries to fill such vacancies. The Amir was able to obtain ample numbers of jezail muskets, and some modern muzzle-loading rifles, as well as field guns. A large purpose-built military cantonment was constructed just outside Kabul at Sherpur, as the main military base, armoury and training depot. The formation and development of this new model Afghan army was

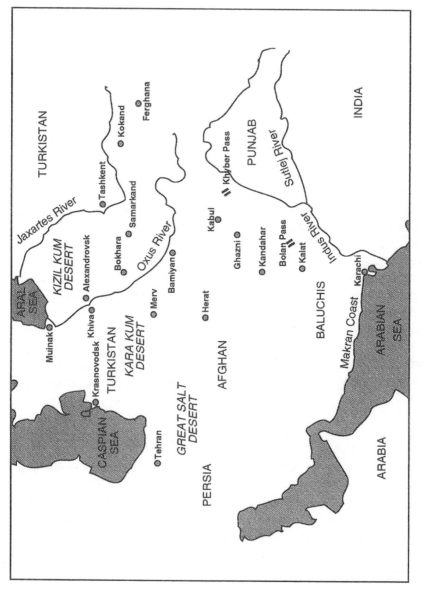

The Chess Board – For the Great Game
19th Century

watched by the British authorities in India with anxiety and displeasure.

More on the Great Game

During the second half of the 19th Century, the Russians expanded into Turkistan. In 1865, they took Tashkent by storm, and remained in possession; the following year they seized Bokhara, where a Russian delegation had been imprisoned; Samarkand was occupied and annexed in 1868; and finally in 1873, the long-delayed prize of Khiva fell to them (*Hopkirk*).

During this period of Russian expansion Amir Sher Ali remained fairly quiescent. He had not protested when a British military garrison was established at Quetta, which he still laid claim to; nor did he complain when the Khan of Kalat was persuaded to accept a British Political Officer. Throughout this time there had been a Vakil (an Indian representative) at the Amir's Court in a liaison role.

Meanwhile, impressed by the Amir's developing army, and playing on his illusions of grandeur, the Russians tried to persuade him to turn against the British, and march to recover his traditional Afghan territories, offering to support him with 30,000 troops. Additionally, the Russians tried to persuade the Amir to declare himself the 'Grand Muslim Khan', and to assume religious influence, under their suzerainty, over their recent gains in Turkistan. Perhaps the Amir toyed with these suggestions, but the Russian situation, in the European context, changed, and the Czar suddenly went cold on him.

Anglo-Russian Understanding

Discussions in government circles in both Britain and India over strategy to be adopted in the Afghan region and Turkistan had mainly centred on whether to match the Russians step by step by pushing forward over the Hindu Kush into the upper basin of the Oxus river, or to leave it as a convenient land barrier. In January 1873, the Anglo-Russian Understanding was signed, dividing the so-called 'neutral area' between the Afghan region and Turkistan between Britain and Russia, with the Afghan area remaining within the British sphere of influence; but the agreement foundered.

Demand for a British Mission in Kabul

The Viceroy of India, Lord Northbrook, wanted to send a diplomatic mission to Kabul, to explain the Anglo-Russian Understanding to the Amir, and also the British arbitration decision to award the province of Seistan to Persia, and not to the Amir. The Amir refused this request, and instead sent his own representative, who met the Viceroy at Simla in July of that year. The Amir refused to open up his territory to the British.

Amir Sher Ali was nervously trying to play the British and Russians off against each other in order to maintain his territorial integrity. But he had problems. When the Russians occupied Khiva, a large group of Khivans took refuge in the Amir's northern Badakhshan area, from where they operated hit-and-run raids on Russian military posts. The Amir became anxious in case the Russian military should be provoked into hot-pursuit tactics into his territory, or use the situation as an excuse for further southward advances. Additionally, the Amir's hostile nephew, Abdur Rahman Khan, was living in Tashkent as a Russian political 'pensioner', and was suspected of touting for Russian support to muster an army to march on Kabul, and seize the throne his father, Mohammed Afzal, had once briefly held.

Russo-Turkish War

In April 1877, Russia declared war on Turkey over the 'Bulgarian issue', which quickly ended in a Russian victory, sealed by the Treaty of San Stefano, which the British government refused to recognise. The resultant wave of anti-Russian feeling in Britain brought the word 'jingoism' (meaning blustering patriotism) into the English vocabulary.

Treaty of Berlin

Russian reaction to the British anti-Russian attitude was to complete the occupation of the upper Oxus basin. In April 1878, three large Russian military columns formed up at Tashkent, Alexandrovsk and in the Ferghana valley respectively, preparing to move towards the Afghan region (*Hopkirk*). Bismarck, the German Chancellor, stepped in and persuaded the British and Russians to sign a 'peace with honour' agreement on 13 July 1878, which became known as

35

the Berlin Treaty. Accordingly, the three Russian military columns in Turkistan halted.

The Act of War

Meanwhile, an uninvited Russian diplomatic mission left Tashkent, to arrive at Kabul in August. With three large Russian military columns liable to march at any moment, the Amir was perforce polite and tactful. On hearing of the arrival of the Russian mission in Kabul, Lord Lytton, the Viceroy, demanded that the Amir receive a similar British mission. The Amir refused and, moreover, stated that if one were dispatched, it would be stopped by force. Thinking perhaps he would call the Amir's bluff, Lytton ordered a British diplomatic mission to set out for Kabul. On 21 November 1978, Faiz Mohammed Khan, Governor of what is now the Afghan frontier province of Nangrahar, turned the British mission back as it neared Ali Masjid, at the eastern entrance of the Khyber Pass, and so triggered off the Second Anglo-Afghan War.

19th Century Advancement

While in many respects warfare in the sub-continent and adjacent regions was much the same as it had been for years, significant 19th Century inventions had made their appearance. One was the telegraph system of communication that had reached Bombay and spread to major government and military centres, and meant instant, or nearly instant, communication between them and the India Office in London. British Viceroys, Cs-in-C, and commanders of field armies on active service, no longer had virtually unfettered discretion of action. The telegraph could be a spur, a curb or means of harsh criticism, but most significantly it enabled the British government to issue direct orders that had to be obeyed.

The military took to the telegraph system for its own use, and it became the practice of field columns as they advanced to erect telegraph lines behind them, and so remain in touch with higher authority and their comissariat. Also, it enabled HQ, India, and its subordinate HQs speedily to receive intelligence from a battlefield. Otherwise, the heliograph remained the quickest means of communication; while the age-old dispatch-rider still fulfilled basic communication needs.

The other 19th Century invention was the railway. The great

Indian railway system was fast taking shape, and was used whenever possible by the military for transportation purposes. However, away from the railway system, the military still had to rely upon animal transport, while infantry still marched on foot. A few narrow-gauge railways made their appearance, often snaking out from main railway lines, many constructed by the military to serve outlying garrisons.

Two other factors should be appreciated when comparing the first Anglo-Afghan War, with the second. First, in the second War, most of the troops, both British and Indian wore khaki-coloured uniforms, instead of their former 'red coats'. A drawback was that the new khaki-coloured pith helmet, the 'topee', blanched quickly in the sun, making it conspicuous in the field, which was a disadvantage when on active service.

The second factor was that in 1871, the British army had been issued with the breech-loading Martini-Henri rifle, and a little later most Indian units were equipped with the breech-loading Snider rifle. These weapons could fire several carefully-aimed shots a minute. The Afghan army remained mainly equipped with jezails and muzzle-loading rifles, although the Amir had obtained some 7,000 Snider rifles.

British High-Level Friction

Friction developed between the Viceroy, Lord Lytton, and the C-in-C, India, General Sir Frederick Haines, surfacing over the distribution of available troops and guns for the assembling Expeditionary Force. Exasperated, Lytton began to issue orders direct to military commanders, by-passing normal military channels of command, which not only caused internal friction, but made for confusion. The official reason for waging war against Amir Sher Ali was to demand an apology for a slight, and to establish a British diplomatic mission at Kabul.

Three British-Indian Columns

About 40,000 fighting men were distributed into three separate military columns, and several thousand more became involved in the logistic back-up to oppose the Afghan army, which still numbered about 50,000 men, with some 300 guns, most of the latter being retained at the Sherpur cantonment (*Army in India*). A word of

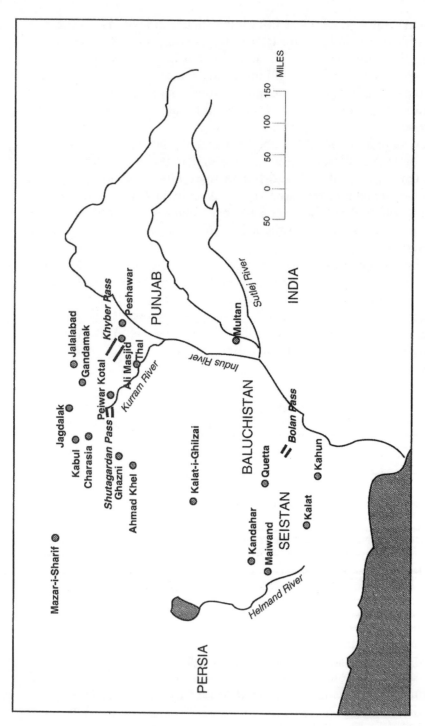

Second Anglo-Afghan War
1878-82 – Afghan Region

caution should be added regarding military strengths, as even official sources sometimes tend to vary slightly, and at times they seem to be too well 'rounded off' to be accepted as being absolutely accurate.

One column, the Kandahar Column, commanded by Lieutenant General Donald Stewart of the Bengal Army, and comprising about 17,000 troops with 92 guns, basically formed into two divisions, mustered at Multan, in the Punjab, with orders to move through the Bolan Pass to Quetta, and thence to Kandahar. This column, without undue hindrance, arrived at Kandahar on 8 January 1879, to find the Amir had just withdrawn his Afghan army garrison from that city.

Another column, the Kurram Column, commanded by Major General Frederick Roberts, also of the Bengal Army (who had won the Victoria Cross in the Indian Mutiny fighting), with about 7,000 men and 18 guns, was ordered to move into the Kurram Valley. The third column, the Peshawar Valley Field Force, commanded by Lieutenant General Sir Samuel Browne, of the Bengal Army (also an Indian Mutiny Victoria Cross recipient, who had lost an arm in action), consisting of 16,000 men and 48 guns, formed up at Peshawar, Browne is the acknowledged originator of the 'Sam Browne' belt still worn by British officers today.

Browne at the Khyber Pass

Browne's first task was to force the Khyber Pass, which was blocked by a fort at Ali Masjid, held by Faiz Mohammed Khan, who had about 4,000 Afghan soldiers and 24 guns (*Army in India*). It should be mentioned that estimates of Afghan numbers were made by the victors. Browne's column was first in action, the forward elements moving into the Pass towards the fort on 20 November 1878. After darkness fell, Browne sent out two flanking brigades, one to seize and hold the Rohtas Heights, which overlooked the fort, and the other to threaten Faiz Mohammed Khan's rear communication through the Pass, and to block his retreat. Both brigades got lost during the night, and when General Browne lined up his other formations ready to advance at dawn on the following day, they were nowhere to be seen.

An artillery duel broke out between opposing sides, which had little effect on the Ali Masjid fort, but caused British gunners to run out of ammunition, as ammunition-wagons could not get forward through a traffic jam of bullock-carts that had built up at the mouth of the Pass. Hordes of armed tribesmen began to appear along the crests of the Pass, causing the impatient Sir Louis Cavagnari (leading the diplomatic mission to Kabul) to urge Browne to attack quickly 'or they will attack us' (*Heathcote*).

In the afternoon, General Browne gave the order to advance towards the Ali Masjid fort, but progress was slow, and when it became obvious his infantry would not reach it in daylight, he gave orders to withdraw, his troops retiring in some confusion. Afghan artillery had pre-registered targets, and their precise shooting caused many British casualties, indicating that Afghan artillery skill had improved considerably.

At dawn the next morning (22 November) the two missing brigades reappeared above the Ali Masjid fort, frozen and tired. However, when he saw them, Faiz Mohammed Khan quickly withdrew his force, marching right back to Jalalabad. Browne followed slowly, reaching that city on 20 December, only to find that the Afghan army had pulled out the previous day. Lytton was said to be infuriated by Browne's conducting of the Khyber Pass action, referring to him as an 'incompetent' (*Heathcote*).

Roberts's Column

Meanwhile, Roberts's column had entered the Kurram Valley from Thal, just on the Indian side of the border, and the furthest point reached by the telegraph system. Having occupied most of it, he found that the two-mile-wide pass at the head of the valley was blocked by an Afghan army contingent, its defences based on a feature known as the Peiwar Kotal. Robert's intelligence was faulty, he being under the impression that the Afghan force was quite small, consisting of only a few units in the act of withdrawing before his advance. On 27 November, Roberts moved the major part of his force forward and made camp, but Afghan artillery open up the same evening, accurate shooting causing a British withdrawal.

On the night of 30 November, Roberts decided to take the larger part of his column on a right-flanking march over unknown, rough, frosty terrain, taking four guns carried on elephants. In the darkness, some of his units had difficulty in keeping direction, and in touch with each other. He also had a minor sepoy mutiny to handle on this night march, which he resolved by hanging a mutineer on the spot.

At dawn, on 1 December, it was seen that a deep ravine blocked Roberts's advance, but British artillery soon found their targets, including the Afghan camp site, causing the Afghans to withdraw.

Roberts won the Battle of Peiwar Kotal for the cost of only 21 dead (*Army in India*).

Death of Sher Ali

Realising that his new model army had not been able to prevent British military columns penetrating his country, Amir Sher Ali turned to the Russians for help. They refused, having no intention of becoming involved in war with the British in the Afghan region in mid-winter. In any case, the Russians considered the Amir to be too pro-British to be trusted. Advised by the Russians to make peace with the British, the Amir offered to accept a British diplomatic mission on a temporary basis, but did not apologise for turning one back previously; nor would he agree to grant an amnesty to the Afghans who had helped the Browne Column get through the Khyber Pass safely. Brushing aside the Amir's offer, the British advance on Kabul continued.

Now thoroughly alarmed, Amir Sher Ali demanded an audience with the Czar of Russia, but this too was refused, so the Amir moved northwards with the departing Russian diplomatic mission, halting at Mazar-i-Sharif. The Russians offered him political sanctuary at Tashkent, but he declined, as this would mean becoming a helpless 'pensioner'. Amir Sher Ali died suddenly at Mazar-i-Sharif on 21 February 1879. His son, Yakub Khan, who had previously been imprisoned by his father for raising revolt against him, was accepted in Kabul as the new Amir, being something of a compromise candidate.

Treaty of Gandamak

Back in India, Lord Lytton at first hesitated to treat with Amir Yakub, believing him to be anti-British and to lack popular support. Lytton seems to have been toying with the idea of 'Balkanising' the Afghan region, but eventually decided to negotiate with Amir Yakub. Negotiations came to fruition with the Treaty of Gandamak (a town some 30 miles south-west of Jalalabad), which was signed on 26 May 1879.

In return for promises of British money, arms and military support in case of need, Amir Yakub accepted British control over his foreign policy. It was agreed that there would be a British Resident (Political Officer) at Kabul; that all Afghans who had helped the British would be amnestied; and that the Amir could handle all domestic affairs without British interference. The telegraph line would be continued to Kabul; and both sides agreed to promote trade and commerce.

Territorially, the British did well out of the Treaty of Gandamak and enclaves around the Khyber Pass, the Kurram Valley, Quetta and the Bolan Pass, came under British influence. British-Indian troops were to leave all other parts of the Afghan region as soon as possible. However, their evacuation in places was delayed by an outbreak of cholera on the return route, which severely strained the military medical service.

Murder of British Resident

Sir Louis Cavagnari, with a small military escort, proceeded to Kabul to take up his post as British Resident, and for a while it seemed the Afghan region was settling down under the new Amir; but appearances were deceptive. On 3 September 1879, Afghan soldiers from the Herat Regiments came to the Bala Hissar, the Amir's partly rebuilt fortress palace, to collect three month's arrears of pay, only to be told that as revenues had yet to be collected, they would have to be content with one month's pay on account. This angered them; rioting ensued, and when General Daoud Khan, the Afghan C-in-C, appeared to try to calm them down, he was 'pulled from his horse and trampled underfoot' (*Heathcote*). Suddenly, the anger of the rioting Afghan soldiers turned against the British Resident; the military mob attacked the British Residency, and some Afghan soldiers fired artillery at the building. Cavagnari and his staff were killed.

British Reaction

When news of this disaster reached Lord Lytton, all British withdrawal from the Afghan region ceased. General Roberts's column, the only one readily available, became the avenging sword. Lytton's instructions to Roberts were brief and to the point—to march quickly to Kabul and execute all culprits. In private letters (*Heathcote*), Lytton urged him to extract heavy retribution, writing: 'There will be more clamour at home over the fall of a single head six months hence, than over a hundred heads that fall at once'. Roberts marched off with about 7,000 troops and 18 guns, the official fiction being that he was going to assist Amir Yakub restore order.

On 25 September, high-ranking envoys from Amir Yakub arrived at Roberts's camp, pleading that he should not march to Kabul, but instead let the Afghans settle their own internal problems. They were sharply rebuffed. Roberts marched on, and two days later reached the Shutagardan Pass to find Amir Yakub, Musa Jan (the Amir's son) and General Daoud Khan waiting for him. Again, Roberts was urged not to continue his march on Kabul, and again he refused abruptly. The Afghan VIPs remained in Roberts's camp.

Battle of Charasia

One of Amir Yakub's entourage, Nek Mohammed Khan, was sent back to Kabul, ostensibly to quieten the populace. Instead, he appeared a few days later with '13 regiments of Afghan troops' (*Heathcote*), and a horde of supporting armed tribesmen, to establish a line of defences along the Charasia Heights, about 10 miles due south of Kabul, thus blocking Roberts's advance. On the morning of 6 October 1879, Roberts launched his attack, a strong flanking assault along the line of the Heights, which was completely successful, gaining victory for the loss of only 18 men (*Army in India*). The new, rapidly withdrawing Afghan army, had yet to develop determination in defence. Nek Mohammed Khan fled to seek sanctuary in Turkistan.

General Roberts in Kabul

Roberts arrived at Kabul on 8 October, and settled his troops into the Sherpur cantonment, thereby taking possession of most of the Afghan army's guns and other military stores. Retribution was immediate and deadly; gallows were erected in front of the damaged Embassy Residency; rewards were offered for information about those who had borne arms against the British; and any Afghan within 10 miles of Kabul with a weapon in his possession was executed. General Roberts was later criticised for his actions by the British Liberal Press, which was opposed to this colonial war, and for executing Afghans whose only 'crime' had been to fight against an invading enemy.

Later, General Roberts would only admit to hanging 87 Afghans (*Forty-One Years in India*), justifying his acts by the barbaric way Afghans had treated British soldiers. In fact, however, a great many more Afghans must have been executed. On 13 October, General

Roberts held a Grand Victory March through Kabul. Two days previously Amir Yakub had abdicated, and was hurried off to become a 'pensioner' in India. Lord Lytton ordered Roberts to burn Kabul to the ground, but its solid masonry buildings did not lend themselves to such means of destruction. However, there was some bitter Afghan reaction, fanned by the Mullahs, and British requisitioning of crops to feed the troops, leading to local shortages and hardships, caused further resentment. Groups of armed tribesmen began to harass British-Indian troops as opportunity offered.

Roberts Besieged at Kabul

Meanwhile, a group of Ghilzais had attacked the small British garrison left at the Shutagardan Pass, but were driven off. Two further attacks were subsequently quashed. A British relief column arrived which dispersed the tribesmen, but the garrison was withdrawn into Kabul, where General Roberts was coming under hostile pressure.

Roberts's intelligence, not always reliable, indicated two Afghan armies, supported by armed tribesmen, were approaching Kabul. General Roberts first sent a strong contingent to deal with the one approaching from the north which, on 10 November, met and scattered the Afghan troops, but did not defeat them. The other Afghan army, commanded by Mohammed Jan Khan, estimated to be about 10,000-strong was approaching from the direction of Ghazni.

Roberts decided to make a pincer attack on the Ghazni army, using two brigades, one commanded by Brigadier General Baker, and the other by Brigadier General Macpherson. A small mounted force, of 300 lancers and four guns (*Heathcote*), commanded by Brigadier General Dunham Massy, was to remain outside the anticipated battle area. However, instead of following the route laid down for him, Dunham Massy took a short-cut across country, and stumbled on Mohammed Jan Khan's Ghazni army—which was not quite where Roberts had expected.

Dunham Massy fired his guns and conducted a fighting withdrawal. Hearing sounds of gunfire from an unexpected quarter, General Roberts, with a small escort, galloped across country to see what was happening, becoming involved with Dunham Massy's withdrawal, and only narrowly escaping with his life. British detachments withdrew back into the Sherpur cantonment.

Roberts blamed Dunham Massy for this considerable set-back, but many sympathised with him, claiming he had actually saved the British garrison at Kabul from disaster, as the Afghan Ghazni army had, in fact, slipped through Roberts's planned pincer movement. Roberts later admitted that he had no idea so many Afghan soldiers were marching against him (*Forty-One Years in India*).

The Afghan Ghazni army closed in on Kabul, basing itself on high ground overlooking the Sherpur cantonment. To pessimists, it seemed as though a repeat of the January 1841 disaster was about to occur. But this time the British leadership was of better quality, and fortune favoured them. Winter was setting in and many armed tribesmen were beginning to disappear to their home villages; the cantonment was well provisioned, and the defenders were armed with breech-loading Martini-Henri and Snider rifles.

The Afghans launched their major attack on 23 December 1879, and it was held by the steady and accurate fire of British and Indian riflemen. The fighting continued throughout the night until dawn, when the attackers began to withdraw. A British relief column was nearing Kabul, reaching the cantonment that day (24 December). The Afghan 'body count' was 'over 1,000 Afghan dead left on the battlefield' (*Heathcote*).

Elsewhere in the Afghan region, the Peshawar Valley Field Force, now under command of Major General Bright, had reached Gandamak. Lytton had written 'Thank God, we have got rid of Sir Samuel Browne at last' (*Heathcote*). At Kandahar, General Stewart had reformed his column, and in October had sent a large force to make a demonstration in the direction of Kalat-i-Ghilzai, the Ghilzai tribal centre, whose fortress commanded the route between Kandahar and Kabul.

Battle of Ahmad Khel

On 1 March 1880, responsibility for the defence of Kandahar was transferred to the Bombay Army, and General Stewart handed over to Lieutenant General Primrose. Stewart collected his Bengal Army units and began marching towards Kabul. Hordes of Ghilzai tribesmen harassed his flanks, and also systematically looted Hazara villages as they passed through them. Eventually, on 19 April Stewart found his route blocked by a force of some 15,000 soldiers and Ghilzais, at Ahmad Khel, some 20 miles west of Ghazni.

The Afghans launched an attack; in the fighting, elements of

British-Indian formations gave way, and some units had to 'form square', the traditional last-ditch defensive tactic. However, the day was won by disciplined shooting of Martini-Henri and Snider rifles. The Afghan body count was 'over 800', for the loss of '17 men killed' (*Army in India*). The Afghans later admitted they had lost over 1,100 men in this battle, a reversal of customary estimates of Afghan casualties, when British commanders were sometimes suspected of slight exaggeration. Stewart wrote: 'Some of the cavalry did not do so well, nor did some of the other troops'. (*Heathcote*) On 21 April, Stewart reached Ghazni, which surrendered after only slight resistance. He then marched on to Kabul where, being senior to General Roberts, he took command.

Viceroy Lord Ripon

A general election in Britain brought about a change of government, and a new Viceroy for India. He was Lord Ripon, who arrived at Simla in June 1880. He decided to withdraw the British-Indian Expeditionary Force from the Afghan region completely, no doubt influenced by economic factors. The original cost estimate for the campaign had been the equivalent (calculated in rupees) of about £5 million, and was already exceeding £17 million.

The situation in the Afghan region was that a strong British-Indian force was in Kabul, while to its north hovered the Russian-supported candidate for the Amirship, Abdur Rahman, with a reputed 200 riflemen, gathering tribal support; and Herat was held by Ayub Khan (a son of Amir Sher Ali), who also harboured designs on the Amirship; while Sher Ali Khan (not to be confused with Amir Sher Ali), a nephew of Amir Dost Mohammed, had been installed as Wali (Governor) at Kandahar by Lord Lytton.

Battle of Maiwand

In April, Wali Sher Ali Khan's Afghan troops at Kandahar mutinied, and the mutinous troops, under Nur Mohammed Khan, took common cause with Ayub Khan, of Herat. The Wali asked for British assistance, and General Primrose, at Kandahar, sent one (of his two) brigades, under Brigadier General Burrows, to restore the situation, but instructed him not to go beyond the Helmand River without further orders.

Burrows's brigade clashed with the much stronger Afghan force, led by Ayub Khan, which had joined up with the mutineers, led by Nur Mohammed Khan, on 27 July (1880), near the village of Maiwand. Outnumbered in men and guns, Burrows's brigade began to withdraw, a withdrawal that became a rout and then a disaster; his force was pursued for some miles before Afghan discipline snapped, and Afghans broke off to return to loot the British baggage train. At the Battle of Maiwand, Burrows lost over '1,000 dead and two guns' (*Army in India*).

On 8 August, Ayub Khan and his Afghan troops, together with Nur Mohammed Khan's mutineers, reached Kandahar, and laid siege to that city, during the course of which General Primrose ejected the civilian population, estimated to number about 15,000. A large British sortie was made from the Kandahar garrison, on 16 August, which was ambushed near the village of Deh Kwia, at a cost to the British-Indian force of over 100 lives. Survivors scrambled back into the city in disorder.

Kabul to Kandahar

Lord Ripon recognised Abdur Rahman as Amir, on 31 July 1880, and gave orders for the final evacuation of Kabul, which got under way on 11 August. The new Amir kept his promise to do his best to ensure a safe and uninterrupted passage for British-Indian troops to Peshawar, and officially only one sepoy was lost in this withdrawal.

Previously, on 8 August, General Roberts had formed a military column, of about 10,000 troops and, with the best pack-animals available, was ordered to march rapidly to relieve Kandahar. Anxious to restore his military reputation, which had been somewhat dented by events in Kabul, Roberts pushed his column hard, reaching Ghazni on 15 August. He then moved on to reach Kalat-i-Ghilzai a week later, arriving before Kandahar on 31 August.

General Roberts's march from Kabul to Kandahar, 313 miles in 20 days, was something of a military record, considering the terrain and the fact that that heavily-laden infantry had to march on foot. Some of his contemporaries, perhaps a little envious, (professional jealousy not being unknown amongst professionally-orientated sepoy generals), thought he was making too much fuss about this exploit of endurance, pointing out that the march had taken place at harvest time, when many tribesmen, who would otherwise have been harassing him, were in their villages gathering the crops. Roberts found the garrison at Kandahar demoralised (*Forty-One Years in*

India); the British flag had not been flown for days, and he complained that 'not a Band turned out to play us in, not a cheer was raised to welcome us' (*Heathcote*).

As General Roberts's column approached Kandahar, Ayub Khan's Afghan forces had withdrawn to take up positions on a feature called the Baba Wali Kotal, near the village of Pir Paimal. On the afternoon of 31 August, Roberts sent out strong reconnaissance detachments, which accurately located the Afghan dispositions. Without waiting for the expected arrival of a military column from the Bombay Army, (*Heathcote*) General Roberts, an officer of the Bengal Army, launched his attack the following day. Once again, Afghan troops were not at their best in defence, and the day was carried, largely because of the effect of Martini-Henri and Snider rifles. The Afghan 'body count' was over '1,200 men for the loss of 40 soldiers and sepoys' (*Army in India*). The chastened Ayub Khan withdrew with the remnants of his Afghan troops and tribesmen towards Herat.

The Final Evacuation

Wali Sher Ali Khan of Kandahar was persuaded to accept a comfortable exile in India, and Lord Ripon agreed that Kandahar should revert to the suzerainty of Amir Abdur Rahman. The Amir's appointed Governor arrived at Kandahar on 16 April 1881, and the British-Indian garrison marched out on 21 April. It was officially stated that the Second Anglo-Afghan War formally ended on 23 May 1881, and that the whole of the British-Indian Expeditionary force had been withdrawn from the Afghan region.

The human military cost must have been considerable, but we do not seem to know exactly what it was. One authority (*Hanna*) put the casualties at about 40,000, but did not categorise them or say how this figure was arrived at. Another authority (*Robson*) wrote: 'I have found no detailed record of casualties on the British side'. It seems that somehow, someone at GHQ. India was at fault. In addition, the loss of thousands of camels and draught bullocks was an economic disaster for the local areas from which they had been requisitioned.

The ostensible British aim, to install a British Resident in Kabul, was not accomplished, as Amir Abdur Rahman refused to accept one. Neither did the British accomplish their underlying aim of expanding their influence and trade into the region.

Concluding Comments

In the Second Anglo-Afghan War, as in the First, the British-Indian Expeditionary Force had its triumphs in battle, its failures and disasters, with reputations of Generals being enhanced or ruined. General ('Bobs') Roberts, who had a flair for publicity, came out of this war as the popular hero, to the British public at least, even if less so to his brother sepoy generals. Certainly, Roberts's presence on the battlefield seemed to inspire confidence, although he also could be less than generous at times, as the unfortunate Dunham Massy could vouch for. The real winners of this war were the breech-loading Martini-Henri and Snider rifles, and the disciplined direction under which they were employed.

On the British side, the leash on Viceroys, authorities in India, and Generals in the field, was tightened by the telegraph system which linked them to the British government of the day and its policies. Handicaps were high-level hesitation, lack of decisiveness at times, a cost-conscious attitude, and the deceit of ignoring conventional channels of military command.

On the Afghan side there was a lack of positive direction, compounded by top-level intrigue. This war was fought much as the First had been. In effect, the fledgling Afghan Army barely existed, being untrained and lacking in discipline, which nullified the possession of the small number of breech-loading rifles. Afghan commanders still basically relied upon their household troops, while much of the other military muscle consisted of Jezailchis and armed tribesmen. Afghan senior military leadership was undeveloped and unco-ordinated.

3

The Third Anglo-Afghan War: 1919

Amir Abdur Rahman consolidated and ruled his country with an iron hand, crushing dissidence with terrible cruelty, becoming known as the 'Assassin'. He stamped out the periodic crime waves that swept through his provinces; criminals were either stoned to death or impaled on stakes, while sometimes robbers were hung in cages near the scene of their crime and left to die of starvation. Trying to encourage trade, *Bazaaris* (merchants) caught cheating had their ears severed and displayed above their stalls.

Amir Abdur Rahman also tried to improve his Afghan army and to replace the 'forced levy' from villages under which every eight men had to provide and support a conscript for two years, a system by which soldiers were properly paid, fed and clothed. It was said that he also obtained money to pay his soldiers by robbing trade caravans in Turkistan, and imposing levies on merchants. Conscripts still came mainly from the non-Pathan groups, and many of them, due to poverty, stayed on in the army. A Pathan officer class began to develop. The army acquired more breech-loading rifles, but a very tight control was maintained over ammunition, very few rounds being issued to soldiers, and hardly any for training purposes.

The Afghan-Russian Agreement: 1885

Afghan borders with both Russia and British India were settled during Amir Abdur Rahman's reign. The Russians were in the final phases of colonising Turkistan, and Merv was occupied by them in 1881. As Russian influence and annexation crept toward Afghan territory, disputes arose with the Amir, and on 30 March 1885, Russian military forces attacked the oasis on Pendjdeh, claimed by the Afghans, killing two Afghan soldiers and wounding many more. The Amir sought British military aid, but the British government, reluctant to fight a campaign against the Russians north of the Hindu Kush, declined.

Meanwhile, an Anglo-Russian Boundary Commission (1884-85) was at work, and as tension between Afghans and Russians subsided, the Afghan-Russian Agreement was signed in September (1885); this defined their common frontier, which was mainly along the Oxus river.

The Durand Line: 1893

Next, under a Convention signed by Indian Administrator, Sir Mortimer Durand, in Kabul in 1893, the frontier between Afghanistan and British India was defined by the so-called 'Durand Line'. The Amir's territory could now be more properly referred to as 'Afghanistan', rather than the more indefinite 'Afghan region'. Under this Convention the areas of Chagai, Baluchistan, New Chaman and Waziristan were ceded to the British. The western Afghan border had been defined in an agreement with the Persians in 1857 (and a later one in 1904).

The Durand Line extended for about 1,500 miles, running from the Pamir mountain range in the north, to the Arabian Sea in the south, in the mountainous northern and central sectors cutting through and dividing tribal regions. There are over 200 mountain-pass border crossing points, the best known being the Khyber Pass. Neither Britain nor Russia wanted their respective colonial territories to march with each other in the Turkistan-Afghanistan region, and so a narrow strip of remote mountainous territory, basically an elongated valley lying between the Hindu Kush and the Pamirs, and known as the Wakhan Strip, was given to Afghanistan, a gift only reluctantly accepted by the Amir.

Anglo-Afghan Treaty: 1905

Amir Abdur Rahman died in 1905, and, unusually for Afghanistan, was peacefully succeeded by his son, Habibullah. Shortly afterwards the Viceroy of India, Lord Curzon, carried out an administrative reorganisation of north-west British-Indian territory, creating the North West Frontier Province, much of which became 'tribal territory'. Regular troops were withdrawn from these areas and replaced by locally-enlisted paramilitary militias, commanded by British officers, and armed and trained as light infantry.

Amir Habibullah continued a selective friendship with Britain, but was more cautious in his relations with the Russians. The visit of a British mission to Kabul resulted in the Anglo-Afghan Treaty of 1905, confirming British control over Afghan foreign policy, in return for a large cash subsidy and permission to import arms for the Afghan army through British India. A Tri-National Convention, of Afghanistan, Britain and Russia, settling their respective boundaries with Persia, and with each other, and confirming previous agreements, was signed in 1907. British-Russian relations were improving.

First World War: 1914-18

During the First World War, probably because the Amir was not sure which Great Power would win, Afghanistan managed to remain neutral. Amir Habibullah did receive a Turkish military mission, accompanied by a German officer, which arrived in Kabul in September 1915. The Turks tried to persuade the Amir to join a Muslim *Jihad* against Britain, Russia and France, but he found excuses for not becoming involved in such an enterprise, fearful the end result would be failure. It was said that Habibullah did agree to launch an attack on India, but only if the Turks produced a large army to help him, together with military aid and arms for his Afghan army, and a very large financial reward—virtually impossible demands. In frustration, the Turkish military mission left Kabul in May 1916. German attempts to influence the Amir also failed.

The Russian Revolutions: 1917

The Russian Revolutions of 1917, and the accession to power by a Bolshevik government, with new revolutionary policies, brought a period of instability to the Turkistan region, so recently 'pacified' by Russian arms, and caused a rash of nationalism to develop amongst the Khanates. In October 1917, the 'Protectorates' of Khiva,

Kokand, Tashkent and Ferghana declared their independence from Soviet rule, which caused them all to be classed as 'counter-revolutionaries'.

The peoples of the Khanates were still tribal, some largely nomadic, with only a small proportion engaged in stock-breeding and cotton-growing. An estimated five per cent of the people were Russian, being mainly officials and technocrats, railway and government employees, and traders. By this time the Russian railway system had extended from Krasnovodsk (on the Caspian Sea), through Merv, Bokhara and Samarkand, to terminate at Tashkent, which enabled Red Army formations to be quickly brought into Turkistan, to bring the counter-revolutionaries to heel. An idea was floated in Turkistan to form a 'League of Free Muslim States in Central Asia'. Amir Habibullah showed an interest in this project, and discussed the matter with the Khan of Bokhara. In early 1919, Habibullah began to question British control over his foreign policy.

Amir Amanullah

On 19 February 1919, Amir Habibullah was murdered in his tent on a hunting expedition by a Colonel in the Afghan army, the motive most probably stemming from a blood-feud, although there were rumours that the Soviets were responsible, because they wanted to prevent Habibullah lending his weight to the tentative League of Free Muslim States in Central Asia.

Quick succession changes followed. Nasrullah Khan, brother of Habibullah, assumed the title of Amir, having obtained the support of the nominal Heir Apparent, Inayatullah Khan, both of whom were in Jalalabad, the winter capital, at the time. However, Amanullah (Habibullah's son), being Governor of Kabul, and having the treasury, arsenal and a large part of the Afghan army under his direct control, also declared himself to be Amir. Lacking military means, both Nasrullah Khan and Inayatullah Khan backed down, and both went to Kabul to give their allegiance to Amanullah.

Amir Amanullah was young (26 years of age), forceful, energetic and a convinced nationalist. He appointed as Foreign Minister (a new appointment in Afghanistan) Mohammed Tarzi, his father-in-law, also a dedicated nationalist, who had been educated in Turkey. Mohammed Tarzi had founded Afghanistan's only newspaper, *Siraj-i-Akbar*. The Amir appointed General Salah Mohammed, also a dedicated nationalist, to be the new C-in-C of the Afghan army.

On 3 March 1919, Amir Amanullah wrote to the Viceroy of India, announcing his accession as Amir of 'Free and Independent Afghanistan', and offering to negotiate a commercial treaty with the British. At a Durbar in Kabul on 13 April, Amir Amanullah declared Afghanistan to be 'fully independent, both internally and externally'. He appointed an Ambassador to the Khan of Bokhara (then struggling for independence against the Soviet Red Army), and said he would also send one to Persia.

British-Indian Weaknesses

During the First World War, the Indian army (excluding British units and elements) had swelled to a strength of over half-a-million men, by recalling reservists and enlisting volunteers 'for the duration only'. In early 1919, although seemingly strong in numbers, this army was weak in capability, as the reservists and 'duration only' volunteers were in the process of demobilisation; 'over 124 battalions and 80 squadrons' were still overseas (*Official Account*); many units were dispersed on internal security duties, and some had already reverted to the pre-1914 custom of taking 'block leave' for a couple of months or so, the sepoys being dispersed to their villages. It was said that 'while India was full of soldiers, they were chiefly to be found in the depots' (*Heathcote*).

A wave of nationalism, bringing with it riots and disorders, swept across the sub-continent in March and April 1919, affecting especially large cities, and troops had to be deployed 'in aid of the civil power'. The most notorious incident occurred at Amritsar, in the Punjab, on 11 April (1919), when Brigadier General Dyer ordered Indian sepoys to open fire on a prohibited assembly which had refused to disperse. Some 375 people were killed.

This heavy death toll shocked public opinion both in Britain and India, and Dyer was mildly censored for over-reacting. However, his supporters believed his action had prevented the outbreak of another Indian Mutiny, arising from widespread discontent in the Indian army. It was said that if similar firm, decisive action had been taken initially at Meerut in 1857, it would have prevented the Indian Mutiny spreading.

The Afghan Army: 1919

With new-found boldness in foreign policy matters, Amir Amanullah wrote to the Viceroy in India, criticising British handling of the internal security situation in India in general, and at Amritsar in particular, and said he was moving troops towards his frontier with India to ensure the virus of discontent did not seep into his country.

In early 1919, the Afghan army, now wearing khaki uniform for active service, was still about 50,000-strong (*Official Account*), consisting of 38,000 infantrymen, armed with modern Martini-Henri or Snider rifles, formed into 78 battalions, about 8,000 'sabres', or cavalrymen, in 21 units, and about 4,000 artillerymen to serve some 260 breech-loading guns, mainly the Krupp 75mm (maximum range—4,500 yards) and the 7-pounder (maximum range—3,500 yards). Only a few modern guns were horse-drawn, and most of the artillery pieces still had to be moved in the old traditional way, yoked to oxen or carried on elephants.

The Afghan army had a few old Gardiner machine-guns, (operated by turning a handle), and plenty of old muzzle-loaded cannons. Additionally, the arsenal at Kabul contained 15,000 small bore rifles and 400,000 Martinis, the Afghans having taken full advantage of the Treaty of 1905 to stock up. The arsenal was able to repair weapons, produce shells and ammunition (but not fuzes), and a 'Black Powder' factory at Bawali, near Jalalabad, produced sufficient gunpowder for the army's needs; but cordite cartridges had to be imported through India.

A rank structure had been established but the shortage of professionally-trained medium and junior grade officers, and the barely-trained non-commissioned officer class, were decided weaknesses. There was still no higher formation than the battalion, which averaged about 500 men, and so any assembly of military force was just a collection of battalions and cavalry units, without co-ordination. The few staff officers were mainly at GHQ at Kabul. Afghanistan had been divided into 10 military districts, each with a small detachment of troops with an internal security role, while by far the largest part of the Afghan army remained at Kabul.

Two Afghan military practices are of interest. The first was that along the main routes in the country there were fortified supply depots every 12 miles or so (a day's march apart) which, in theory at least, contained supplies for a given number of soldiers on the march for a given number of days, thus enabling fairly large bodies of troops to be deployed quickly. It is not known how thoroughly this system of provisioning was maintained, and inspected.

The other practice was that all camels had to be registered, to be subject to requisitioning as required, it being said that this system worked better than the conscription of men. Reserves continued to be armed tribesmen, mustered as required. In 1912, when an insurrection broke out at Khost (in Paktia province) against Amir Habibullah, about 4,000 regular soldiers, 18,000 armed tribesmen and 8,600 camels were mustered to march off to quell the rising, relying on the relay of provisioning posts of food, fodder and ammunition.

The introduction of modern, long-range rifles had caused a change in Afghan military tactics, away from the traditional massed wild charge designed to overwhelm the enemy quickly, after which control was lost and looting became the first priority. New tactics concentrated on individual concealment, engaging the enemy at a distance, and the maximum use of artillery.

British India: Arms and Morale

In India, all units, both British and Indian, were now armed with the .303 Lee Enfield rifle, which had amply proved its value for rapid aimed fire in Europe during the First World War, supplemented by the Vickers machine-gun and the rapid-fire Lewis gun. Artillery used during the 1919 war was mainly the 15-pounder gun, and 4.5-inch and 3.7-inch howitzers. Artillery was still basically British-manned, although there were a number of Indian-manned mountain batteries (the Indian artillery arm was not reformed as such until 1936).

Communication in the field was by telegraph and field-telephone, supplemented still by the heliograph, signalling flags and the dispatch courier, both mounted and on foot. As regards recent inventions; there were no tanks in India at the beginning of 1919, but there were a few motor-transport companies, some armoured car squadrons, and a score or so of RAF aircraft. The Afghans had none of these military advantages.

Previous wars fought by the British in this part of the world had been waged by long-service British soldiers, well-trained and well-disciplined, with officers thirsting for action and acclaim; the same could be said in general for Indian troops, although there had been exceptions. Morale, therefore, had been invariably high. But in 1919, there was a difference: morale tended to vary from unit to unit, both British and Indian, and was usually lower in those with a large proportion of re-called reservists and 'duration only' volunteers. Many British soldiers were chafing at the shortage of shipping

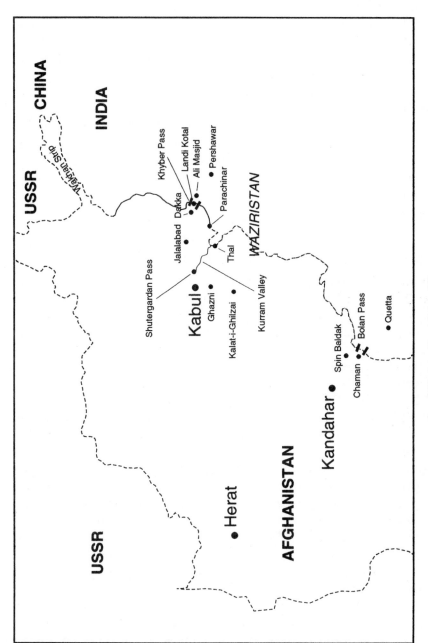

Third Anglo-Afghan War
1919

available to take them home, while Indian sepoys, also wanting to go home quickly, were chafing at demobilisation delays.

When the Third Anglo-Afghan War began, homeward-oriented British personnel were less than enthusiastic at having to fight against a country of no interest to them, and which certainly could be no threat to Britain. Not all British infantry units in India had been trained, or acclimatised, in mountain warfare. A large number of British troops from the campaign in Mesopotamia, on their way home when this war was about to begin, had been detained in India due to shortage of shipping, and were formed into Special Service Battalions, one brigade of which was sent north-west to Rawalpindi, only to be broken up as detachments were drafted to reinforce other units.

The Afghans Move First

On 3 May 1919, a detachment of Afghan troops crossed the border into British-Indian territory to occupy the small village of Bagh and the water springs outside the village of Tangi, which gave them control of the water supply to the pumping station below in the Khyber Pass, and also the water supply to Landi Kotal, just to the east, where two companies of Indian troops were stationed. A few Indian labourers were killed, and the Third Anglo-Afghan War had begun.

It is doubtful whether Amir Amanullah really wanted a war with the British. It is more probable that he had not thought the consequences through, and simply wanted an abrasive frontier situation to develop, to divert the minds of his own people who were becoming restive under his modernisation projects. He had already imprisoned Nasrullah Khan (soon to die in prison), and a few other opposition diehards. He was also probably satisfying his own ego by proving to himself that he really was, and could act as, an independent Ruler.

Amanullah was also hoping his action would encourage 'revolutionary activists' in India, and make the situation more difficult for the British authorities, who would, he hoped, soon have a massive internal security problem on their hands, with no time or resources to spare to muster an army to march against him. In fact, the opposite occurred, as even revolutionary activists in India, however anxious to get rid of the British, did not relish the thought of being 'liberated' by wild Afghan tribesmen, whom they suspected of being far more interested in loot than furthering the cause of decolonisation.

First Battle of Bagh

Contingents mustered for the Third Anglo-Afghan War became known as the 'Trans-Indus Force'. Meanwhile, Afghan soldiers remained in possession of Bagh and the Tangi Springs, their main Northern Army Group, with artillery, being at Dakka, some nine miles to the rear. On 7 May, a British battalion arrived at Landi Kotal, which was only about a mile from the forward Afghan positions, and well within range of Afghan guns. The British unit had been carried up from Peshawar in 67 motor transport vehicles (*Official Account*). Rushing troops into action in motor vehicles was an innovation in this part of the world.

The battle began at dawn on 9 May, when the British unit began an attack to recover Bagh and the Tangi Springs, but as the troops moved forward a large gathering of hostile armed tribesmen appeared on the northern flank, and companies of the unit had to be detached to take action against them. The remainder of the unit continued the advance and succeeded in seizing Tangi Springs, but failed to take Bagh and its adjacent crags. Finding the Afghan positions had been reinforced, they had to 'dig-in' to hold what ground they had gained, only managing to do so as RAF aircraft appeared overhead to bomb the Afghan positions.

The Royal Air Force

A little earlier, on 6 May, three RAF planes had made their first reconnaissance over Afghan territory, returning with bullet holes in their fuselages. The next RAF raid, (9 May) was on the Afghan camp at Dakka, where Afghan officers were distributing rifles, ammunition, blankets and other stores to Pathan tribesmen. When the RAF aircraft appeared, the Afghan officers ran for cover—to emerge when the planes had gone, to find the Pathans had taken all the rifles and other materials and disappeared into the hills.

In this raid '1½ tons of bombs were dropped and 1,151 rounds of ammunition fired. Enemy casualties were estimated to number about 600 men. The Afghan GOC (Naib Salar Khan) Governor of the Jalalabad Military District, was wounded, losing a foot, and his brother, the Malik (recognised elder), was amongst the dead' (*RAF*

Sources). The aircraft were from No. 31 Squadron, and had flown from an airfield at Risalpur, about 30 miles east of Peshawar.

The RAF were using BE-2C Bristol Fighter aircraft, which had a maximum speed of 72mph at 6,500 ft, a ceiling of 20,000ft, and could remain airborne for about 3½ hours. Due to the plane's slow rate of climb after take-off, RAF pilots soon had the unusual experience of being shot at by Afghan rifle-fire from mountain crest-lines above them.

At the request of the Viceroy, a small detachment of the Royal Flying Corps (RFC), (which became the RAF on 1 April 1918), had arrived in India late in 1914, consisting of five Bristol Fighters, but owing to priority demands for pilots and aircraft for the European theatre, the build-up in India was very slow. Already, RFC Bristol Fighters had taken part in operations against tribesmen in both Baluchistan and Waziristan during 1916-17.

By early 1919, there were about 24 serviceable Bristol Fighters in India, then already considered obsolete for European warfare (*RAF Sources*). The RAF in India complained continually of 'parsimonious' support, mentioning shortages such as lack of tyres. There was also high-level argument as to whether RAF aircraft were 'in support' or 'under command', as well as the perhaps more understandable lack of appreciation of the potential strategic and tactical uses of military aircraft. It is likely that few, if any, British senior officers in India in those days had ever flown in an aircraft, and accordingly had only novelty interest in them.

Second Battle of Bagh

Major General Fowler (GOC, 1st Division) arrived at Landi Kotal and took command of the situation. Reinforcements were brought up by motor transport, and by 11 May, he had assembled six infantry battalions, 18 field guns and 22 machine-guns (*Official Account.*) An attack was launched at dawn that day, with a battalion covering either flank, the other units moving forward in the centre against Afghan positions at Bagh, a bayonet charge driving them from their forward lines of 'sangars' (small stone and rock-built defensive positions). One battalion charged right through to capture the Afghan artillery in the rear, and as the Afghans withdrew they were bombed by the RAF. The whole Afghan camp was seized for the cost of eight dead, while the 'body count' of Afghans, who also lost five guns and all their transport animals, was 65. (*Official Account*).

Peshawar Uprising Pre-empted

Amir Amanullah, who seems to have had a taste for psychological and insurrectionary warfare, planned a mass uprising of the Pathan population in Peshawar on 8 May, to coincide with his abrasive frontier activity. His chief secret agent was Ghulam Haidar, the Afghan Postmaster at Peshawar, who was already covertly distributing subversive literature to 'nationalist' leaders and agitators in India, explaining the Amir's cause, and urging them to rise up against British rule, in conjunction with the Amir's offensive. It was reputed that Ghulam Haidar had already gathered several thousand young activists, ready to cause disturbances and manipulate the mobs. Pathan tribal elders had become suspicious of Amir Amanullah, and were disinclined to join him in raising civil insurrection, but there were plenty of willing young hotheads.

Forewarned, on 7 May, the authorities forestalled the scheduled uprising by placing detachments of troops at each of the 16 gates of the walled city (which is about two miles in length and averages about 1,200 yards in width) during the afternoon siesta period. Water supplies were cut off, and an ultimatum given that unless Ghulam Haidar, and other named suspected Indian revolutionaries, were handed over to the police, the people of Peshawar would remain confined within their walled city without drinking water. By evening all the 'wanted' men had surrendered and, with the aid of armoured cars, the planned uprising was pre-empted. The following day motor transport companies brought in more reinforcements.

The Afghan War Plan

Once committed, Amir Amanullah called a Loya Jirga, a Grand Assembly of tribal and Islamic leaders and representatives of other groups, at which he declared a *Jihad* against Britain, promising amongst other things that Karachi would become an Afghan port. This was only the third such Loya Jirga in Afghan history, the first having been 1121, and the second in 1747, when Ahmad Shah had proclaimed himself 'King'. Amanullah's 'war plan' was to advance on three fronts against British India; through the Khyber Pass with his Northern Army Group, commanded by General Salah Mohammed, his new C-in-C; down the Kurram Valley with his Central Army Group, commanded by General Nadir Khan, his recently superseded C-in-C; and against Quetta, with his Southern

Army Group, commanded by Abdul Kudus Khan, his Chief Minister.

The Battle for Dakka

In the north, skirmishing along the frontier line began on 13 May, and General Fowler sent an infantry brigade into the Khyber Pass which, as it moved forward, established a line of protective pickets along the crests on either side, continuing until the open Dakka plain was reached. A complete cavalry brigade rode through that part of the Khyber Pass on 15 May, without opposition, to establish camp near Dakka, a large village, and was joined by other infantry formations. The camp site had been selected for its logistical, rather than its tactical, advantages, and was vulnerable to Afghan artillery fire. Fowler himself rode through the Pass, criticised the camp's location, and ordered that it be moved to a more secure and easily defended position.

On 17 May, a cavalry scouting party ran into a large group of Afghan soldiers advancing to attack the Dakka camp. The British cavalry charged the Afghans, momentarily halting them. This was later written up as the 'last cavalry charge in action of the British army', it being thought that machine-guns had made such tactics obsolete. By evening Afghan shells were striking inside the British camp area, horse-lines especially being targeted. Many horses were hit and others broke lose to gallop off into the hills. Eighty-seven horses were lost in all, as well as 10 soldiers (*Official Account*). The British camp was subjected to sniper fire throughout the night.

It was decided to attack two positions from which Afghan guns were firing the following morning at dawn. Two infantry units made a night march which brought them to the foot of the crests by daylight, when they began a slow climb. When the soldiers were within a 100 yards of the crests, Afghan defenders opened rapid and accurate fire, catching them completely by surprise, and in the open. Attacking troops hastily scrambled down the hillsides, while six guns supporting the British attack ran out of ammunition.

Motor transport rushed reinforcements and ammunition to the battlefield from Landi Kotal, enabling the assaults on both Afghan-held positions to be resumed. In the course of this fighting one unit mistakenly attacked the HQ of another. The RAF came into action, and both positions were successfully stormed. Harassed by aircraft, Afghan troops rapidly decamped, abandoning seven guns. British casualties were 28 killed and 137 wounded (*Official Account*).

The Khyber Rifles

During the fighting for Bagh and Dakka, British forces had come under occasional sniper fire from the locally-recruited paramilitary, Pathan militia, the 'Khyber Rifles', whose attitude was considered to be unreliable, and even hostile. Further trouble was curtailed by disarming and instantly dismissing many militiamen. It was suspected that many were about to desert with their rifles, as a rumour had spread amongst them that the Khyber Rifles were to lead the next assault, when British guns would be turned on them.

The situation in the Khyber Pass became unstable as groups of armed tribesmen began ambushing small parties of British and Indian troops, sniping at them from a distance, and cutting telegraph and field-telephone lines. The mood, both in London and New Delhi, became aggressive, and it was decided to send a British-Indian force to occupy and annex Jalalabad, to deprive the British-Indian tribal areas of subversive support from fellow Pathans on the western side of the Durand Line.

An infantry division and a cavalry brigade were detailed for this task, but there were provisioning problems due to shortage of motor transport, as this task force needed rations and stores for three months; and there were communication problems, radio transmission being in its infancy in this region. It was not expected the task force would be able to march until the end of May at the earliest.

Meanwhile, the narrow gorge in the Khyber Pass approaching the Ali Masjid fort had become the scene of a perpetual traffic jam of both animal-drawn and motor transport, through which soldiers on horse or foot had to struggle. The disbanding of the Khyber Rifles caused the system of local militia policing in the region to collapse, and the area was soon swarming with aggressive groups of anti-British armed tribesmen.

The Southern Front

When the war began, the Afghan army on the southern front had five units of infantry and one of cavalry stationed at Kandahar, two units of infantry at Kalat-i-Ghilzai and one at Spin Baldak. The Afghan commander of the Southern Army Group, Abdul Kudus Khan, was reported to be on his way with reinforcements of 1,500 men, but seemed tardy in journeying. On the British side, Lieutenant General Wapshare had an infantry division (4th Division), and a cavalry brigade at Quetta; and two infantry brigades at New Chaman, and was well positioned to block any Afghan thrust towards the Bolan Pass. One RAF squadron, No. 114, was allocated to the southern front.

Wapshare decided on aggressive action. His first target was the Afghan fort at Spin Baldak, situated on a commanding mound, impressive in size and design, and originally constructed in the reign of Amir Ahmad Shah. Its one main weakness was that its walls could not withstand modern artillery bombardment. Spin Baldak was just six miles inside Afghan territory, opposite New Chaman, and roughly half way between Kandahar and Quetta.

Battle for Spin Baldak

Wapshare began his attack at dawn on 27 May, when two cavalry units and a small group with machine-guns made a detour to get behind Spin Baldak to cut its communications with Kandahar. Then his main attacking force of four infantry units, some with machine-guns, advanced under a 'creeping barrage', a technique operated, and perfected, many times on European battlefields in the First World War. One British Territorial infantry unit, on coming under Afghan artillery fire, got down on the ground and 'would not respond' (*Official Account*). Another regular unit had to be quickly rushed forward to take its place in the actual assault, unfortunately only to be hit by an RAF bomb, which breached part of the wall of the fort, but also killed 15 attacking troops.

After a six-hour artillery bombardment, the assault was successful, and the fort was seized and occupied. Of about 600 Afghan soldiers holding it, 186 were killed and 176 taken prisoner, the remainder making their escape by moving between two cavalry units, each of which thought this route was the responsibility of the other. (*Official Account*). Wapshare left three infantry units at Spin Baldak, and withdrew the remainder of his force to New Chaman. He had, however, been only allocated two RAF aircraft.

The Central Front

The British commander on the Trans-Indus Central Front was Major General Eustace, who basically had four infantry units, with sub-units of cavalry, engineers and artillery (four mountain guns and 3-inch mortars). Many of his troops were young, inexperienced and anxious to return home in one piece. Facing him was General Nadir Khan, commanding the Afghan Central Army Group, still trusted by Amir Amanullah in military matters, with about 3,000 soldiers, mainly based on Matun, an Afghan border town on the Kaiku River, which flows southwards to join the Kurram River.

Not having sufficient force to hold the line of the Tochi River, some 30 miles south of Matun, Eustace decided to reinforce the British outpost at Parachinar (near the Peiwar Kotal), and to strengthen his garrison at Thal, on the Kurram River. Waziristan territory just to the south of Thal, was policed by locally enlisted North Waziri and South Waziri militias, which had already shown signs of unreliability.

Without consulting the political authorities, Eustace withdrew all the Waziri militiamen from their posts, ordering the destruction of all government stores they could not bring in with them. Already, many Waziri militiamen had deserted with their arms to join General Nadir Khan's Central Army Group, a few even shooting their British officers. By the evening of 26 May, the whole of Waziristan was in open revolt. Major General Eustace was roundly condemned for his decision, but judging by the example set by the Khyber Rifles, had he not done so the situation might have become much worse.

The Battle for Thal

RAF aircraft were dispatched from Risalpur to Kohat, to carry out bombing raids against rebellious Waziris, which caused General Nadir Khan to lose much of his expected support. On 27 May 1919, the Afghan General's military detachment of some 3,000 men, supported by twice that number of armed tribesmen, emerged into the Kurram Valley from the north-west, having surmounted the Shutagardan Pass, his artillery (two howitzers and seven field guns) carried by elephant train. Nadir Khan had a flair for the spectacular, was good at improvisation, and perhaps wanted to upstage the General who had superseded him as C-in-C. He slowly approached Thal, and camped before it.

Thal, being just inside a corner angle of the British-Afghan frontier, was protected by rivers on three sides, the confluence of the Sangroba, Kurram and Ishkhalal Rivers. Both the telegraph and a railway ran from Thal some 60 miles eastwards to Kohat. The cantonment perimeter consisted of about five miles of defensive works and trenches, held by four infantry units, all Indian, and a cavalry sub-unit. There was just one bridge across the Sangroba River.

General Nadir Khan commenced his artillery bombardment of Thal on 28 May, causing considerable damage, setting fire to railway ration trucks, petrol and forage dumps, and hitting the radio installation. During the night, the armed Frontier Guards protecting the adjacent water-pumping station deserted with their arms. In the six-day siege of Thal, a number of Afghan attacks were repulsed by the garrison, but food, ammunition and water began to run out, and casualties were mounting. Some 90 men were killed and 100 horses lost (*Official Account*).

Dyer to the Rescue

A reinforcement division moving up from Lahore (in the Punjab) and intended originally for the Dakka area, was diverted, and one of its brigades, commanded by Brigadier General Dyer, (not to be confused with Dyer of Amritsar fame), was detailed to relieve Thal, the remainder of the formation going on to Kohat, which Eustace had left virtually undefended.

On the way to Thal, the enterprising Dyer collected more units, five of them infantry, and sub-units of cavalry and armoured cars. In addition to using the railway line, Dyer also had 62 motor transport vehicles (*Official Account*). Also collecting some artillery units, he loaded the guns, gunners and ammunition on to the motor transport. He also loaded on to the trucks, suitably trimmed huge tree trunks, which, when covered with a sheet, resembled guns, thus giving the impression he had a large artillery force.

At Togh, about 27 miles east of Thal, Dyer assembled his *ad hoc* force, and gave a rousing address to his assorted troops, who included veterans and many, both British and Indian, who were anxiously awaiting demobilisation. He told them that their comrades at Thal, under siege, outnumbered and in dire straits, were waiting for them to come to their rescue. Morale was instantly raised, and the Dyer force marched towards Thal on 30 May.

The following day Dyer saw his route was blocked by two groups of Afghan army troops, supported by large numbers of armed tribesmen. The northernmost group, with four guns, was estimated to be about 2,000-strong, and that to the south of it, about 4,000-strong. On 1 June, Dyer fired his guns at the larger Afghan group, which soon scattered and fled, as subsequently did the smaller group when the guns were turned on it. Dyer then marched quickly to Thal to take command.

Dyer now had about 19,000 troops at his disposal, 13 guns and 22 'dummy' guns on trucks. Without wasting time, he ordered four infantry units to move out from the Thal cantonment in 'order to advance' to battle, under a 'creeping' artillery barrage, against General Nadir Khan's soldiers and armed tribesmen, also deployed in battle formation.

As soon as the advance had begun, a messenger from General Nadir Khan arrived at Dyer's HQ, saying the Amir had ordered a cease-fire, pending negotiations with the British, and asking that his message be acknowledged. Dyer's response was: 'My guns will give an immediate reply'. The sight of advancing forces was regarded with dismay by the Afghans, and General Nadir Khan said: 'My God, we have the whole artillery of India coming up against us' (*Heathcote*). He immediately gave the order to withdraw and, harassed by cavalry, armoured cars and RAF aircraft, the Afghan force rapidly moved away, halting, some three miles distant, to make camp.

The RAF came into action to bomb the repositioned Afghan camp, while Dyer reorganised his force and made ready for pursuit. On 4 June, a British cavalry patrol found the Afghan camp abandoned, everyone in it having withdrawn the previous night. The cavalrymen rounded up some 300 camels which had been left behind, and returned to Thal with them, and the news of the decampment. A stronger British force arrived at the abandoned Afghan camp site later that day, only to find that in the meantime it had been thoroughly looted by local tribesmen. Dyer was making ready to pursue General Nadir Khan and bring him to battle, when he was ordered to halt, as an 'armistice' had been concluded with the Afghans on 3 June 1919.

The RAF Contribution

The sudden armistice was brought about largely by the RAF, still operating mainly from its airfield at Risalpur. On 17 May 1919, mustering all available airworthy aircraft, it mounted a bombing raid on Jalalabad, when '332 bombs were dropped, mainly on enemy troops on the ridge, and the rest on Jalalabad' (*RAF sources*). Heavy casualties were caused, there was panic in the city, many inhabitants fled, and their empty shops and homes were looted by opportunity-seeking tribesmen. Jalalabad was again raided by the

RAF in a similar manner on 20 May, and again four days later, when government buildings were hit, and about 2,000 soldiers were caught in the open on a parade ground. One bomb practically destroyed the tomb of Amir Habibullah.

Meanwhile, the RAF was planning to bomb Kabul but, being some 140 miles from Risalpur, this was beyond the capabilities of the Bristol Fighters. Four Handley Page V-1500s were flown out to India from Britain, but only one made it to the North-West Frontier Province, the others falling victim to accident and engine trouble. The Handley Page aircraft, specially designed to bomb Berlin, was a twin-engine bi-plane, having a speed of 90mph at 8,000ft, and an airborne duration of about six hours.

The RAF raid on Kabul was carried out on 24 May (1919), by the single remaining Handley Page aircraft, piloted by Captain Robert Halley, with Lieutenant William Villiers as Observer, and three other crew members, striking the city at dawn. Twenty bombs were dropped, four of which damaged the Amir's Palace, another destroyed Kabul's only ammunition factory, and yet another hit the tomb of Amir Abdur Rahman (*RAF sources*).

Negotiations

Amir Amanullah had been making overtures for a cease-fire since 15 May, while at the same time continuing to criticise British handling of its internal security problems in India. Prevaricating and playing for time, he claimed (falsely) that his troops had not set foot on British Indian soil, insisting that British forces had invaded his territory, which was true. The British regarded these Afghan feelers as ploys to put them off-guard, in the hope they might cease operations, and even withdraw their forces. Within the Trans-Indus Force, which rose to a strength of 340,000 men, there was a strong determination amongst the military leadership to pursue the war with vigour. The Generals in the field certainly did not want a cease-fire at this stage, and Brigadier General Dyer's response to General Nadir Khan's overtures had expressed the mood of the moment.

However, the C-in-C, India, General Sir Charles Monro, saw the problem from a completely different angle, believing that if the war was continued his resources to pursue it successfully would be inadequate. In reality, he was concerned with another factor, which was not aired in public—a doubt as to the calibre of some of the

British and Indian units, some of which had already given cause for anxiety in action. General Monro feared that if the war were taken deep into Afghanistan, bearing in mind the improved capability of the Afghan army, weak links might result in a major British defeat that would severely shake British military prestige in India, which was already rumbling with discontent.

Lord Chelmsford, the Viceroy, replied to Amir Amanullah's request for a cease-fire, welcoming the offer, but refusing to admit that the British had started the war, and demanding that Afghan troops be withdrawn 20 miles from Trans-Indus Force units. On 11 June, Amanullah wrote again to the Viceroy, accepting negotiations, saying he was sending a peace delegation, but complaining of continued bombing by the RAF.

Peace negotiations eventually began, Afghan delegates arriving at Rawalpindi on 26 July. The British were still convinced that Amanullah was playing for time, possibly hoping for Soviet assistance, so that he could continue the war. The Afghan delegates demanded that Waziristan be ceded to Afghanistan, as the British seemed unable to control it. There was argument over the size of the British cash subsidy, and a demand that the Amir be accorded the title of 'King'.

On 1 August, the British threatened to resume hostilities. The British government in London had a sudden change of mood, becoming displeased with the abruptness with which the negotiations had commenced, and Lord Chelmsford and others were criticised for being too conciliatory towards Amanullah. Some in Britain wanted to treat Amir Amanullah as they had just treated the defeated German Kaiser, and pack him off into exile.

The Treaty of Rawalpindi

Eventually, the Treaty of Rawalpindi was signed by British and Afghan representatives on 8 August 1919, thus ending the Third Anglo-Afghan War. It was agreed that the Afghans would be allowed to control their own foreign policy, the issue on which the war was fought (and lost) by Britain.

The Abrasive Cease-Fire

While negotiations were haltingly in progress, there was hostile action on all three battle fronts, which in theory should have been quiet and peaceful: armed tribesmen sniped at, attacked and generally harassed units of the Trans-Indus Force, while the RAF countered with bombing and machine-gun sorties. In these operations, due to anxiety for the safety of RAF pilots and crew should they be brought down or have to make a forced landing while flying over hostile tribal territory, personnel were issued with a document, printed in Pushtu and Dari, promising high rewards for their safe return. In RAF jargon, these became known as 'ghooli-chits'. In one incident, when a plane had to make a forced landing, motor transport trucks, with machine-guns on board, successfully raced armed tribesmen on horseback to the scene to rescue the pilot.

Both General Nadir Khan, commanding the Afghan Central Army Group, and Minister Abdul Kudus Khan, commanding the Afghan Southern Army Group, made little pretence of adhering to the cease-fire, actively encouraging armed tribesmen to attack and harass British forces. In typical Afghan fashion, Abdul Kudus Khan, the Amir's 'trusted First Minister', let it be known to the British that he would not be averse to a separate agreement with them, and that if Amanullah was forced to abdicate, as some British were advocating, he would be delighted to become a pro-British, anti-Bolshevik candidate for the Amirship.

Concluding Comments

In this month-long war, the Afghan army had in certain aspects shown distinct improvement on previous performance but, while the bravery of Afghan soldiers could not be questioned, determined resistance and steadiness under shell fire continued to be weak points. There were, however, exceptions. Generally, Afghan drawbacks remained much the same, including inept generalship, lack of a professionally-trained officer cadre, and of a field staff organisation. Artillery capability had improved considerably, but guns still lacked flexibility and mobility.

On the British-Indian side on certain occasions the calibre of some units was questioned, and there was an uncertain morale factor, hitherto hardly experienced. The Afghan army lacked two major assets possessed by the Trans-Indus Force—motor transport and aircraft, although from the British point of view, both were in very short supply. Had the Afghan army possessed these two advantages (and a sound staff organisation) the story of the Third Anglo-Afghan War might have been different.

The tiny RAF element in India was undervalued, under-supported and under-recorded. The fact that it had to make do with obsolete aircraft provoked protesting letters to *The Times*, pointing out that under demobilisation processes in Britain the latest RAF aircraft were being burnt and their engines sold for scrap, while they were urgently needed in Afghanistan. One ship loaded with 'war supplies' for the Third Anglo-Afghan War, did reach Bombay during the conflict, only to find that crates containing 'new aircraft' had been left behind on the dockside at Marseilles.

Despite faint, low-level praise by Army GHQ, India, for their activities (contained in a single paragraph on page 133, of the *Official Account*), the RAF instilled fear into both the Afghan army and the tribesmen, and above all into the Amir who, having heard of British plans to bomb Berlin during the First World War, and anticipating such an RAF bombing blitz on his own capital, and other Afghan cities, decided to settle for negotiations. Certainly, there can be no doubt that the RAF played a major part in the Third Anglo-Afghan War.

4

Afghan Political Development

In August 1919, after achieving what he considered to be a fairly satisfactory peace agreement with the British, and having gained control over his own country's foreign policy, Amir Amanullah turned his attention to his northern border, beyond which Muslim Khanates were striving to maintain their precarious independence against the Bolsheviks, then embarking upon civil war campaigns to bring all parts of the former Imperial Russian Empire under their control. In October, Amir Amanullah sent a detachment of some 400 Afghan troops to occupy the city of Merv, in Turkistan, ousting Bolshevik officials. He also offered assistance to Ferghana if its Khan would join an Islamic Central Asian Federation.

However, Amir Amanullah's moment of opportunity had passed because of his preoccupation with the Third Anglo-Afghan War, and Bolshevik army divisions were already moving southwards. The Red Army sacked Kokand, and after a two-month siege overcame Tashkent. The Soviet General (later Marshal) Frunze then moved a Tartar brigade into the Ferghana Valley, which extinguished its hope of retaining independence. The Afghan military detachment at Merv was withdrawn. By 1923, Bokhara and other Turkistan Khanates were firmly in Bolshevik hands, although pockets and drifting groups of *Basmachi* (Bandits), as the Soviets called the insurgents, remained active for another decade. About half-a-million refugees from Soviet Turkistan sought sanctuary in Afghanistan and settled in its northern provinces.

Amanullah the Reformer

Abandoning his dream of leading an Islamic Central Asian

Afghanistan Provinces

Federation, Amir Amanullah had perforce to give thought to the defence of his country as, beyond his northern frontiers, Red Army formations were moving southwards on the heels of fleeing refugees. Fearing the Soviets might move into Afghanistan in hot-pursuit, the Amir hastily concluded an agreement with them in 1923, renouncing all support for the *Basmachi*. A Soviet military mission arrived in Kabul, followed by a British one, and at intervals other foreign embassies also appeared in the capital. In 1926, the Afghan-Soviet Treaty of Neutrality and Non-Aggression was concluded.

At a Loya Jirga in 1926, Amanullah assumed the title of 'King' (*Pasash*), a title he had already been accorded by the British under the Rawalpindi Treaty. King Amanullah strove to modernise his backward country and to force his people into the 20th Century, establishing secular schools, attempting to ameliorate the position of women, and to modify the oppressive land tenure system. For example, he ordered his ministers to wear western dress, and his wife (Queen Soraya) appeared in public unveiled. These policies offended a great number of people, especially those with vested interests in the old ways.

Opposition to Amanullah's modernisation policies deepened. A son of ex-Amir Yakub led a rebellion against him in 1924, which Amanullah crushed with extreme cruelty. General Nadir Khan, in recognition of his services in the Third Anglo-Afghan War, had been reappointed C-in-C of the Afghan army; and in 1924, was appointed Afghan Ambassador to France; however, he resigned two years later in protest against Amanullah's modernisation policies, remaining abroad.

King Amanullah spent the first part of 1928 touring Middle Eastern and European capitals, where he was received with royal pomp and ceremony, but on his return home from this ego-satisfying grand tour he found his country in open opposition to his reforms. An insurgent movement had surfaced, and an armed force was marching on Kabul, arriving there in December. For their safety, British citizens in Kabul were hastily evacuated to Peshawar by RAF aircraft. A few rudimentary airstrips were appearing in Afghanistan and, while still very much a novelty, aircraft were slowly becoming a familiar sight to Afghans.

Too late, King Amanullah tried to back-track on reform, but hostile pressure was too great, and on 14 January 1929, he was forced to abdicate in favour of Inayatullah Khan, his brother, and withdraw to Kandahar. King Inayatullah held out in Kabul for only three days, before departing on an RAF flight to Peshawar. A Soviet-supported candidate, Bacha-i-Saqa, known as 'the Bandit' because of his reputed previous activities, was established as 'Ruler' in Kabul. The Soviets blamed the British for Amanullah's downfall, which was officially denied. The Soviet Ambassador in Kabul at the time afterwards wrote: 'The tragedy of Amanullah's case lay in the fact that he undertook bourgeois reforms without the existence of any bourgeoisie in the country'.

King Nadir Shah

In March 1929, General Nadir Khan returned to Afghanistan from exile by way of India and, raising an army, drove Amanullah from Kandahar. He then marched to Kabul to defeat the 'Bandit King' in October, establishing himself as King Nadir Shah. The 'Bandit King' was publicly executed.

King Nadir Shah's comparatively short reign was generally one of stability and consolidation during which, in 1931, he forcibly brought Herat into his Kingdom. His policy was not only one of international neutrality, but of almost complete withdrawal from the modern world. Afghanistan remained a stationary Middle Ages 'time-capsule'. In 1933, King Nadir Shah was assassinated. The British and the Soviets blamed one another, each denying its involvement; the real motive was obscure, and perhaps a family blood-feud was the root cause.

Mohammed Zahir Shah, one of King Nadir Shah's sons, came peacefully to the Throne of Afghanistan, being generally accepted by majority of the population. Then only 19 years of age, King Zahir Shah began a slow, cautious programme of reform.

The Afghan Army

From 1919 to 1933, the Afghan army had been deliberately neglected, having devolved into little more than a collection of small infantry units and, owing to the cost of horses and their upkeep, a declining number of cavalry units. Artillery and ammunition were still kept mainly in the Sherpur cantonment armoury at Kabul. Neither Amirs nor Kings had wanted the army to become too efficient lest it attract ambitious contenders for power to subvert sections of it for their own political purposes.

A Turkish military mission arrived in Kabul in 1937, to reorganise the Afghan army, which then had a strength of about 60,000 men, being either conscripts with a two-year service obligation (each province having to produce a quota of men), or volunteers on short-service engagements. The Turks formed a command structure of divisions and brigades, with HQs and supporting staff officers, and began to regularise the officer corps. A military academy was established to educate and train officer-cadets; and a small air force began to take shape.

Afghanistan remained neutral in the Second World War, although under British pressure King Zahir Shah was persuaded to expel German and Italian nationals from his country. The British suspected an Afghan bias against the Allies in favour of the Axis Powers. After the war, Afghanistan became a member of the United Nations, but still retained its isolationist stance.

Pakistan Appears

When the British withdrew from the Indian sub-continent on 14 August 1947, Partition brought into being the new Muslim state of Pakistan, which became Afghanistan's eastern neighbour. Initially, Afghanistan refused to recognise Pakistan, or the Durand Line as its eastern boundary, and indeed at first blocked Pakistan's admission to the United Nations.

Afghanistan claimed the North-West Frontier Province and certain other territory, including parts of what is now Pakistan's Baluchistan Province, which would have given it access to the Makran coast. Pakistan took possession, by force when necessary, of all former British-Indian territory, west of the demarcation line drawn under the Partition agreement. For example, territory of the 'independent' Khan of Kalat, was forcibly occupied by Pakistani troops, the Khan fleeing into Afghanistan.

The Baghdad Pact

As the Cold War between NATO and the Warsaw Pact countries developed its tentacles reached out to south-west Asia, and NATO allies tried to cobble together a defensive band of pro-Western and anti-Soviet states to contain part of the USSR's southern frontier. The Baghdad Pact, as this defensive coalition became known, embraced Iraq, Iran (the new name for Persia decreed in 1935), Pakistan and Turkey (as well as Britain). The inclusion of Afghanistan would have completed the defensive arc. Consequently, American aid was given generously as bait, financing a number of projects, including the completion of some 2,500 miles of tarmacked strategic roads between the major cities; the Darla Dam, near Kandahar; and two large airfields, one, at Bagram and the other at Kandahar. King Zahir Shah took what Western aid he could get, but remained stubbornly neutral.

The accession of Pakistan to the Baghdad Pact worried the Afghan King, who called a Loya Jirga, which met in November 1955, to consider its strategic implications. It was agreed that Afghanistan should stay out of this military alliance, and that the Afghan Prime Minister, Daoud Khan, should make contact with the USSR as a counter-balance. Previously, the Soviet Union had been regarded as a Godless outsider by Afghans, and diplomatic relations were kept on a strictly formal level.

The Afghan Prime Minister was also authorised to reopen the former Afghan demand for a plebiscite to be held in Pakistan's Pathan territory, in furtherance of an 'independent Pushtunistan', which the Afghans thought would want to merge with Afghan Pathan territory.

Soviet Influence

Significant Soviet influence in Afghanistan can be traced to the visit of the two Soviet leaders, Bulganin and Khrushchev, in December 1955, immediately after the Loya Jirga decision. Afghans agreed to accept Soviet military and economic aid, and a Soviet military mission arrived in Kabul in 1957, with a remit to reorganise, modernise and re-equip the Afghan army and air force.

Small quantities of Soviet weaponry and equipment began to arrive, including T-34 tanks (the first tanks ever to appear in the country), guns, military vehicles, field radios and combat aircraft. By 1960, the Soviet military mission had swelled in number to about 500 military advisers, technicians and instructors. The Afghan army also increased in strength to about 100,000 men, still formed into static divisions, with some 30,000 reservists.

In November 1963, an agreement was signed that concluded demarcation of the 40-mile Soviet-Afghan frontier along the eastern edge of the Wakhan Strip, where it adjoined China. Later, in August 1965, the Soviet-Afghan Treaty of Neutrality and Non-Aggression (signed in 1926) was extended for another ten years.

The Soviets took over the maintenance of the strategic northern route from Kabul to Mazar-i-Sharif, and on to the Oxus river (now called the Amu Darya) at Pata Kesang, across which lay the Soviet town of Termez, just north of which was the Kalif railhead, on the Soviet railway system. In August 1964, the Soviets completed the two-lane Salang Tunnel on the northern route, through the Hindu Kush, a project which had taken six years. It was now possible for vehicles to use the whole of the route throughout the year, whereas previously, the route went over the Salang Pass, which was snow-bound during winter months.

In September (1964), the Soviets agreed to assist the Afghans to build a plant to produce nuclear energy for peaceful purposes, and to train Afghan personnel to service it. In return the Soviets accepted huge quantities of Afghan natural gas from the Shibargham field, in Jowzjan Province, laying a 60-mile pipeline to the Soviet border, which was completed in 1967.

Afghan Air Force

The Soviets provided help for the Afghan Air Force (AAF), which had previously been deliberately neglected in case it fell into politically unreliable hands, and which had about 30 old British and Italian aircraft. AAF bombs were securely lodged in the Sherpur armoury. The first Soviet aircraft to arrive in Afghanistan were a batch of 40 MiG-15s, and these were later followed by 32 MiG-17 fighter planes. By 1960, the AAF had over 100 Soviet combat aircraft and six helicopters. Meanwhile, the Soviets were improving airfields, bringing in ground-control equipment, constructing accommodation and storage facilities, and laying down other airfields near main cities.

A Constitutional Monarchy

Winds of enlightened political change were slow to reach Afghanistan, one of the first breezes bringing about a constitutional monarchy, in August 1964. This debarred from political office all members of the Royal Family (descendants of King Nadir). Previously, a monarch's relatives had served as Cabinet ministers, often dominating governments. A Loya Jirga, held in September, confirmed this decision.

People's Democratic Party of Afghanistan

At Soviet instigation, the first modern political party in Afghanistan, the Khalk (meaning People or Masses), was secretly formed on 1 January 1965, the Secretary General being Mohammed Taraki, a writer and journalist. Its full title was the People's Democratic Party of Afghanistan (PDPA), *(Jamiyat-e Demokrati-e Khakq-e Afghanistan)*. The PDPA developed a typical Communist party structure, with an orthodox Marxist-Leninist orientation.

Within a year there had been a split within the PDPA, one part becoming known as the Khalk, led by Mohammed Taraki, who was in favour of abolishing the monarchy as a first step towards a socialist state; and the other as the Parcham (Flag or Banner), led by Babrak Karmal, who thought the time was not yet ripe for such action. The two wings of the PDPA developed separately, and in hostility towards each other.

President Daoud

On 17 July 1973, while King Zahir Shah was away in Italy, a claimed 'bloodless' coup (actually eight people were killed), led by Mohammed Daoud, a cousin of the King, and a former Prime Minister, took place. Daoud declared his country to be a Republic, and himself to be President.

Daoud called a Loya Jirga, which in January–February 1974, approved republican status, and confirmed Daoud as President for a term of six years. It also confirmed the use of Dari (Farsi) and Pushtu as the two official languages; and declared that legislation would be guided by the Koran.

The watching Soviets pressed the PDPA to give full support to President Daoud, but Mohammed Taraki, leader of the Khalk faction, refused to do so, while Babrak Karmal, of the Parcham faction, did co-operate. This caused the split within the PDPA to become a break.

President Daoud tried to keep his country non-aligned, cheerfully accepting aid from the Soviet Union, Western nations, Iran, Kuwait, and others. For example, the Shah of Iran paid a French company to carry out a feasibility study for the construction of a 1,200-mile railway network to link main Afghan cities. Daoud visited Moscow, concluded economic agreements, and called upon the Soviets to continue arming and training the Afghan army and the AAF. The

Soviets took full advantage of this opportunity to bring Afghan officers and technicians to the USSR, not only for professional and technical training but, even more important, for Soviet indoctrination. One authority (*Hyman*) stated that over 7,000 Afghans had received military training in the USSR, or Czechoslovakia, in the period 1961-70.

In August 1975, President Daoud announced a Land Reform Law to establish an administration to implement proposed limitations to land holdings, and for the creation of agricultural co-operatives. Land reform was badly needed in Afghanistan as the limited amount of arable land was in the hands of a few powerful and arrogant land-owners, who had an economic stranglehold on the country. This law catered for the transfer of land to landless peasants, but left riparian rights with the former owners.

This law also made no provision to help peasants who acquired holdings with seed, tools or loans, while landowners, reluctant to be deprived of their estates, put difficulties in the way of distribution, irrigation and marketing of produce. President Daoud introduced other reforms, some of which further upset religious and traditional leaders. He had inherited severe economic problems, compounded by drought and famine in the three years preceding the 1973 coup, which necessitated international relief aid being sent to Afghanistan.

Political Resistance

Back in September 1973, a 'plot' against President Daoud had been discovered, when a number of people were reputedly executed, and many others imprisoned. The change of regime to that of republican was certainly not popular with every one in the country, and became less so as Daoud, supported by the Parcham faction of the PDPA, began to initiate, and implement, Communist-pattern policies. This caused what was originally thought of as a 'Bring back King Zahir Shah' campaign, which soon turned into an 'Islamic anti-Daoud' resistance movement.

At first, the form of this resistance movement was shadowy and indefinite as it tended to swirl around individual personalities, often in opposition to each other, and it developed into two broad, but separate, streams. One derived from the ideology of the extreme Muslim Brotherhood (*Akhwanul Muslimin*), which operated in certain Middle East countries, and whose objective was to conduct a *Jihad* against the Daoud regime, according to the Sharia (Islamic law), to turn Afghanistan into an Islamic state. Its followers became known as 'Fundamentalists'.

The policy of the other broad stream was also to fight a *Jihad* against Daoud, but in a different way, using Afghan customs and means to achieve a traditionally independent Afghan country, several of its members initially being Royalists. Followers of this broad stream became known as 'Traditionalists' (or later as 'Moderates'), as they believed that, while Islam guided personal lives, community problems should be solved in the Afghan way.

Tiny resistance groupings were led by young, educated, ambitious politicians who, in vocal opposition to the Kabul government in what was becoming a closed Communist-type repressive atmosphere, had perforce to operate from exile in Pakistan; several later became well-known leaders in the Afghan Mujahideen movement. A little surprisingly, many local Mullahs, extremely influential over rural, uneducated youth, regarded the Muslim Brotherhood as 'revisionist', and so tended to veer away from Fundamentalist resistance groups, tending instead to favour Traditionalist ones. Afghan resistance seemed to develop into a four-sided struggle, with Fundamentalists differing with Traditionalists, and both pitched against the two competing wings of the PDPA.

Pakistan

After the 1973 Afghan coup, diplomatic relations were severed by Pakistan because of the Communist nature of the Daoud regime, and were only restored in 1977, when Prime Minister Zulfikar Ali Bhutto released the veteran 'Pushtunistan' resistance leader, Abdul Gaffar Khan, from detention. During that period, relations between Afghanistan and Pakistan were bad, each accusing the other of instigating hostile insurrection, and sheltering the other's dissidents.

In the early 1970s, Pakistan was faced with rebellion in its Baluchistan Province, mainly over the imposition of civilian central administration in areas that had never before been subjected to one. The Pakistan government had to mount military campaigns to enforce its 'pacification' process. During one such campaign, between May 1973 and October 1974, Pakistan accused the Kabul government of actively assisting Baluchi 'rebels'. General Zia, who came to power in Pakistan in July 1977, disliked the Left-leaning Daoud government, and was deliberately cool towards it, although maintaining the restored diplomatic relations.

The Saur Revolution

President Daoud was identified by the Soviets as being the obstacle to their ambitions in Afghanistan, and they instigated his removal. First, they persuaded the Khalk and Parcham factions of the PDPA to reunite, persuading the Parchamis to stop supporting Daoud.

On 27 April 1978, the so-called 'Saur (April) Revolution', mounted by the PDPA, violently overthrew President Daoud. An assault on the Presidential Palace was led by Colonel Abdul Qadir, in which President Daoud, some 30 members of his family, several of his Ministers, and his C-in-C were killed. The death toll was said to be 73, but was generally considered to be much greater. Some 4,000 people were detained, several of whom were alleged to have been executed in the notorious Poli Charki prison, outside Kabul.

Mohammed Taraki, Secretary General of the PDPA, and leader of the Khalk faction, now came to the fore, appointing himself Chairman of the 'Armed Forces Revolutionary Council', (and later President), which on 30 April, proclaimed the existence of the 'Democratic Republic of Afghanistan'. Mohammed Taraki formed a government that included members of both the Khalk and Parcham factions. Both Babrak Karmal (a Parachami) and Hafizullah Amin (a Khalki) became Deputy Prime Ministers, but the power behind the scenes came to be the Khalk-dominated PDPA, and its Central Committee.

Mohammed Taraki later said (*Kabul Radio*) that when he took over after the Saur Revolution he found there were 12,330 political prisoners detained by the previous regime, and went on to admit he was still holding 1,400.

Mohammed Taraki followed a non-aligned policy, but also accepted aid from whoever would supply it, turning closer towards the USSR, which initially embraced his regime with open arms. He instituted drastic social and economic measures, including land reform, women's rights and education, thus continuing to offend those with vested interests in maintaining the *status quo*. On such issues, he insisted he was not anti-Islamic.

Mohammed Taraki's land reform measures included limiting the acreage an individual could own, and sharing out the remaining portions of larger estates amongst landless peasants. Land distribution aroused the hostility of many, who had previously been indifferent to the Kabul government, especially in areas where central authority rested very lightly.

A new national red flag, crested with a 'star and wheat-sheaf', was introduced. The President visited Moscow, and concluded several economic agreements, and on 4 December 1978, signed the standard Soviet Friendship Treaty.

The Islamic anti-Daoud resistance movement swelled in anger and strength to become anti-Taraki and anti-Communist. There were numerous incidents and clashes between insurgents in open revolt against the Kabul government and Afghan security forces in the countryside, especially in the eastern provinces of Paktia and Kunar, during the summer of 1978. Insurgent attacks were also mounted in Kabul, a city in which curfews were frequently enforced. On 1 June, seven Afghan political parties came together in a coalition, known as the National Salvation Front (*Jub Najat-e-Milli*). This unrest continued on into 1979 and, in March that year, Mohammed Taraki appointed Hafizullah Amin to be his Prime Minister, (and, later, in July, also Minister of Defence), with a brief to crush dissidence with severity.

PDPA In-fighting

So far the PDPA was a comparatively small organisation, narrowly recruited mainly from the Kabul-educated élite, who included teachers, civil servants, army officers and politically-orientated intellectuals. One authority (*Dupree*) put its membership as low as 5,000, and others as high as 12,000, although Mohammed Taraki later claimed it was over 18,000. Although the Soviets had persuaded the Khalk and Parcham factions to work together for the downfall of President Daoud, it had not been a happy arrangement, even though both went along with the fiction of being united. The Soviets hoped that once Daoud was eliminated, the two factions would forget the past and co-operate amicably.

This was not to be. Mohammed Taraki, the Khalk leader, could not forget that Parchamis had supported Daoud. Quarrels between the two were constantly erupting, sometimes ending with a shoot-out. Ethnic composition of the respective factions only exacerbated friction. Broadly speaking, the Khalk faction consisted mainly of Pathans, and was strong within the officer corps, but weaker in government service, while the membership of the Parcham included Hazaras, Qizilbashias, Tadjiks, Uzbeks, and other minorities, who were drawn more from government service than the armed forces.

There was a bout of open fighting between Khalkis and Parchamis in July 1978, with the Khalkis emerging victorious; thereafter purges against Parchamis began, many being dismissed from their posts, and some arrested. Rumours of executions were rife. In August, practically all Parchamis were removed from senior political appointments and government service positions, and a number of Parchami leaders, including Babrak Karmal, fled to the USSR, and thence to Eastern Europe. The Soviets increased their military strength and posture along the northern border of Afghanistan, indicating that they would intervene if there were a counter-revolution.

Death of American Ambassador

Previously, in February 1978, the American Ambassador, Adolph Dubs, had been kidnapped by members of the small Maoist group, National Oppression, (*Settem-e-Milli*), based in the far north-eastern Badakhshan Province, (*Urban*) whose platform was furthering the interests of ethnic minorities. He was being held in a hotel bedroom in Kabul and, although asked by the Americans not to do so, Afghan security forces stormed the room, overcame the terrorists and fatally wounded Dubs. The terrorists had hoped to blackmail the USA into aiding their cause. The CIA alleged this had been a KGB plot, which was denied, but it caused the USA to withdraw its Peace Corps workers and severely reduce its aid programme. Under the Carter administration relations between the USA and Afghanistan were abrasive and poor, owing to President Carter's accusations of human rights abuses in that country.

There was already a CIA presence in Afghanistan, and it was said (*Urban*) that its covert activities increased after this incident. Soviet interest in Afghanistan also increased, and a large consignment of Soviet arms and equipment arrived in March 1979, including armoured vehicles and helicopters. The following month, Soviet General Yepishev, a Deputy Defence Minister, with a high-ranking military team, arrived in Afghanistan. Mohammed Taraki admitted that there were '1,900 foreign advisers in Afghanistan, of whom 1,100 were Soviet' (*Kabul Radio*). There were probably more, including a few Soviet troops. Afghanistan was becoming a pawn in the Cold War.

An Islamic *Jihad*

On 12 March 1979, the insurgent National Islamic Liberation Front, based in Pakistan, called for a *Jihad* against the Kabul government, and the same day there was a resistance uprising in Herat, where Afghan and Soviet troops (the latter not yet officially in Afghanistan) took 10 days to restore order, at the cost of probably 5,000 dead. This was the first time Soviet troops had been openly employed to help Afghan forces quell internal disturbances. Several Soviet advisers and their families perished in the Herat uprising.

The Iranian government, then in the throes of its own Islamic Revolution, closed its frontiers with Afghanistan to prevent an influx of Afghan refugees. The Kabul government accused the Iranians of sending soldiers in disguise to assist insurgents at Herat, and expelled the Iranian Consul General.

In September, there was a mutiny at Ghazni by elements of the 14th Infantry Division, and again Soviet troops had to assist the Afghans to restore order. By this time discontent was spreading through the Afghan armed forces, not only because of the effects of the PDPA quarrel, but because Mohammed Taraki's Communist-type reforms seemed to them to be anti-Islamic. Torn by conflicting military, Islamic, political and family pressures, soldiers were increasingly deserting often with their arms, and already some units had become 'unreliable'.

The Hafizullah Amin Coup

The Kremlin leadership watched anxiously as insurrection seemed to spread throughout the Afghan countryside. The Sovietisation of the Afghan armed forces was in progress, but was slow-moving, and it would be some time before they would be conditioned to counter organised internal resistance successfully on their own. The Kremlin saw the Kabul government slipping away from its grasp.

The Soviets identified the Afghan Prime Minister, Hafizullah Amin, as the catalyst, as he was forcing the pace of reform too fast, and with much too heavy a hand. When persuasion to get the Prime Minister to ease the pressure failed, the Soviets decided to eliminate him. However, a personality clash suddenly erupted between President Mohammed Taraki and his Prime Minister, who, reading the writing on the wall, struck first.

Precise details of Hafizullah Amin's coup against President Taraki in September 1979, are still subject to speculation. It seems there was a private shoot-out in the Presidential Palace at Kabul, probably on 14 September, in which Mohammed Taraki was fatally wounded, and several others, including two Ministers, were killed. Kabul Radio announced on 15 September that President Taraki had resigned for health reasons, and had appointed Hafizullah Amin to succeed him as Khalk leader. The following day it was announced that Hafizullah Amin had been appointed President.

It is believed that Mohammed Taraki died on 17 September, but it was not until 9 October, that Kabul Radio officially reported his death after a 'long illness', although no specific date was mentioned. Tass, the Soviet news agency, later reported, again without mentioning a date, that Mohammed Taraki had been killed by three Afghan officers on the orders of Haifzullah Amin, and his body secretly buried. Other versions were also current.

Although saddled with an Afghan leader they certainly did not want, the Soviets continued to give aid and support to Afghanistan, and in October-November 1979, probably as the result of General Yepishev's visit, at least one large arms delivery was received, which included '30 Mi-24 helicopters, 800 modern tanks, 800 armoured personnel carriers (APCs) and a number of guns' (*IISS*). Soviet anxiety deepened when it was seen that President Hafizullah Amin seemed to be shaking off Afghan's almost traditional policy of non-alignment and neutrality, and extending political contacts with the USA, and other Western nations.

The Hafizullah Amin coup gave impetus to the insurrection that was making fumbling progress in Afghanistan and soon spokesmen for the resistance groups based in Pakistan were claiming that several Afghan provinces were already under insurgent control; that the Soviet Embassy in Kabul had been attacked (on the 4 October) when six Soviet personnel died; and that Afghan army units were launching offensive operations in the eastern part of the country. By this time the Islamic leadership in Iran was openly encouraging Shia Fundamentalist resistance movements into activity in western Afghanistan; Pakistan, being officially neutral, was more cautious and restrained, but unofficially sympathetic and helpful to the Afghan resistance movement.

Afghanistan: December 1979

In December 1979, Afghanistan was still a very backward country, barely developed in economic terms, still struggling into the 20th Century, still without railways, and with only 3,000 miles of hard-surfaced, all weather roads throughout its some 450,000 square miles of terrain. The main forms of communication were the telegraph system and, to a lesser extent, the telephone. Transistor radios had become fairly common, but Kabul Radio, the national transmission station, was government-controlled, and the few newspapers were subject to heavy censorship.

Afghanistan had been divided into 28 provinces, each with a Governor appointed by the Kabul Government. A census in June 1978, showed the population to be 15,540,000, of which only 11.7 per cent lived in urban areas. The largest city was Kabul, with a population of 600,000, and the three cities of Herat, Kandahar and Mazar-i-Sharif each exceeded 200,000; other cities were much smaller, although individual estimates tended to vary.

A university had been established in Kabul in 1932, and secular education was, up to secondary standard in cities and elementary standard elsewhere, in theory, free. Religious education was in the hands of the Mullahs. Very few Afghan women were educated at all, which was not the fault of recent Kabul governments, but of protesting religious leaders. In April 1979 President Mohammed Taraki had launched a major campaign to teach one million people, including women, to read and write, which was received with hard hostility by the Mullahs.

In the Western sense, industry had barely made its appearance in Afghanistan, being confined to natural gas production, cement works and cottage industries, which included carpet-making and textiles. About 80 per cent of the work force was employed in agriculture, cash crops being cotton, oil seeds and fruit. The average income of an Afghan worker was estimated to be the equivalent of US $100 a year (UN figures).

Afghanistan's main trading partner was the Soviet Union, with India coming second; and the main trade routes from Kabul were north to the USSR, east through the Khyber Pass into Pakistan, and from Herat into Iran. Afghanistan was thought to be mineral-rich, as deposits of copper, lead, coal, iron-ore, asbestos, bauxite, silver and chromium, had been discovered, but as yet no comprehensive mineral survey had been made, although Soviet exploration teams had been operating in the country since 1976.

Taxation was becoming a heavy burden on the people, its far-reaching net including taxes on land, factories, grazing, businesses, mineral-mining, and co-operatives, as well as levies on income, and the wealth of certain individuals. Taxes could still be collected in kind, although the 'Afridi' had become the monetary unit.

Reduced somewhat by desertion and avoidance of conscription, the Afghan armed forces were probably about 90,000-strong, and were handicapped by a deeply-divided officer corps. There was a nominal reserve of about 150,000 men. The country was divided into Military Districts, encompassing static divisions. The army was now largely Sovietised in structure, military doctrine and training, and equipped with 'export' models of Soviet weaponry. (*IISS*). It lacked the mobility required to counter insurgency, its policy being mainly retributive, and in frustration it often used a very heavy hand. Military loyalty to the central government had become suspect in many formations, as apart from individual desertions, on occasion whole units had mutinied, deserted with their arms, surrendered to the insurgents or even joined them.

The Afghan Air Force, with a probable strength of about 10,000 all ranks, had about 160 Soviet combat aircraft, all 'export' models, lacking the latest sophisticated improvements, and where possible flown jointly by Soviet and Afghan pilots, the latter being seldom allowed to fly solo (IISS). The Gendarmerie, the Sarandoy, which had an internal security role, was about 30,000-strong (IISS).

5

The Soviet Military Invasion: 1979

D-Day for the invasion of Afghanistan by the Soviet 40th Army was 27 December 1979, when three Soviet motor rifle divisions commenced crossing the Amu Darya (Oxus river) at the Shir Bandar-Qizil Qala (Pata Kesang) ferry crossing point where, in the preceding hours of darkness, Soviet military engineers had erected a 750-yard pontoon bridge, to facilitate movement southwards along the northern route to Bagram and Kabul, and south-west to Herat. CIA sources estimated that 350 tanks and 450 other armoured vehicles crossed the bridge, which remained in constant service for many months. The following day, two more Soviet motor rifle divisions began crossing the Amu Darya, followed by a further two, and within a week some 50,000 Soviet troops were deployed to the principal Afghan air bases and garrisons throughout the country.

The Soviet military invasion of Afghanistan was well-planned, well-organised and well-operated, although it must be said that Afghan opposition was negligible. Subsequent Afghan opposition to the Soviet occupation is another story.

Reconnaissance for this invasion and its ground planning had been carried out by General Ivan Pavlosky, a Soviet Deputy Defence Minister, who spent three months in Afghanistan (August-October 1979), a period covering the latter part of the Taraki regime, and the beginning of that of Hafizullah Amin. His opinion was that the Kabul PDPA government could not survive alone, no matter who headed it, due to the degree of hostility it had generated among so many sections of the population. President Brezhnev was concerned about the survival of the PDPA regime but cared little about President Hafizullah Amin, who was showing too great a deviation from the Moscow line by contacting Western powers.

The other senior Soviet commander involved in this Soviet military invasion was Marshal Sergei Sokolov, who as Commander of the Soviet Southern Theatre of Military Operations, was in overall charge, and he established a Soviet staff group for the operation at Tashkent, in the Turkistan Military District. The 40th Army soon lost its numerical designation and became known as the 'Limited Contingent of Soviet Forces in Afghanistan' (LCSFA).

Previously, the Soviet military mission in Afghanistan had been increased in strength from about 1,500 personnel to over 5,000. Its task was to ensure that nominated Afghan air bases, and certain other garrisons, were firmly under its control by D-Day. During the hours of darkness of 7-8 December, one fully-equipped Soviet airborne assault brigade was airlifted into the Bagram air base, some 40 miles north of Kabul. On the night of 20 December, it moved out to secure the vital Salang Tunnel, about 30 miles to the north, remaining there to ensure the unhindered passage of invading Soviet ground troops.

On 24 December, a massive Soviet air-lift had brought in another two Soviet airborne assault brigades to the Bagram air base, involving '180 sorties of Antonov-12 and Antonov-22 transport aircraft, escorted by about 100 combat aircraft, mainly MiG-21s (*CIA sources*). The ground invasion itself was given strong air cover by both combat aircraft and helicopter-gunships, although this proved to be unnecessary as the Afghan air force had been successfully grounded by the Soviet military mission, and Afghan army formations confined to barracks. Afghan military mutterings came later.

Moscow's priority for the invasion of Afghanistan was not of the highest and, apart from Soviet air force contingents and airborne troops, other formations had to be produced from adjacent Turkistan and Central Asian Military Districts. The selected seven motor rifle divisions were in a low category state of readiness, and had to be brought up to 90 per cent strength in manpower, weapons and vehicles. Reinforcements were either drafted in from other formations, or were recalled Muslim reservists.

Also, a special brigade of Soviet Muslim soldiers had been assembled, it being thought that, as co-religionists of the Afghans and speaking dialects akin to theirs, they would be both an example to the Afghan population of successful collaboration with the Soviets, and of help to the Soviet Psychological Warfare Branch (Psy-Ops), in 'hearts and minds' activities. The Soviets had not really anticipated serious resistance, but did feel that a gigantic show of military force would give confidence to the Kabul government, hearten the Afghan military, and intimidate Afghan 'rebels'. However, they did fear 'either a Western counter-stroke, or a major revolt by the Afghan armed services' (*Urban*).

President Babrak Karmal

Meanwhile, in Kabul, Hafizullah Amin had been persuaded by Soviet advisers to move to the Darulaman Palace, a military HQ on the southern outskirts of Kabul city; on the afternoon of 27 December, the final part of the Soviet plan was put into operation: presumably to capture the President, and spirit him away for trial, or into exile. What precisely happened is still not clear. Some insist that there was opposition to the Soviet Spetsnaz unit detailed for this task, and in the cross-fire the President was killed; others insist that Hafizullah Amin was killed in a shoot-out between Khalki and Parchami military personnel in the Darulaman Palace.

Statements made by prisoners released after Hafizullah Amin's death indicated their belief that he was planning a blood-bath on 29 December, in which many Parcham detainees were to be executed. Another theory was that the President, who had survived two assassination attempts already that month, was planning an attack on the compound in Kabul where Soviet personnel lived, in which some Soviets would inevitably have been killed, giving him an excuse openly to call for American military assistance to counter an anticipated Soviet reprisal. The CIA seemed to be of the opinion that the Parchamis had been set up to eliminate Hafizullah Amin. Hafizullah Amin had received a university education in the USA, was fluent in English, but spoke no Russian, which fuelled Soviet suspicions that he sought American involvement in Afghanistan.

The sudden death of Hafizullah Amin meant the Soviets had no Afghan President in Kabul to give a formal welcome to incoming Soviet military formations. But they had catered for this eventuality, and one was already speeding on his way. Babrak Karmal, leader of the Parcham faction, recalled hastily from exile in Eastern Europe, arrived at Bagram air base, probably on 28 December, to be rushed, reputedly riding in a T-72 tank, with a Soviet (not Afghan) military escort to Kabul.

That evening, Kabul Radio announced that Babrak Karmal had been elected President by a newly reshuffled Revolutionary Council, now with a predominance of Parchami members. That broadcast was made from Termez, just north of the Amu Darya, on Soviet soil. Otherwise dates and timings of Babrak Karmal's steps to power remain blurred and suspect. It is sufficient to say that he was brought into Afghanistan at some stage after the Soviet military invasion had actually begun. President Brezhnev was smugly satisfied, his military grip on Afghanistan was accomplished, and a suitably compliant puppet president had been installed.

Soviet Motive and Opportunity

Brezhnev wanted a friendly, sympathetic Afghan government on his southern border, and Babrak Karmal's remit was to unite the PDPA, work to soften the inherent prejudice and xenophobia of the feudal, tribal and Islamic Afghan character, and persuade the Afghan people to develop a socialist style of society. He hoped ultimately to lure Afghanistan into becoming an 'equal and willing partner in the Commonwealth of the Soviet Socialist Republics' (*Tass*). Brezhnev regarded the Iranian-Afghan-Pakistan bloc as forming an important 'arc of influence' over which he wanted the USSR to have exclusive control.

The USA and its Western allies, on the other hand, regarded these three countries as forming an 'arc of crisis', over which they were striving unsuccessfully to obtain paramount influence. The Soviet military invasion suddenly turned Afghanistan into a valuable pawn in the East-West superpower Cold War struggle—which seemed like a belated continuation of the old Great Game of the 19th Century.

It is an understatement to say that in December 1979, this region was in a state of instability. In Iran, in February that year, Khomeini's Islamic fundamentalist revolution had ousted the Shah, America's 'Policeman of the Gulf', but was in turn savaged by its own diverse factions. The Shah's armed forces, once the best equipped in that region, were emasculated, deprived of conscript manpower, and confined to barracks, incapable of producing an effective expeditionary force. Afghanistan was in a state of barely suppressed festering revolution against the PDPA government, which would have been unlikely to retain power without Soviet active support.

In Pakistan, General Zia had seized power in 1977, governing his four disparate and discontented provinces, in which political unrest was endemic, by military dictatorship. Pakistan had received little American aid, or other support, since its 1971 war with India, which resulted in East Pakistan becoming Bangladesh. In 1979, when President Carter suspected Zia was working to produce a nuclear warhead, US military aid ceased completely, much to the satisfaction of Pakistan's giant neighbour, India, with which it had fought three wars since the Partition of the sub-continent in 1947.

Had the Shah, with his large armed forces, remained in power, and had Pakistan's large, well-trained and well-disciplined forces been equipped with modern aircraft and other weapons, it is unlikely the Soviet military invasion would have taken place, as the prospect of fighting the armies of two such anti-Communist governments would have deterred Moscow from embarking upon such a venture. The main Soviet advantage was its predominant air strength. Brezhnev considered Jimmy Carter to be a weak President, who would be unlikely to resort to the military option in an American presidential election year (1980). What other nation would be willing, and able, to march to the aid of Afghanistan? India was friendly towards the USSR, and would be more likely to join that superpower than not, in the hope of territorial gain.

China was the only other possible danger to the USSR, especially now the Karakorum Highway, linking China and Pakistan, was open, and Brezhnev expected the Chinese to supply arms to Pakistan, and to Afghan dissidents. But he also knew that although the Chinese armed forces were numerically huge, they had hardly any expeditionary potential. The Sino-Vietnamese War (February-March 1979) had shown the Chinese army to be shambling and incompetent, and had turned into a Chinese débâcle. Brezhnev saw his opportunity, and took what was probably the last major strategic decision before his terminal illness began to affect him; certainly Soviet policy in respect of Afghanistan did not change during his lifetime.

Surprise Attack

It is often claimed that modern satellite surveillance methods and electronic detection equipment make it almost impossible for one country to mount a large military invasion against another without this becoming obvious in advance. In theory this may be so, provided both have the essential detection apparatus, but in practice such warning, so obvious in hindsight, can be misread, overlooked or ignored amidst the welter of information clutter, mostly trivial, that is continually pouring into intelligence centres.

The American CIA insists that it had detected, and monitored, the Soviet military build-up north of the Amu Darya river since early in December 1979, but that its reports had not been taken seriously. It is hard to apportion blame, but whoever or whatever the cause, President Carter was taken completely by surprise and, apart from feebly protesting to the USSR on 28 December, seemed to be at a loss as to what to do next. It was not until 20 January 1980, that the US President announced a boycott of the forthcoming Olympic Games due to be held in Moscow, and then he was only partially able to persuade his Western allies to follow his example.

Fumblingly, Carter began to develop and strengthen what became known as the US Rapid Deployment Force (RDF). Next, he rushed to make friends with the previously cold-shouldered President Zia of Pakistan, crudely throwing money at him by offering him military aid to the tune of $400 million. This was rejected by Zia, with his now famous comment: 'That's just peanuts'. Zia put a far bigger price on his friendship and co-operation, one of $2.6 billion. He wanted some US F-16 combat aircraft, at that time prestige planes for a Third World country. He wanted to use half the money to replace his ageing weaponry, which included Chinese-made combat aircraft and tanks, and the other half to redeploy his armed forces along his Afghan frontier, away from their stance against India.

Lacking sophisticated detection equipment, President Zia had also been taken by surprise by the Soviet invasion of Afghanistan, and hastily rushed a few divisions of troops to his western border. Pakistan had no formal diplomatic relations with the Kabul government, having severed them at the time of the Saur Revolution, in 1978, but in all other respects, especially trade, relations between the two countries were fairly normal. The joint frontier (1,500-miles long) remained open, and Afghan refugees continued to cross into Pakistan, where they were accorded 'sanctuary and humanitarian aid'. At this stage Zia had not yet come out openly in support of the Afghan resistance movement.

The Iranian leadership had also been taken by surprise by the Soviet invasion. Wary, suspicious, unsure, beset with conflicting internal pressures and not wanting their armed forces to clash with those of the USSR, the Iranians closed their frontier with

Afghanistan, refusing to accept any more refugees. In February 1980, Shia Afghan refugees in Iran were refused permission to establish a radio transmitter on Iranian soil.

Western opposition against the Soviet action was marshalled in the United Nations but on 8 January 1980 a Security Council Resolution (which would have been mandatory on all members), calling on the Soviets to withdraw from Afghanistan immediately, was vetoed by the USSR. However, on 15 January, a General Assembly Resolution (which was only recommendatory) was approved, condemning the Soviet aggression, and calling for instant withdrawal. A second General Assembly Resolution in a similar vein was approved on 20 November. Meanwhile, on 11 January, M. Pérez de Cuéllar had been appointed as Personal Representative of the UN Secretary General to liaise on the Afghan issue.

A meeting of Foreign Ministers of the (then) 42-member Islamic Conference Organisation (ICO) was held at Islamabad (Pakistan), at which Afghan membership was suspended until all Soviet troops had pulled out. Brezhnev remained deaf to appeals to withdraw his forces, proposals to allow Afghanistan to be 'neutralised', or requests to talk to representatives of the Afghan resistance movement. The Afghan pawn was firmly in Brezhnev's hand, and he meant to hold on to it.

Status of Forces Agreement

The Soviet military build-up continued smoothly and swiftly; equipment, ammunition and stores flooded into Afghanistan by air and road. Soon airfields were crowded with Soviet military aircraft and helicopters, and parks were packed with tanks and other vehicles, signs that the Soviets were preparing for a long stay. The Soviet military presence was 'legalised' by a Status of Armed Forces Agreement, signed in April 1980, catering for the temporary occupation of a Limited Contingent of Soviet Forces.

The Soviets claimed their military invasion had been in response to an invitation by President Babrak Karmal (who had actually been brought in by them after it had happened), under the terms of the Afghan-Soviet Friendship Treaty of 1978, to protect the country 'in the face of provocation from Afghanistan's external enemies', meaning the USA, China and Pakistan (*Kabul Radio*). Brezhnev later also occasionally quoted Article 15 of the United Nations Charter, in justification.

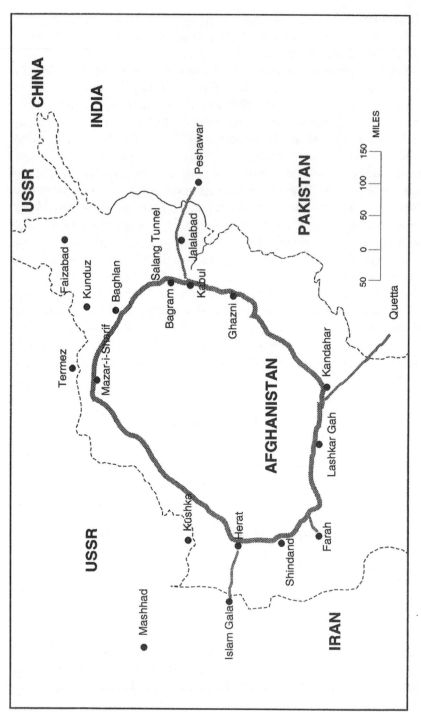

Afghanistan Strategic Routes

Soviet Strategy

Soviet armed forces, trained and conditioned to fight a major war against sophisticated enemies on a European battlefield, arrived with their full complement of tanks, arms and equipment for such a conflict, and were at once out of their element in mountainous, largely barren Afghanistan. They did not expect to have to fight, but just to provide firepower back-up for the Afghan army, which would combat 'rebels' on the ground. The Soviet strategic plan was that Soviet forces would occupy the main air bases, garrisons, government centres and key points, and use aircraft, helicopter-gunships, armoured vehicles and artillery, to keep open the roads linking them, assisting the Afghan army as necessary. The Soviets did not want to make themselves unduly unpopular with the Afghan people, and so sought to avoid clashing with the 'rebels' themselves as far as possible.

Before many weeks had passed the Soviets had two big disappointments. The first was that their brigade of Soviet Muslim troops, widely dispersed to work with Afghan formations actually fighting the 'rebels', instead of persuading the 'rebels' to lay down their arms and accept Kabul-type socialism, became sympathetic to Resistance aims, and began to help them, initially passing on information about impending sweeps, searches or attacks. This help progressed to providing 'drops' of arms, ammunition and food for the Resistance fighters, and some Soviet Muslims even gave their own arms. When they realised what was happening, horrified senior Soviet military commanders quickly sent this formation out of Afghanistan before it could do any more damage. They also began to thin out Soviet Muslim reservists within the formations, and replace them with Slavic conscripts.

The Afghan Army

The second big disappointment was the unreliability of the Afghan army. The Soviet military invasion caused a flood of anti-Soviet hatred across the country, affecting most sections of society, and this had a dire effect on the Afghan armed forces. Already the Afghan government's hold on certain major cities was tenuous, being barely controllable by day, while at night large sections were openly in insurgent hands. The Soviet arrival simply increased the existing hostility of the majority against the PDPA regime and its collaborators.

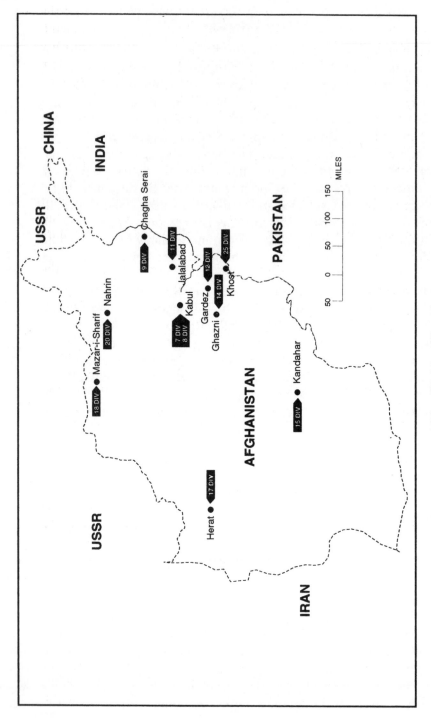

Afghan Divisional Locations
1980

The arrival of the Soviet armed forces strained the loyalty of the Afghan officer corps, already deeply rent by the Khalk-Parcham feud, but it had a more devastating effect on Afghan soldiers, already reluctant to fire on their own countrymen in case they became involved in a blood-feud, and who were now additionally expected to collaborate with, and take orders from, a foreign invader to act against their own people. Desertion increased, the deserters invariably taking their arms with them, either to use for the Resistance, or to sell on the black market. In February 1980, an amnesty offer was made to deserters to try to persuade them to return to their units, but this brought little response; neither did a later scheme for a 'voluntary call-up' for six months only, instead of the two-year obligatory conscription. The strength of the Afghan army during 1980 declined to 33,000 soldiers (*US State Department*).

As the full enormity of the Soviet military invasion dawned on the Afghan army, minor mutinies became frequent, and sometimes complete Afghan units, or sub-units, deserted with their arms to Resistance groups. In February, there was an insurgent rising in Kabul which Afghan troops refused to put down, and Soviet forces had to be brought in to quell it. The Soviet response was to deprive the Afghan army of its tanks, guns, missiles, rockets and mines (which included SAM-7s, RPG-7s, AGS-17 grenade-launchers and 122mm rockets), and impound them under Soviet guard. Some Afghan units were disbanded and others simply disarmed, but a number did continue to be reliable and so were included in Soviet operations, or left to fight against Resistance groups on their own.

The Soviets realised they would have to embark upon a gigantic training and indoctrination programme for the Afghan army, and that in the meantime Soviet troops would have to take on many of its tasks. To avoid conscription, many young Afghans were joining the streams of refugees heading for Pakistan.

Soviet Troops

Western reports indicated that young Soviet troops were bewildered by the terrain and the Afghan people, took time to acclimatise, and were in doubt as to precisely why they were in Afghanistan, having been told they had come to fight the Americans, Chinese or Pakistanis. Soviet regimental officers do not confide war aims, strategy or role to their soldiers, but hide behind Communist clichés;

and in any case they knew remarkably little about the 'enemy', meaning the 'rebels'.

It took Soviet conscripts some time to become conditioned to their new environment, and the more they saw, the less they liked it. Young Soviet regular officers were more enthusiastic, having mostly volunteered for a tour of duty in the country to gain battle experience at an early age, which they hoped would subsequently enhance their promotion prospects. The Soviet army had not seen any real active service since 1945 (which makes one wonder how medium-ranking officers could become so bemedalled without ever having seen a shot fired in war). However, it did have a long-forgotten experience of anti-insurgent warfare in the Turkistan region in the 1920s, and also of partisan warfare in the Second World War.

Soviet Offensive: March 1980

In March 1980, the Soviets launched a Spring campaign designed to clear Resistance fighters from the eastern provinces, and so block illicit supply routes from Pakistan; and also to clear the north-eastern province of Badakhshan, inhabited by several thousand Tadjik exiles from Soviet Turkistan, who had been startled into restive rebellion by the appearance of their former colonial masters. The Soviets also took strong action, using heavy fire-power, bombing insurgent positions, and harassing with rocket and machine-gun fire from helicopter-gunships, to rid Afghan cities and provincial capitals of Resistance occupation, partial occupation, or containment. Parts of Herat and Kandahar occupied by insurgents were heavily bombed and many buildings destroyed. In June, martial law was declared in both cities, which meant strict curfews, mass detentions and frequent searches. Insurgent disturbances also began to surface in Jalalabad.

By similar heavy-handed means, the Soviets strove to keep the main strategic roads between cities open. Resistance positions were bombed and machine-gunned, while villages and crops were razed to give Soviet aircraft good fields of vision. Helicopter-gunships flew above armoured vehicle-escorted road convoys, with bomber aircraft on call. Despite this Soviet use of fire-power, ambushes on roads were frequent, as the nature of the terrain, with narrow winding defiles through which roads passed, lent themselves to this tactic. In April, eight senior Soviet officers, including three Generals, were killed in one road ambush near the village of Kirga, on the Kabul-Jalalabad road.

A good hard-surface double-track road linked Kabul in a huge circle with Ghazni, Kandahar, Lashkar Gah, Shindand, Herat and Shibargham which, for convenience and clarity, can be referred to as the Circular Road. This road had off-shoots from Kabul to Jalalabad; Kandahar to Quetta (in Pakistan); to Farah and Zaranj and southern Iran; Herat to Islam Gala (in Iran); and from Herat north to Merv (in the USSR). The so-called Northern Route ran from Kabul, through Bagram and the Salang Tunnel (1.7 miles in length) to Mazar-i-Sharif, and then north to the Amu Darya.

At night the Soviets did not operate on the ground outside their own perimeter defences, or garrisons, and so the strategic roads came under control of Resistance fighters, who during the hours of darkness emerged to lay mines, destroy bridges and culverts, prepare dawn ambushes and intimidate the civilian population. Strategic roads were soon littered with damaged or burnt-out Soviet armoured vehicles and other debris of the insurgency, while alongside the roads were razed villages, smashed irrigation systems, and scorched-earth fields.

During the Spring of 1980, Resistance groups emerged from valleys in the provinces of Kunar, Laghman, Nangrahar, Logar and Paktia, to lay ambushes and attack government vehicles on the Northern Route. [The term 'government forces', unless otherwise stated, covers both Soviet and Afghan units.] Also, the natural gas pipeline from Shibargham eastwards to Mazar-i-Sharif (which had developed into a natural gas industrial town), was disrupted several times by sabotage, but damage was repaired so quickly that the Resistance seemed to give up on this target, and left it alone for a while.

The Soviets invited fraternal military experts in insurgent warfare from Vietnam to advise on how to counter Resistance tactics, and a Vietnamese delegation visited Afghanistan. Marshal Sokolov rejected out of hand its recommendation to use small sub-units of Special Forces, supported and supplied by helicopters. Like most Soviet Generals, Sokolov had an inherent dislike of guerrilla warfare, believing that partisans should be eliminated and areas depopulated where necessary, exemplified by Stalin's policies in the Second World War. Soviet ground forces in Afghanistan momentarily retained their conventional formations and conventional tactics as far as was possible.

Soviet Reorganisation: July 1980

In July 1980, the Soviets divided Afghanistan into seven military districts, each under the command of a Soviet General paired with an Afghan General or senior Afghan government official; each district had a detachment of Special Forces commandos at its disposal, and a number of Mi-24 helicopters. The Limited Contingent of Soviet Forces in Afghanistan now probably numbered about 85,000; deployed in four divisions and a few independent brigades. In the reorganisation, most of the main battle tanks and heavy weapons, much of the unnecessary support units and equipment, and certain Divisional HQs had been sent back to the USSR.

The Soviet Mi-24, first introduced into Soviet service in 1973, had steadily developed into a formidable attack-helicopter, nick-named the 'Flying Tank' by Soviet troops. Carrying a four-barrel 12.7mm rotary cannon, it also had an array of missiles and rockets under its short stubby wings (*IISS*), and could carry eight fully-equipped soldiers. Shoulder-held anti-aircraft missiles, like the SAM-7, were generally ineffective against the lightly armoured Mi-24D model, and it was not until June 1985, when two deserting Afghan pilots flew two of these types to Pakistan, that Americans were able to work out how to penetrate their electronic defence system. With top fighter cover, Mi-24 helicopter-gunships spearheaded Soviet 'search-and-destroy' operations during the first four years of the Soviet occupation.

The Soviet Air Force

By mid-1980, the CIA estimated that there were over 320 Soviet combat aircraft deployed in Afghanistan, including 100 MiG-21s, 30 MiG-23s and 70 Mi-24 helicopters. There were also a number of air force squadrons north of the Amu Darya, including some with long-range bomber aircraft. The Soviets brought in modern landing and communications equipment to upgrade Afghan air bases, established new air bases and airfields, and accumulated stocks of bombs, rockets, missiles and high-octane fuel. Afghan air bases given priority by the Soviets included those at Bagram, Farah, Herat, Kabul International (the air base was alongside, and used, civilian runways), Lashkar Gah and Shindand.

To counter increasing American naval projection into the Indian Ocean and the Arabian Sea, in the Spring of 1980, the Shindand air base was adapted to operate Soviet long-range naval reconnaissance missions. Also, specially-equipped ECM-ELINT (Electronic Counter-Measures—Electronic Intelligence) versions of the Antonov-12 and Antonov-22, usually with Ariana (Afghan civilian air-line) markings, flew from this base. When the Iran-Iraq War broke out in September 1980, these missions were intensified. Early in 1981, five pre-production SU-25s (a STOL attack aircraft) were sent to Bagram air base for testing (*IISS*), after which a 15-plane squadron of SU-25s was formed there.

The Afghan Air Force

The Afghan Air Force (AAF) had also deteriorated, although not to the same extent as the army. Afghan pilots, and to a lesser extent air crew and technicians, had been carefully selected, given lengthy training in the USSR, and were generally considered to have become Sovietised. However, collaboration with a foreign enemy against their fellow countrymen affected the AAF, and there were desertions. CIA sources estimated that over 1,000 air force personnel deserted in 1980, and another 1,000 in 1981.

Soviet pilots were introduced into Afghan squadrons to fill gaps caused by defections, and in two-seater aircraft there was invariably one Soviet pilot. Otherwise rigid restriction of fuel was the Soviet security measure. Two Soviet MiG-19 squadrons were attached to the AAF. About 40 Afghan aircraft were destroyed in 1980, mostly on the ground by sabotage, but also through Resistance raids on air bases. The AAF also received a few Mi-24 helicopters. The main handicap of the AAF was a shortage of technicians. Ariana still functioned but in a very reduced capacity, as many of its pilots and crews had defected.

Soviet Starvation Tactics

The initial Soviet aim was quickly to break the will of the Resistance groups by hitting them hard whenever they would stand and fight. In 1980, a few of them, with misguided enthusiasm, charged into battle whereupon Soviet fire-power caused them many casualties. Soviet initial operations highlighted several problems. One of them was the narrowness of the many fertile valleys in which large numbers of people lived and worked; another was the dearth of tracks suitable for motorised traffic, apart from the few strategic roads.

103

This made it difficult for the Soviets quickly to concentrate sufficient military force against Resistance targets, as only limited numbers of vehicles could be squeezed into some of the valleys, and once inside they were invariably deprived of manoeuvre. Once in the valleys, Soviet tracked-vehicles became strung out in single file, vulnerable to Resistance flanking attacks and ambushes from higher ground. An early Resistance tactic was to allow a Soviet column to enter a valley along a single track, and then destroy the last vehicle, thus trapping the whole column. Another problem was that Soviet tracked-vehicles quickly churned up the roadways, making them impassable for their own motorised support vehicles.

To overcome these problems, the Soviets instituted what became known as their 'starvation policy'. Having insufficient troops available to pursue Resistance fighters right into the valleys to bring them to battle, they blockaded the broad entrances of the main valleys in which there were active Resistance groups by means of 'blanket bombing', artillery barrages, and the use of assault helicopters to terrify the inhabitants into either moving further up into the less fertile reaches, becoming refugees, or flocking into the cities. The mouths of the valleys became Free Fire Zones, in which crops were burnt, live-stock killed and irrigation works destroyed. Any person found in a Free Fire Zone became a legitimate target for government forces' guns and bombs. The real objective was to protect strategic roads from attacks from the branching valleys.

Autumn Offensive: 1980

Getting their second wind, in the Autumn of 1980, the Soviets began to launch a series of aggressive 'sweep-and-destroy' operations into some of the main valleys that harboured large Resistance groups. For this purpose over 6,000 Soviet troops were mustered, and as many 'reliable' Afghan units as were available, supported by bomber-aircraft, helicopter-gunships and mobile artillery. The first such operation, known as 'Panjshir-1' (*Urban*) and commencing in late August, went into the long narrow Panjshir Valley (in Kapisa province), which had strategic significance because the crossroad town of Gulbahar was at its mouth, only some five miles from the Northern Route, just south of the Salang Tunnel. The major town of Charikar was on the northern Route (some 12 miles from Gulbahar), south of which lay the Resistance-infected Shomali Valley and Plateau.

The Soviet-Afghan force moved through the Free Fire Zone into the Panjshir Valley but, as the valley narrowed and vehicles were confined to a single motorable track, the way ahead was increasingly blocked by boulders while rocks periodically rained down on the Soviet-Afghan column. Bulldozers were constantly clearing the track ahead as Resistance fighters were kept at bay by helicopter-gunships. Determinedly, but very slowly, the column pushed forward, but after two weeks it ground to a halt and, to avoid being trapped, had to withdraw completely. The operation was absorbing too much manpower and too many military resources for no apparent gain; and the casualties of men and vehicles had mounted at an unacceptable rate.

A similar operation was launched in September into the Kunar Valley (Kunar province) to protect the Kabul-Jalalabad road by blocking Resistance infiltration from Pakistan, and this had a somewhat similar result. Two more large Soviet-Afghan operations were launched into two large valleys in Paktia province in October, but both terminated within two weeks with nothing to show except more casualties. One more similar attempt was made in November, to clear a valley in Logar province, immediately south of Kabul, but this had barely started before it had to be aborted due to the onset of winter weather, together with another incursion into the Panjshir Valley.

In all these operations the Soviets had made liberal use of bomber aircraft and helicopter-gunships to clear valley floors, causing the inhabitants quickly to take to the hills on either side to shelter in caves, or to disappear into smaller side valleys. As soon as the aircraft departed, Resistance fighters reappeared to take aggressive action against strung-out government columns. The Soviets had intended these operations to be aggressive but in reality they were defensive. Soviet air mobility and technical superiority were countered by Resistance 'foot-mobility' that quickly took fighters where neither tracked nor wheeled vehicles could follow. It was stalemate from the start.

As Winter closed in, the Soviets ceased ground operations, contenting themselves with reactive bombing, shelling and helicopter-gunship missions, concentrating on protecting their bases and encampments, and securing strategic roads, along which heavily-escorted government convoys moved in daylight hours only. One CIA source estimated that Soviet casualties in 1980 were just over 5,000, but gave no figures for losses of vehicles. Neither did it mention Afghan army casualties as Afghan soldiers, although sometimes small in number, were involved in all operations, usually being sent into action first by the Soviets.

Soviet Generals sat back to reflect on their lack of success. Conditioned and trained for fast-moving mobile warfare in European terrain, their troops were uneasy and stifled when penned up in narrow valleys. Despite patchy good work by Afghan units in Soviet-commanded operations, generally the Afghan army proved to be more disappointing than Soviet Generals had feared and, as there was no sign of any policy change from Moscow, they realised that Soviet units would have to bear the brunt of ground fighting in 1981.

Parchamis v Khalkis

President Karmal had not taken seriously his Moscow remit to heal the PDPA rift and instead set about making his Parcham faction dominant in both government and military circles. Parchami detainees were released, and many restored to their former appointments or positions, while imprisoned Khalkis remained in gaol, to be joined by more Khalkis as Karmal quietly carried out purges. However, all Khalkis could not be made to disappear from the public scene overnight, and so the two factions had ostensibly to try to get on with one another as best they could.

This proved difficult. For example, in October 1980, two Afghan armoured regiments at Poli Charki, one commanded by a Parchami officer, and the other by a Khalki, fought a mini-battle against each other. Soviet troops had to be called out to separate the two regiments, and it was some 10 days before a semblance of discipline was restored.

The defection rate amongst Afghan army officers was surprisingly small, although precise figures are hard to come by, and so there must have been substance to the claim that they had been 'well-Sovietised'. The Afghan officer corps was on the way to becoming a class apart, believing it knew what was best for the country, and impatient of backward, dragging feudalism and tribalism. There were many defections, of course, but reasons often included in-house factional quarrelling, pique at unfavourable promotion decisions, or malicious treatment of Khalkis by the now dominant Parchamis. The Military Academy at Kabul was readjusting to running three-month crash courses to produce junior officers.

Afghan conscript soldiers, on the other hand, deserted in droves whenever opportunity occurred during the first two years of the Soviet occupation, as indeed they had been doing since the Saur Revolution. Military service remained very unpopular, and was avoided whenever possible. In an effort to boost military manpower, the age of call-up for conscription was lowered progressively from 21 to 19 years, and authority given to retain conscripts after their obligatory service had expired, and also to call-up reservists.

There remained a small but dedicated core of professional soldiers who perhaps in other circumstances would be regarded as mercenaries, and who were attracted to active military service, liked military life, and for reasons that may have included poverty, unemployment, or being unable to return to their village or tribe, were content to be long-service soldiers. This small professional core kept the Afghan armed forces viable and active. One scheme that did have some success was that a number of these professional soldiers were eventually commissioned as junior officers, and sent on short training courses to the USSR. Throughout, the Afghan armed forces were woefully short of junior leaders.

Soviet Psy-Ops

Soviet Psy-Ops personnel worked to obtain the support of the Afghan people on what might be termed 'hearts and minds' lines. For example, a 42-hours a week radio programme in both Dari and Pushtu was instituted, explaining that the Soviet armed forces had been invited into Afghanistan to help protect the country from 'Western imperialism', and would be withdrawn as soon as this external danger subsided. The other aspect of Soviet Psy-Ops was to undermine the will of the Resistance groups, and those in opposition to the Kabul government, which was done by reviving old feuds, both family and tribal, instigating quarrels between groups, casting doubts on the competence and loyalty of Resistance leaders, and spreading black propaganda and rumours to cause alarm and instability.

The Kabul Government

President Karmal regarded his term of office as the second phase of the Saur Revolution, which had abolished the country's former Constitution. To fill this gap, in April 1980 he introduced a document entitled '*The Basic Principles of the Democratic Republic of Afghanistan*', specifying the structure and functions of government, which would serve as a makeshift temporary Constitution. He also abolished the national red flag with its star and wheat-sheaf emblem, reverting to the generally more acceptable black, red and green tricolour.

In an effort to rally popular support for his own government, Karmal, in December 1980, formed the National Patriotic Front, designed to attract a wide range of ethnic and political elements. In June 1981, he announced that the unpopular land reform conditions would be reviewed and that, in the meantime, families with sons serving voluntarily in the armed forces would receive priority in land distribution. The same month, Karmal reorganised the National Patriotic Front into the National Fatherland Front (NFF), which he hoped would become a mass organisation embracing all sections of Afghan society.

Defection of Afghan ministers and other leading citizens continued to plague President Karmal during 1981, as he struggled to hold his government together. He had to contend with both inefficiency and corruption, and established a Special Department within the Prime Minister's Office to deal with this monumental task, but it was only a cosmetic measure. Karmal also made a special effort to obtain the support of Islamic leaders, most of whom had been deeply offended and alienated by President Hafizullah Amin's policies. Those in detention were released, and all Islamic leaders given government help.

In April 1981, Karmal established the Supreme Council of the Ulema to further Islamic teaching, to hold Islamic conferences and discussions, and to arrange visits for Afghan clerics to Islamic centres in the USSR. Karmal also tried to woo the tribes and ethnic groups and, in May, established a Ministry of Border and Tribal Affairs; in June, he enlarged the ruling Revolutionary Council to give it a pan-Afghan look, and suggested a scheme for localised government, based on a hierarchy of village councils, rising to provincial level.

President Reagan: 1981

The outbreak of the Iran-Iraq War caused considerable anxiety, not only to the USSR, because it might spill over into Afghanistan and was prompting the USA to take a greater military interest in the region than formerly, but also to President Karmal, who feared an eastward spread of Khomeini's Shia fundamentalism and remembered that Iran still harboured age-old territorial claims to parts of Afghan territory. The governments of both the USSR and Afghanistan became cautious, precise and correct in their dealings with Iran.

In the USA, in January 1981, Ronald Reagan succeeded Jimmy Carter as President, and that month American hostages held in the American Embassy in Tehran were released. Both Brezhnev and Karmal breathed more easily, as both feared that a new American President might want to take the military option to force their release, which would have brought American troops to the borders of both Afghanistan and the USSR.

Reagan worked to revive US military strength and prestige, and gave immediate attention to expanding and upgrading the US Rapid Deployment Force and to projecting US power into the Gulf and the Arabian Sea. Reagan also took up the cause of the Afghan Resistance organisations, which now had their political HQs in Pakistan, promising them badly-needed arms and other military aid. In June 1981, Reagan, needing a strong, viable ally in the southern Asian dimension of the superpower conflict, offered more generous military aid to President Zia and the following month agreed to let Pakistan have US F-16 aircraft. This brought Reagan into conflict with India, which protested vigorously at the rearmament of Pakistan, its old enemy. Previously, in January, Zia had proposed at the Third Islamic Summit, held at Taif (Saudi Arabia), that there should be Tripartite Talks between Pakistan, Afghanistan and Iran.

Ministry of the Interior Forces

Because of the aggressive activities of certain Resistance groups in penetrating, and even taking over, parts of cities and towns, and a wave of assassinations of political leaders and government officials, forces under the control of the Ministry of the Interior were expanded. This included the Gendarmerie (Sarandoy), which had become responsible for security in Kabul, and began to expand to other major cities for the same purpose; it was intended to free Afghan military formations for a more mobile role against Resistance groups. The part-time 'home guard' militias, known as Revolutionary Defence Groups, were also expanded and were slightly better organised. Towards the end of 1980, a new paramilitary body, known as the Border Force, was formed under the Ministry of the Interior, and its detachments were positioned in sensitive border areas to monitor illegal crossing routes.

Unreliable Reporting

Soviet and Afghan communiqués were heavily censored, and so were immediately suspect in the West, as were their excessive claims of successes in the field, and casualties inflicted on the 'rebels'. In November 1981, the editor of the *Afghan News Media* defected to Pakistan and, when questioned by CIA officers, stated that the whole Afghan media was completely manipulated and controlled by Soviet 'advisers', who deliberately issued misleading bulletins. However, the communiqués put out by the various Resistance HQs, reporting battles fought and won, and the numbers of Soviet soldiers killed, were even less credible, invariably lacking verification. Nevertheless they tended to be heeded by the West, because they were saying what the West wanted to hear. Indeed, these misleading reports were often endorsed by the CIA, one suspects for this reason. It is true, however, that the CIA suddenly became handicapped in its information-gathering role in mid-1980, when the bulk of Soviet signals traffic in Afghanistan was switched to 'hardened' land-lines (*Urban*), and so it was desperately short of reliable intelligence. As Western journalists were progressively restricted, and then barred, by President Karmal, the outsider's window on events in Afghanistan became, to say the least, opaque.

As reliable hard news about events in Afghanistan became scarce, the world's media came to rely upon, and frequently quote, 'Diplomatic sources in Kabul'; but as foreign diplomats were themselves strictly confined to the capital, the information produced was merely bazaar gossip of doubtful validity. Because of these drawbacks in the early years of the Soviet occupation of Afghanistan, the CIA and other American analysts continually liken the situation in Afghanistan to the American experience in Vietnam, which further confuses the picture, as there were so many different factors in the respective struggles.

Operations in 1981

In February 1981, Mohammed Rafi, the Afghan Defence Minister, boasted that 'the back of the Resistance is broken ... it will all be over within six months' (*Kabul Radio*); but the abrasive stalemate continued throughout the year, and beyond. However, during this period Soviet and Afghan armed forces did gain a greater control over some of the cities, and the roads between them, at least in daylight hours. The government garrison at Kandahar remained besieged by Resistance fighters in its Chowee cantonment area, and at one period lost control of the 18-mile road out to the air base and airport. A large part of the province of Herat remained firmly in Resistance hands, and several attacks were made on the Afghan garrison which, in December 1981, lost all control of Herat city, only regaining it late the following month.

At Ghazni, the defecting Afghan garrison was attacking by Soviet and Afghan troops, and in the fighting the Soviets lost a number of armoured vehicles. Rumours and counter-rumours of victories, defeats, ambushes, air raids and heavy casualties abounded in the eastern provinces adjacent to Pakistan. In June, the Resistance captured its first Soviet air force pilot when his aircraft was brought down, and he was smuggled into Pakistan for a propaganda display to the Press.

During 1981, the Afghan Resistance began to change tactics from traditional mass tribal charges to guerrilla hit-and-run tactics. The Soviets continued to rely upon massive fire-power and bomber aircraft, 'starvation' tactics, depopulating certain areas and creating Free Fire Zones alongside roads. Many inhabitants fled to the cities and population centres, outside which Displaced Persons Camps (DPCs) were constructed, thus enabling the authorities to exercise some measure of control. These DPCs, on which many internal refugees, being divorced from their land, had to rely entirely for food and shelter, especially in the winter months, assisted the enforcement of conscription, and enabled deserters to be identified and arrested; they were also a fertile ground for alleged 'press gang' recruitment.

The Soviets still mounted occasional all-arms 'search-and-destroy' operations into certain valleys, including yet another into the Panjshir Valley, against the tough Resistance group there, which periodically ambushed convoys on the Northern Route, and sabotaged culverts. Penetration attempts into valleys were again only partially successful.

Fighting tended to focus on Gulbahar, parts of which changed hands several times. There was almost continual skirmishing on the Shomali Plateau, just north of Kabul, where large Free Fire Zones had been created on either side of the Northern Route. Lack of success in the Panjshir Valley, which became something of a prestige Resistance base, prompted Marshal Sokolov to visit Afghanistan with a team of Soviet Generals, after which the strength of the Limited Contingent of Soviet Forces in Afghanistan was increased.

In June, there was a protracted battle in the Paghman area, some 12 miles north-west of Kabul, in which at one juncture some 300 officer cadets from the Military Academy at Kabul were thrown into action on the government side. Reportedly, 200 of them went over to the Resistance, and most of the remainder were captured by 'rebels', to be killed when government forces withdrew from that area. It was later announced, (*Kabul Radio*) that the Military Academy, which then probably had about 4,000 officer cadets on crash courses, had become deeply involved in the Parcham-Khalk feud, and was to be closed down. In fact, it was taken over by the Soviet military mission, and its location changed.

In all Soviet-Afghan operations, as had become customary, Afghan units were placed in the forefront of the battle, but there were few reports of them actually refusing to fight. Like traditional mercenaries they did not seem to mind who they were fighting. By this time, the Soviets had become convinced that their new T-72 main battle tanks were fairly useless in Afghan terrain, and most of them, together with their crews and maintenance teams, had been withdrawn. One batch of about 100 tanks and 8,000 soldiers was sent back to the USSR and considerable publicity, but this was soon found to be a routine troop rotation, as reinforcements took their place. Remaining Soviet tanks stayed on vehicle parks.

The Wakhan Strip

In June 1980, Soviet troops had entered the Wakhan Strip, which brought them to the 40-mile long Afghan-Chinese border. The Soviets and the Chinese already share a 3,125-mile joint frontier, parts of which are in dispute, so the significance was simply that the Soviets were able to block this small back-door arms route from China to the Resistance in Afghanistan.

The Soviets (and the Indians) had a far more worrying problem, that of the all-weather Karakorum Highway, linking Rawalpindi, (adjacent to Islamabad) through the Huntsa Valley and over the Himalayan Karakorum mountain range to Kasgar, in China, which had been opened in 1978. This was the first land access route between the two countries, and the nightmare was that hundreds of thousands of Chinese soldiers could be trucked along it within hours to reinforce Pakistan, if required — although Brezhnev became less worried when he saw the Chinese military shambles in their war against Vietnam.

More Soviet troops were packed into the Wakhan Strip during 1981, and a strong base was established at Ishkashim, the Pass controlling the entrance from Afghanistan, where, according to the CIA, ballistic missiles were being installed, targeted on Pakistan. The 3,000 or more inhabitants of the Strip fled into Pakistan, and Soviet border guards, under KGB direction, controlled this section of the Chinese frontier. On 16 June 1981, a Soviet-Afghan Border Agreement was signed covering the Soviet occupation of the Wakhan Strip, but no details were released; this caused the Americans to allege that the USSR had annexed this piece of Afghan territory.

Pakistan-Afghanistan Hijack

On 2 March 1981, a Pakistan Air Lines Boeing 720, on an internal flight from Karachi to Peshawar was hijacked just before landing at Peshawar by three men armed with pistols and grenades. The pilot was forced to fly the aircraft, which had 148 people on board, to Kabul International Airport, where, with hostages and hijackers still on board, it remained on the tarmac apron for several days, surrounded by Afghan security forces.

The hijackers were members of the 'Al Zulfikar' terrorist group, led by Murtaza Bhutto, son of Prime Minister Ali Zulfikar Bhutto, who had been executed in Pakistan in 1979; this group was regarded as the 'military arm' of the People's Party of Pakistan. Murtaza Bhutto had been in Kabul for several months, allegedly organising terrorist exploits directed against President Zia of Pakistan. He was allowed to go on board the hijacked airliner to speak to the terrorists—and is alleged to have given them more weaponry.

Murtaza Bhutto demanded, in exchange for the safe release of the aircraft and all on board, the freeing of over 90 people detained in Pakistan. President Zia refused. On 8 March, the terrorists shot and killed a passenger, a Pakistani diplomat, and then threatened to kill three American passengers if the demands were not met. Zia agreed to release 54 political prisoners, and the exchange was made at Damascus airport on 25 March. The three terrorists and some of the released Pakistani detainees returned to Kabul, where they were given sanctuary.

In December 1981, Britain, France and West Germany severed civilian air links with Afghanistan in protest against the Kabul government's continued refusal to extradite Murtaza Bhutto and other terrorists to Pakistan for trial. By this time, international Western civilian airline flights into Kabul had anyway been reduced to one weekly flight to and from London.

Chemical Warfare

In December 1981, the CIA alleged there had been an accident involving chemical warfare materials in Afghanistan; and later in March 1982, it was also stated (*US Presidential spokesman*) that '3,042 people had died in 47 gas attacks between mid-1979 and mid-1981'. However, doctors of the French organisation *Médecin sans Frontières*, working in Afghan hospitals reported they had not seen any evidence to support these allegations. A US State Department bulletin explained that the material identified was 'Yellow Rain' (Trichothevebe-mycotoxin). Yellow Rain had been used by Americans in Vietnam, and this probably influenced American thinking.

6

The Mujahideen: 1982-83

When the National Islamic Front called for an Afghan *Jihad* against the Kabul government in March 1979, Afghan Resistance fighters became known as Mujahideen (Holy War warriors). When the Soviets invaded in December that year, the *Jihad* was extended to them. During the period 1978-79, it was estimated there were about 30 separate Mujahideen groups, a number that probably increased to over 40 after the Soviet arrival. Most of them were small, locally-based and insignificant, but over the months they were absorbed by larger groups, some surviving in obscurity, others simply dissolving.

Almost all the Mujahideen groups espoused Islam as part of their platform, and the few completely secular groups soon foundered. For example, the Chinese-supported 'Shola Java' group, operating in the Wakhan Strip, was exiled to Pakistan when the Soviets depopulated that territory; it then briefly split into two parts, the 'Sama' and the 'Nama', before disappearing completely.

The Peshawar Seven

Eventually seven major Mujahideen groups came to dominate the scene, each having a strong political leadership, a well-developed political administration and an active public relations element. It was suspected that their claimed support by activists in the field in the interior of Afghanistan was exaggerated. All were based in Pakistan, and accordingly had access to the world media—but decidedly less access to Afghanistan.

Afghan Mujahideen groups, large and small, were fiercely

115

independent and reluctant to co-operate with each other, let alone submit to another's leadership. This independence, a sturdy characteristic, proved to be a disadvantage during the long-drawn out struggle. All groups were committed to ejecting the Soviets from their country, and to removing the Karmal government, but each differed as to how exactly this should be done. Absence of united leadership mean that there was no agreed central strategy and so throughout the conflict Mujahideen efforts were disjointed.

In August 1979, four of the major Mujahideen groups formed a loose coalition, but could not produce an accepted national leader. In March the following year, six of the major groups formed themselves into the 'Islamic Alliance for the Liberation of Afghanistan', to lobby for international support, arms and money, but each continued to claim it alone represented the Mujahideen fighters in Afghanistan. It had no better fortune.

By 1982, seven major Mujahideen groups became known as the 'Peshawar Seven', or the 'Seveners' (*Haftganah*) although in the course of their separate evolutions their designations tended to alter, and also to suffer from mistranslation. They were:

    1. The *Hizb-i-Islami Afghanistan* (HIA)—known in Afghanistan as the *Akhwanul Muslimin* (Muslim Brotherhood)—was led by Gulbuddin Hekmatyar, a veteran opposition Afghan politican, who claimed to lead the largest Mujahideen group, of some 40,000 armed warriors. Hekmatyar was a Fundamentalist;

    2. The *Jamiat-i-Islami*—(Islamic Association), (IA); it claimed to be the second largest group, with over 20,000 armed warriors in the field; led by Burhanuddin Rabbani, a Fundamentalist;

    3. *Hizb-i-Islami*—(HI) (a break-away from the main *Hizb-i-Islami* group), led by Younis Khalis, a Fundamentalist;

    4. *Islamic Unity for the Liberation of Afghanistan*, (IULA), led by Abdur Rasaul Sayaf, a Fundamentalist;

    5. *Harkat-i-Inquilabi Islami*—(Islamic Revolutionary Movement) (IRM), led by Mohammed Nabi Mohammadi, a Traditionalist;

    6. *Mahaz-e-Milli Afghanistan*—(National Islamic Front of Afghanistan) (NIFA), led by Mohammed Gilani, a Traditionalist;

    7. *Jabhe-ye Nijate Milli Afghanistan*—(National Liberation Front), (NLF), led by Sibghatullah Mujadidi, a Traditionalist.

There were also other unaffiliated Mujahideen fringe groups, and splinters, which tended to be even more insular, remaining to an extent apart from the Resistance mainstream.

In mid-1983, the Peshawar Seven divided into two alignments. The first, the Fundamentalist *'Islamic Unity of Afghan Mujahideen'*, was led by Abdur Rasaul Sayaf, with Gulbuddin Hekmatyar as his deputy, and consisted of:

- Islamic Unity for the Liberation of Afghanistan (IULA)
- *Hezb-i-Islami Afghanistan* (HIA).
- *Jamiat-i-Islami* (IA), and the
- *Hizb-i-Islami* (HI)

The Traditionalist alignment, known as the *Islamic Alliance*, was led by Mohammed Gilani, and consisted of:

- *Harakat-i-Inquilabi Islami* (IRM),
- *Mahaz-ye Nijate Milli Afghanistan* (NIFA), and the
- *Jabhe-ye Nijate Milli Afghanistan* (NLF).

These two alignments were known for some months as the 'Unity' group and the 'Alliance' group. An *IISS* commentator wrote: 'They often appear more intent on establishing their political pre-eminence within the resistance movement than on driving the Soviet forces out of Afghanistan'.

Shia Afghan Mujahideen Groups

Having sufficient problems of its own, the new Islamic government in Iran initially stood back from the Afghan struggle, but after an interval it did recognise the exiled HQs of a number of small, quarrelling Afghan Shia Mujahideen groups, whose fighters were allegedly operating in western and central parts of Afghanistan. They were kept on a very tight political rein, and given very sparse military aid. Afghan refugees moving into Iran, Mujahideen or not, were very restricted, expected to conform rigidly to all national laws, and to work for their keep; Afghan refugees reaching Pakistan on the other hand had political freedom and were eventually fed by United Nations and other charitable organisations.

Mujahideen Strength

The strength of Mujahideen armed fighters in the field was subject to many 'guesstimates' as no one knew for sure just how many there were, how many had arms, or how effective they were. Uncertainty was further compounded by the fact that Mujahideen strength, whatever it was, fluctuated seasonally. It was much less in Winter, and when the crops had to be planted or harvested; but for the rest of the time there were ample men available, especially for opportunity fighting.

In the campaigning seasons, 'guesstimates' of Mujahideen seemed to vary between 100,000 and 200,000, governed perhaps by the numbers of weapons that might be available to them. In some parts of the country there were small, full-time hard cores of Mujahideen, always available for both offensive and defensive duties, but the presence, or otherwise, of these small 'regular' groups depended upon the quality of local leadership, and whether funds were available to pay them so that their families would not starve.

The Mujahideen in the field also lacked leaders capable of uniting the various groups, and persuading them to co-operate with each other. Several people tried to take on this role, but none was successful for long. For example, in the Summer of 1981, four separate Mujahideen groups in Paktia province agreed that their leader should be Younis Khalis, a Mullah who, although rather old by campaigning standards, was full of vitality. This arrangement did not survive long as, when differences arose, aggrieved Mujahideen groups simply ignored his authority, and carried on in their own way. Another attempt was made about the same time to unite Mujahideen groups in the Nimroz, Farah, Herat and Baughis provinces in the western part of the country, under Sibghatullah Mujadidi, also a religious leader, but this did not succeed either. Ambitious political leaders with religious standing or qualifications did not scruple to use these assets to the utmost to attain their goals.

Mujahideen Arms Supplies

As the *Jihad* developed and expanded, the Mujahideen began to appeal for modern arms and ammunition, especially those capable of combating armoured vehicles and helicopters; but they were very slow to arrive. Up until then, the Mujahideen had to rely upon weapons obtained by raiding Afghan army armouries and those brought over by deserters but, latterly, owing to the Soviets having impounded so many Afghan army weapons and disarmed certain Afghan units, these two sources almost dried up. Deserters seldom had arms to bring with them as unit security restrictions were implemented. Ammunition was always in short supply as the

Mujahideen, in their enthusiasm, tended to fire excessively whenever they had the opportunity, without thought of replenishment problems.

The main obstacle to arms supplies to the Mujahideen from external sources, which virtually meant through Pakistan, was the disunity of the Mujahideen political leadership. Leaders of the Peshawar Seven groups had rejected the proposal to declare a government-in-exile, as that would have been an admission they were not in the field fighting with their followers. For example, Saudi Arabia early sent a donation of $25 million to purchase arms, but the money lay in a Peshawar bank for many months, as the Saudis would not release it until some form of Mujahideen unity was achieved.

Timidly, in the latter months of the Carter administration, the USA (through the CIA) began covertly to supply arms purchased in Egypt to the Afghan Mujahideen, some $350 million a year being spent in this way for the first two years of the Soviet occupation (*CIA Sources*). These arms were copies of Soviet AK-47s (Kalishnikovs), RPG-7s, 122mm rockets, mortars and land-mines, but this source ceased when President Sadat was assassinated in October 1981.

A few Chinese-manufactured arms of similar types trickled across the Karakorum Highway into Pakistan for the Mujahideen, but the Chinese wanted hard currency on delivery, so this source was slow to develop. President Zia kept a tight control of all arms coming into Pakistan intended for the Mujahideen in Afghanistan, and detailed his Inter-Service Intelligence (ISI) Branch to control, store and selectively dole out arms to the Peshawar Seven groups, on the basis of their willingness to co-operate. Some of these groups received none at all, others just a few, while the bulk went to Hekmatyar's HIA, despite complaints from the others—and from the CIA.

Soviet Strategy

Throughout 1982-83 neither Afghan government forces, nor the Mujahideen in the field gained any significant advantage. The Soviets no longer sought to seize and hold territory; their ground operations became punitive, rather than empirical; and they had to devise tactics to avoid, and counter, Mujahideen mortar, rocket and sniper fire from higher levels of terrain, such as hill-sides in valleys. They also developed the use of helicopters, especially for quick reaction to an incident, and for putting down assault troops at key points to prevent Mujahideen flanking attacks, and for ambushing retreating Mujahideen.

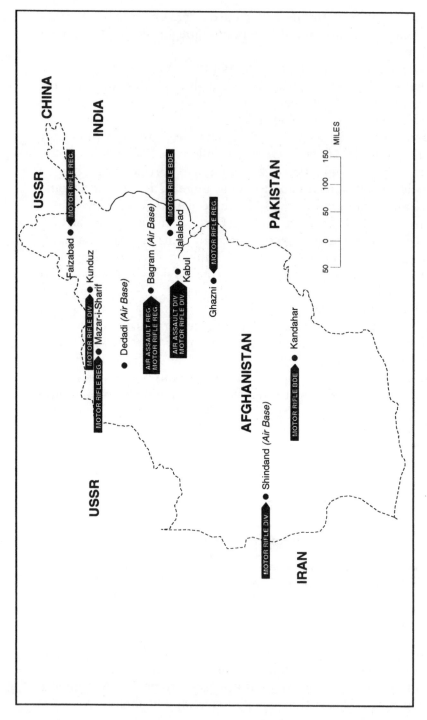

Soviet Ground Deployment
1983-84

The Soviets continued spasmodically their 'search-and-destroy' operations, but although *Kabul Radio* spokesmen repeatedly claimed that in certain areas 'the rebels had been dissolved', this was rarely so; mostly it was a case of tactical withdrawal to home villages to lie low for a while, before reappearing when the time was opportune. During this period, government troops launched a series of 'clearing' operations in the sparsely-populated northern Afghan provinces that bordered the USSR; and also gave special attention to monitoring supply trails from Pakistan into the eastern provinces. The Soviets continued their strategy of maintaining the 'starvation policy', Free Fire Zones, depopulating certain valleys, herding internal refugees into DPCs and keeping the main roads open in daylight hours.

There was an early disaster in the Salang Tunnel on 2 November 1982, caused by a collision inside the tunnel between a fuel tanker and another vehicle. The resultant chaos caused Soviet soldiers guarding the tunnel at either end to assume there was a Mujahideen attack and shoot-out inside the tunnel, and they immediately blocked both entrances. Inside the tunnel fire broke out, and some 400 Soviet and 700 Afghan troops probably perished. The Salang Tunnel did not reopen for nine days. Belatedly, some Mujahideen groups claimed responsibility for this incident, but the truth seems to be that it was an accident caused by human error, compounded by panic. Already, competing Mujahideen groups were falsely claiming responsibility for individual incidents to obtain publicity and credibility.

Soviet Military Strength

The strength of the Limited Contingent of Soviet Forces in Afghanistan by the end of 1983, was probably in the region of 110,000; in fact it barely exceeded that number at its maximum, and was usually below it. The Limited Contingent was still in the process of reorganisation from its European-orientated stance, arms and equipment, to one more suitable to conditions in Afghanistan, with unsuitable formations, units and heavy weaponry being sent back to the USSR.

More airborne formations and special forces brigades were brought in and the ground element of the Limited Contingent of the Soviet Forces in Afghanistan came to consist of four divisions (one air assault and three motor rifle), and up to seven independent brigades or regiments, in fixed garrison locations. Personnel within then rotated, as indeed at times did formations and units, but HQs generally remained static.

Soviet 'field forces' were specially assembled from available regiments and units at a particular moment for a particular operation, and on its completion they were returned to their parent formation. This avoided the logistic burden of moving whole divisions or regiments, with all their weapons, equipment and stores, just for an operation, leaving behind responsibilities which some other formation had to cover while they were away. In 1982, a whole new range of Soviet light armoured vehicles began to arrive in Afghanistan.

A small group of Soviet Generals exercised control over both Soviet and Afghan troops, and dictated military policy. Aware of a long haul ahead, and believing that time was on their side and not on the side of the quarrelling Mujahideen groups, they embarked upon a construction and building programme, including extending and updating air bases, constructing new airfields, storage facilities for fuel, bombs and other ammunition, barrack accommodation and the laying of fuel pipelines. Strategic roads were repaired and widened, bridges were strengthened, and a new all-weather bypass was constructed over the Salang Pass along the old track. Additionally, a sophisticated radio communication network was installed linking all Soviet and Afghan garrisons and outposts, several of which were equipped with modern 'air-ground' control apparatus.

In September 1982, the dual road-rail 'Friendship Bridge' across the Amu Darya was opened, which speeded up the flow of supplies southwards into Afghanistan. This bridge was linked by rail northwards to the Soviet railway system at Kalif, near Termez. Afghanistan still had no railway, but it seems that the Soviets were planning that it should.

Soviet Air Force

The Soviet air force in Afghanistan had been beefed up and by the end of 1982 the combined Soviet and Afghan aerial strength was quoted as '281 fighters, 24 Ilyushin bombers, 220 helicopters (including 48 gunships), and 76 transport and reconnaissance planes' (*The Times*). The aircraft were said to be mainly MiG-21s, but included some MiG-23s, Ilyushin-28s, and Mi-24 and Mi-8 helicopters, the latter being fitted with bomb-racks. Soviet combat aircraft in Afghanistan were rotated from bases in the Turkestan Military District.

One major task assigned to both Soviet and Afghan air forces was constantly to monitor, through aerial photography, a rectangle of joint border terrain, extending about 150 miles from north to south, 120 miles into Pakistan, and another 120 miles into eastern Afghanistan, to detect Mujahideen movement and activity. In one aerial incident in February 1982, a Soviet helicopter, flying from Gardez to Khost, was hit by a SAM-7 missile, crashing near Khost with loss of life, including a Soviet General. The Soviet pilot survived, was taken prisoner, and smuggled into Pakistan to be presented at a Mujahideen Press conference. This was a 'multiple claim' incident, with several groups boasting they had shot the helicopter down, a practice that was becoming fairly common amongst Mujahideen groups.

Informers and Activists

When President Karmal was projected into power, he disbanded President Hafizullah Amin's Khalki-oriented security and intelligence organisation (KAM) and, with KGB help, formed one of his own, known as KHAD ((*Khedemati-e-Dolati*). This was commanded by a Parchami, Mohammed Najibullah, a medical doctor and political activist, who was awarded the rank of General as being compatible with his task. Under Najibullah, KHAD expanded and developed, operating with cruel efficiency. One source (*Urban*) says that by 1982, KHAD had a staff of 18,000, grouped into 182 zones.

The Soviets began using KHAD for Psy-Ops activities. Mujahideen leaders in the field were handicapped by the traditional 'openness' of Afghan society, and because they had both to reveal and discuss operational plans in advance to obtain agreement, which militated against normal military security procedures designed to prevent plans being prematurely leaked, and passed on to the enemy. KHAD informers infiltrated Mujahideen groups to discover their plans, often enabling government armed forces to be forewarned and so to take counteraction in time. If detected, the fate of such informers was painful and deadly. KHAD agents were also planted in Mujahideen groups to stir up internal unrest, to revive old tribal and family feuds, and start new ones.

KHAD informers were also planted in prisons and detention camps, especially the notorious Poli Charki prison, near Kabul, where political prisoners and captured Mujahideen were held, to obtain information and to detect ring-leaders. On one occasion, in December 1982, these tactics caused a major prison mutiny, and a number of people died in the resultant shooting to restore order. In the cities where the Mujahideen had long perfected the traditional Afghan system of *Shahmans* (night letters) secretly conveying instructions and threats by night to homes, KHAD agents played them at their own game, issuing their own *Shahmans* with counter-instructions, false information and threats.

At Soviet instigation, the Kabul government tried to buy loyalty or defection from individuals, tribes and groups with food, money, ammunition or privileges. This method often worked in the short run, but seldom in the longer term, as the individualist Afghan retained a tendency to change sides at whim, or simply to return home for a while. It was a risky and dangerous game. The Minister for Tribal and Frontier Affairs, Faiz Mohammed, who had had some initial success in 'hiring local militias', was killed while negotiating with tribal leaders in Paktia province in September 1980.

The Soviets dropped large numbers of propaganda leaflets from aircraft threatening punishment to anyone helping or co-operating with the Mujahideen PDPA. Political workers were organised by KHAD to go out and preach to the townsfolk and villagers alike in an effort to convert them to supporting the Karmal regime, but they had little success. In June 1982, during one of the several Mujahideen attacks on the town of Gulbahar, at the mouth of the Panjshir Valley, the Mujahideen massacred a group of PDPA political cadres sent to 're-educate' the townsfolk.

Through KHAD, the Soviets almost openly took control of the secular educational system, teachers being bribed, or intimidated, to disseminate PDPA propaganda. The Mujahideen responded by persuading Afghans, on pain of punishment for disobedience, not to send their children to school. The next escalation was that government forces destroyed empty schools, much to the Mullahs' satisfaction.

There was a reverse side to the Soviet-Afghan Psy-Ops campaigns as, so far as they were able, the Mujahideen struck back in a like manner. Mujahideen informers were planted in the armed forces and all government departments, to obtain information and give advanced warning of impending raids, arrests and other counter-insurgency activities.

Western diplomats working in Kabul, and other Westerners

working in the country, occasionally overstepped protocol in their sympathy for the Mujahideen cause, or out of dislike for the Soviet stance. In June 1982, an American antiquarian, Ralph Pander-Wilson, was imprisoned in Kabul for 'collecting information and spreading rumours'; he was also convicted of smuggling ancient gold coins out of the country. In May 1983, a US State Department employee in Kabul was expelled for 'distributing illegal magazines', (*Kabul Radio*); and in the following September two members of the US diplomatic staff were also expelled for somewhat similar reasons.

Afghan Army

Addressing a PDPA Conference on 12 March 1982, the Afghan Minister of Internal Affairs, Mohammed Ghilabzai, boasted that the Afghan army had 'participated during 1981-82 in 1,700 military offensives ... of which more than 800 were carried out without Soviet assistance, in which over 10,000 counter-revolutionaries were killed, and over 4,000 weapons captured' (*Kabul Radio*). Heavily exaggerated and premature, this statement did contain a small element of fact, as the hard core of the Afghan army had all the time been very much in the front line.

Probably, the first all-Afghan military operation, a five-day skirmish in Paktia province, began on 5 October 1982, some six months after the Minister's boastful speech; it was claimed to be successful and to have captured over 40 rebels. The hard core had certainly taken heavy losses, and in December, the Director General of the Afghan Ministry of Defence in Kabul, Colonel Abdul Mannar, defected to Pakistan, and stated that 'over 3,000 Afghan soldiers had been killed in action so far' by the Mujahideen (*Pakistan sources*).

The Afghan army was certainly undergoing a change but this was brought about more by a new Mujahideen attitude than by any measures taken by the Sovietised Afghan officer corps. So far desertion had been an easy way out for reluctant Afghan soldiers, who were urged by the Mullahs to abandon their units and join the ranks of the Mujahideen, who would welcome them with open arms. Initially this was true, especially if the soldiers brought arms with them; even if they did not, they had valuable military expertise and knowledge of local armoury locations.

As the struggle continued, there was a gradual hardening of attitude by the Mujahideen against Afghan soldiers, especially the hard core, which would cheerfully fight against any of them on behalf of the Soviets. Smiles of welcome began to fade from Mujahideen faces as a feeling of deep resentment overtook them. In September 1982, the Mujahideen attacked the garrison at Jalalabad, destroying two helicopters and capturing 72 Afghan soldiers, of whom 37 were executed for fighting against them (*Pakistan sources*).

There had previously been isolated incidents when captured Afghan soldiers or deserters had been tortured and executed, but they had been regarded as isolated incidents in which private vengeance might have played a part. Now the situation was changing, and this new Mujahideen attitude meant that soldiers no longer had the easy desertion option, as they were no longer welcome in the Mujahideen camp. In a tight corner, Afghan soldiers began to choose to stay and fight, preferring a quick death to a long, lingering and painful one. Morale in the Afghan army began to harden, and the Kabul government could now claim with some truth that more Mujahideen were surrendering, while at the same time its own desertion rate had declined considerably.

Desertion had certainly been rife. During a joint Soviet-Afghan search-and-destroy operation into the Panjshir Valley in November 1982, a complete Afghan regiment, with its officers, vehicles, weapons and equipment, deserted to the Mujahideen. This was probably the largest and most blatant example of mass Afghan desertion, and probably the last major one. During 1983, Mujahideen bitterness increased against Afghan soldiers still fighting for the Kabul government and, by implication, collaborating with the Soviet invaders.

In April, the Afghan garrison at Barrim (Paktia province) was partly overwhelmed by the Mujahideen, who reportedly executed 26 captured Afghan soldiers (*Pakistan sources*). During the following week, in other similar incidents, it was said that some 200 Afghan soldiers were executed by the Mujahideen. In August, a group of village chiefs travelling to meet the Soviet-Afghan regional commander to arrange a temporary cease-fire to enable them to gather in their harvest, were all killed by the Mujahideen, which was trying to stamp out such unofficial local cease-fires.

Although the Afghan army had steadily shrunk from its pre-1978 strength, it had retained its form, and its framework of 14 divisions. There had been no reorganisation, and the divisions had retained their designations and locations. The three armoured divisions (the 4th and 13th at Kabul, and the 7th at Kandahar), having been deprived of their tanks and heavy weapons, had shrunk to little more than a small HQ cadre, while the 11 infantry divisions were very much under strength. As the retraining programme progressed and morale improved, and more Afghan units were judged to be 'reliable' once again, impounded arms were returned to them. These included BTR-152s, the older BTR-60 series of light armoured vehicles, 76mm mountain guns, 122mm and 152mm rocket launchers and RPG-7s (*IISS*). The Afghan forces continued to rely mainly upon impressed civilian vehicles for their transport needs, but were beginning to receive Soviet military transport vehicles. One authority (*Urban*) wrote that in 1983, 'a further 1,500 KAMAZ Soviet trucks were received by the Afghan army'. These additions gave it more credible mobility.

In August 1983, the Afghan government brought in new conscription regulations, increasing the length of service from two to three years; reservists over 35 years of age could be recalled for a second time; and university students now had to serve the full three years, instead of only one. Avoidance of the call-up became more difficult as refugees crowding into cities could be rounded up and vetted, and those in the DPCs brought more easily within the catchment process. Desertion still continued, but the rate decreased, and soon the 'break even' position was attained, after which Afghan army strength began to slowly increase as new batches of conscripts were drafted in.

The Parcham-Khalk feud within the armed forces still seethed under a deceptively placid surface, with everyone trying to pretend it did not exist. Violence occasionally erupted. On one occasion the First Deputy Defence Minister, General Khalilullah, was dismissed from office for physically attacking the National Defence Minister, General Qasr; on another, the body of a senior officer was discovered in suspicious circumstances. There were other incidents of a similar nature. President Kamal made an effort to expand the PDPA within the armed forces, especially within the officer corps, to try to bring to heel some of the more independently-minded officers, who tended to be the root cause of disaffection and indiscipline.

AAF Support Role

The Afghan Air Force was also pulling itself up by its bootstraps after crippling initial defections. These continued but at a reduced rate, although one CIA source estimated that a further 2,000 personnel defected in the period 1982-83. AFF aircraft losses continued to be fairly heavy, most of the planes being destroyed on the ground by sabotage or Mujahideen raids. Periodic Mujahideen raids and rocket attacks were made on several air bases, including Bagram, Ghazni, Herat, Kandahar and Jalalabad. It is said that at one stage the AFF was reduced to having only 20 operational aircraft (*Pakistan sources*).

However, as in the Afghan army, a small hard core of dedicated pilots and technicians remained loyal to the Kabul regime and when the Soviets realised this, replacement planes, mainly MiG-21s, but also more Mi-24 helicopters, were sent to the AAF. Aircraft accidents occurred, but all were claimed by Mujahideen groups as 'kills' brought about by their SAM-7 missiles. No doubt SAM-7s in Mujahideen hands did bring down a few Afghan and Soviet-piloted planes, but evidence was usually lacking in support of such claims. One Afghan pilot defected with his aircraft to Pakistan in October 1982, and another in November 1983, but these were exceptions.

The AAF was fully brought into ground-support operations and it became efficient in this role. Operating closely with the Soviet air force, the AAF tended to develop a good inter-service relationship, which was more than could be said for relations between Soviet and Afghan ground forces. Pakistan authorities complained of incursions into their air space by 'Afghan' aircraft; indeed Afghan aircraft and Afghan pilots were largely used for this reconnaissance task, to avoid international complications should Soviet pilots be brought down inside Pakistan territory.

Ground Activity: 1982-83

Beneath the fog of propaganda and claims and counter-claims by both the Kabul government and the Mujahideen, a myriad of small, and sometimes not so small, actions were taking place. The difficulty is to establish accurate details about them, and to pick out a few typical examples without expanding into a tedious catalogue of similarity. Almost constant fighting was in progress in the eastern provinces of Kunar, Nangrahar and Paktia, and in Logar (south of Kabul), the Paghman area and on the Shomali plateau (north of Kabul); and in and around certain major cities. Elsewhere, government and Mujahideen activity was more sporadic, and even less verifiable.

Kabul, the capital, continued to be the main Mujahideen attraction, as enterprising guerrillas crept close in by night to fire

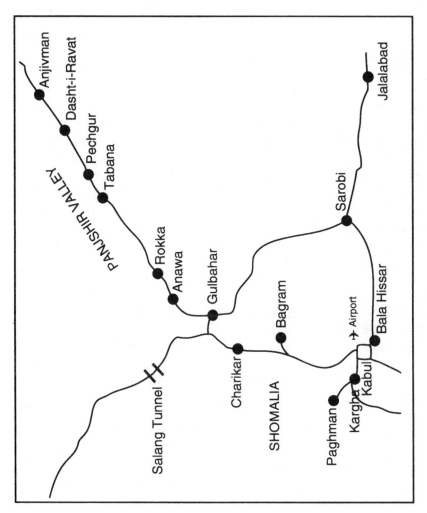

Panshir Valley – Kabul

rockets at the Bala Hissar fortress (HQ of KHAD), the radio transmitting station, government buildings and the sprawling Soviet and Afghan military complexes around the city. In December 1982, the diesel fuel pipeline from Mazar-i-Sharif to Kabul was disrupted on several occasions on the northern outskirts of the city; and in 1983, when the government began to establish a nation-wide electric power grid, the pylons became irresistible targets.

While the heavy military presence in Kabul limited Mujahideen raiding activities, such forays as were made encountered barrages and low-level bombing and strafing sorties on suspected Mujahideen positions in the surrounding ring of low hills. Inside Kabul, assassinations, explosions and sabotage were caused by several diverse factions each seeking their own particular targets, contributing to spasms of violence that resulted in frequent curfews.

Kandahar remained divided, with Mujahideen holding parts of the Old City and adjacent villages and government forces were often besieged in the garrison areas. Several clashes occurred in 1982-83, a major one in November 1982, but the tactical position remained much the same, with government troops having the advantage of air support and air mobility, and the Mujahideen that of ground mobility, especially at night.

A somewhat similar stalemate obtained at Herat, with government troops holding government buildings and the garrison area, and the Mujahideen controlling the Old City and its environs. Soviet special forces were rushed to Herat in January 1982 to prevent the garrison from being overrun, after which government troops launched several operations with negative results. The Mujahideen mounted a strong, but unsuccessful, attack in May 1983, which resulted in government troops conducting a massive house-to-house search, which only temporarily displaced the Mujahideen.

Mazar-i-Sharif, the commercially active 'transit capital of the north', was swamped with troops and security forces, which accounted for the fairly low level of incidents of sabotage and rocket attacks it sustained. One incident occurred in July 1983, when the Soviets took reprisals after citizens had shot and killed four Soviet soldiers, allegedly caught looting, by 'executing 20 city elders' (*Pakistan sources*). The following month, after a Soviet officer had been shot and killed in a street, Soviet troops reacted by firing their tank guns into some buildings.

In Khost, close to the Pakistan border and the main Afghan blocking garrison on a major Mujahideen supply route, a garrison mutiny in January 1983 was repressed harshly. In September, the Mujahideen made a special effort to force open this part of their supply route, managing to overrun the small garrison at Jail, which was regained by government troops the following month, but both Khost and Urgun (another garrison in Paktia province) remained besieged throughout the ensuing winter. Elsewhere, after a mutiny had been quelled at Ghazni, the situation seemed to be fairly quiet, if tense.

The Panjshir Valley

The one resistance fighter in the field who was winning a great deal of publicity in the West was Ahmad Shah Masoud, leader of the Mujahideen group in the Panjshir Valley, who had done so well during the first year of the Soviet invasion. A member of Rabbani's IA, Masoud was a dedicated Fundamentalist whose ultimate aim was to turn Afghanistan into an Islamic state similar to that created by Ayatollah Khomeini in Iran—something his enthusiastic following in the West seemed to overlook. A Tadjik, born about 1956, Masoud was a natural leader, who had qualified as an engineer, and occasionally used that designation as a prefix to his name to emphasise his status. He was one of the few Afghan leaders in the field to appreciate that Western publicity was essential to engender Western support and aid, and probably the only one not to be eclipsed by the individually-publicity-seeking Peshawar Seven leaderships.

Masoud was a good organiser and planner, as well as a good military commander, and had pioneered mountain trails from Pakistan to provide communication channels and supply routes into his valley. He continually invited Western journalists into his domain, consequently obtaining considerable personal international publicity in a world hungry for accurate news of what was happening in the interior of Afghanistan, while other major Mujahideen leaders in the interior, handicapped by geography and less extrovert, were unsung and so unknown.

In May 1982, a combined Soviet-Afghan force in divisional strength, probably over 8,000 men, moved into the Panjshir Valley in yet another search-and-destroy operation, withdrawing after a month's heavy fighting. Masoud's Mujahideen were raiding from the Panjshir Valley along the adjacent part of the Northern Route up to the Salang Tunnel, and also harassing the town of Gulbahar, parts of which continued to change hands. Determined to crush this colourful Mujahideen leader, and to eliminate the threat he posed, the Soviets launched an even larger combined government force in June, which pushed its way into the long, very narrow valley; but this soon petered out, the troops withdrawing in ignominy.

In September, the Soviets launched yet another major expedition into the Panjshir Valley, this time penetrating further than ever before, consolidating certain defensive positions, which they retained even when Winter snow stopped vehicular movement and the main body withdrew. These defensive positions were supplied throughout the winter by helicopter, and were protected by Free Fire Zones.

In January 1983, fortified by the stature gained by his publicity efforts and his impressive resistance record, Masoud did what no other Mujahideen field commander would have dared to do so openly at the time: he negotiated a cease-fire with the Soviets for one year. Soviet Generals, busily preparing for just one more major assault on Masoud's Panjshir Valley, which they thought would completely eliminate his threat, were not too keen on a cease-fire, but were overridden by President Andropov's 'search for a negotiated exit' policy to bring about the withdrawal of Soviet troops from that country.

Masoud promised to stop attacking the Northern Route, the Salang Tunnel, Gulbahar and government military positions within his valley, in return for Soviet promises that his people could emerge from the shelter of their mountain caves to plant and harvest their crops, and save what remained of their live-stock. Masoud justified his action as expedient to ensure his survival and to gain a breathing space to plan and prepare to mount a future campaign against the Kabul government. However, he did send groups of his Mujahideen to operate in the Shomali Valley and in Balkh province.

Despite the fact that the mood of the Mujahideen in the field in 1983 was impregnated with bitterness and vengeance, and that minor local Mujahideen leaders had occasionally been executed for concluding temporary cease-fires with the Soviets for reasons of survival, no criticism was openly voiced against Masoud either by the Peshawar Seven, or the Western media. Masoud still invited Western journalists to visit him, and in return they refrained from dwelling on the fact that he was the only Mujahideen field commander to have accepted a cease-fire arrangement with the Soviets.

The Soviets did not launch any divisional-sized operations during 1983, realising that they were too unwieldy and negative, which may have contributed to a slightly reduced casualty toll. According to later reporting by *Pravda*, the Soviet fatality rate in Afghanistan, including accidents, was 1,948 for 1982, and 1,446 for 1983.

Soviet Prisoners

During the first two or three years of Soviet occupation, Soviet personnel captured by the Mujahideen suffered torture and death, a scant few escaping with their lives by embracing Islam. It was some time before the Mujahideen in the field could be persuaded that Soviet prisoners could be worth more alive than dead, to be bartered for arms that might possibly include modern anti-aircraft weaponry, ammunition or money. Attempts by the International Committee of the Red Cross (ICRC) to persuade the Peshawar Seven leaders to respect the Geneva Conventions regarding the treatment of POWs were met with the counter-argument that as long as the Kabul government treated captured Mujahideen as political prisoners, why should they not use the same methods?

Reports of the Soviet prisoners they held were given a low priority in Mujahideen communiqués, and consequently in most cases no one knew whether Soviet 'missing-in-action' personnel were alive or dead. Information about them did trickle through on occasions, but was generally unverifiable. For example, in October 1982, in an action in the Paghman area, 10 Soviet soldiers were taken prisoner by the Mujahideen, six of whom were killed and four smuggled back to Pakistan (*Pakistan sources*). On another occasion, in December, during a Mujahideen bombardment of the airfield at Mazar-i-Sharif, 16 Soviet civilian workers were seized; 11 were freed by government forces during the action, but the other five were killed by their captors. And, in October 1983, in the course of several actions in the Shomali area, it was alleged that 24 Soviet prisoners were seized, but their individual fate was never made clear.

Red Cross representatives, who had been banned from Afghanistan in June 1980 but allowed to return in August 1982, were ejected again the following October, accused of obtaining interviews with inmates of the Poli Charki prison. However, they did have some success in persuading the Peshawar Seven to allow some Soviet prisoners to be sent to Switzerland for a two-year period of parole (or until the end of the occupation, if sooner), after which they would be allowed to return to the USSR.

Afghan Refugees

After the Saur Revolution in 1978, some 109,000 Afghans sought political asylum in Pakistan (*Pakistan government figures*); and after the Hafizullah Amin coup in September 1979, this number increased to over 400,000. By June 1980, this Afghan exodus had swelled to one million—and reached two million by June the following year. Pakistan provided these Afghan refugees with food and shelter on humanitarian grounds, eventually constructing some 350 Refugee Tented Villages (RTVs); subsequently the UN High Commission for Refugees and other charitable organisations began to contribute towards their upkeep. During 1983, tension erupting between Afghan refugees and local people caused some of the RTVs to be moved away from the vicinity of large cities. Due to wartime security reporting restrictions, less was known about Afghan refugees in Iran, who were thought to number about one million by this time.

International Aspects

In January 1982, Pérez de Cuéllar, (who for two years had been his predecessor's Personal Representative with special responsibility for the Afghan situation) became Secretary General of the United Nations, and under his urging the Proximity Talks between Afghanistan and Pakistan—so-called because respective representatives refused to talk to each other face-to-face, and were in separate rooms, with UN negotiators flitting from one to the other with demands, comments and messages—began in Geneva in June 1982. The Iranians had refused an invitation to attend the Proximity Talks (which were soon adjourned) unless the Afghan delegation included representatives of the Mujahideen, meaning from the Shia Afghan groups under its influence.

In the USSR, the hard policy of President Brezhnev continued until his death in November 1982, when his successor, Yuri Andropov, seemed timidly to put forward his own policy of withdrawal by negotiation; but as the year of 1983 drew to a close there was little sign of it becoming effective. The Afghan problem was simply producing despair, despondency and frustration.

7

The Long Haul: 1984-85

In the USSR, in February 1984, the Soviet leader, Yuri Andropov, died, and was succeeded by another ageing and ailing candidate, Konstantin Chernenko, who in turn died in March 1985. Mikhail Gorbachev, a younger, more vigorous man with radical ideas became the new General Secretary of the Soviet Communist Party. It took him a little while to settle in and put his *glasnost* and *perestroika* policies into practice. In the meantime Soviet policy on Afghanistan continued to stultify, giving all those involved in the struggle the impression there would be no quick solution to the problem. However, as all factions were convinced they would eventually be victorious and that time was on their side and against their opponents, all tightened their belts and settled down for the anticipated 'long haul'—a test of will, stamina and strength.

Soviet Unease

So far the citizens of the USSR had been given few accurate details about what had been happening to their Limited Contingent of Soviet Forces in Afghanistan, since censorship was tight and only bland optimistic platitudes appeared in the Soviet media. However, there seemed to be a vague but growing feeling that things were not going well; rumours of poor Soviet morale trickled back and there was an increasing reluctance among young Soviet conscripts to be drafted there for military service. It was not until December 1984 that the newspaper *Izvestia* carried the first official admission that there were 'serious casualties and shortages at Soviet garrisons in Afghanistan'.

Soviet and East European journalists had been able to visit Afghanistan, but had been kept on a tight rein, their copy being heavily censored so that only comfortable and encouraging reports appeared in the media. The Soviets later admitted in their military periodical, *Krasnaya Zvezda (Red Star)*, that during the first four years in Afghanistan their troops had lacked sufficient physical and psychological training, and that junior officers and sergeants did not display enough aggressiveness and self-confidence in action.

The Soviets certainly did have a troop morale problem in Afghanistan, although perhaps not quite as serious as was claimed by Western media. This centred around lack of motivation, lack of conditioning, and the boredom factor, as a large proportion of Soviet conscripts were engaged in dull routine and guard duty tasks. Young conscripts were often unhappy at being involved in implementing scorched-earth and starvation measures, killing live-stock, demolishing homes in villages and depopulating the valleys.

They were brought into contact with drugs, as opium and heroin were plentiful, cheap and easy to obtain; and many were simply miserable at being far from home. Soviet officers generally did not seem able successfully to address themselves to this vital military issue. On the other hand, morale in special forces formations, which had a high proportion of volunteers, was high, as it was in some units where officers were of a higher calibre.

American Policy

Deeply immersed in the Cold War with the USSR, the US administration had regarded the Soviet military occupation of Afghanistan, and failure to achieve its objective there, as a bonus, and continued to be loudly condemnatory and to demand a Soviet withdrawal; propaganda support was given to the Mujahideen. Enmeshed in the Nicaraguan problem and with vivid memories of the American Vietnam experience, President Reagan was wary of being dragged into another unpopular morass in southern Asia. He was more concerned with the overall stability of the region, where the Iran-Iraq War was still being ferociously fought, Afghanistan was writhing in the throes of Soviet occupation and civil war, and Pakistan was under a military dictatorship, than the cause and plight of the Mujahideen.

President Reagan therefore adopted a policy of maintaining the *status quo*—in effect doing as little as possible—by providing just enough aid to the Mujahideen to enable them to prosecute the war in their own country with sufficient vigour and effort to cause the Soviets to remain in Afghanistan to protect their puppet government, and to drain their resources. He did not want to step up aid to the Mujahideen to such an extent as to make the Soviets decide in despair to pull out, as the Americans had done in Vietnam, or to provoke them into attacking Pakistan, the Mujahideen's spring-board base, as Pakistan was likely to collapse under such pressure, and thus bring about further instability in that region.

Reagan was not happy with the attitude of President Zia. He wanted the Soviets to withdraw from Afghanistan (as did Zia), but to be replaced by a stable pro-Western traditionalist (Afghan-type) government in Kabul; Zia however favoured a Fundamentalist government, which would turn the country into an Islamic state. To avoid provocation, Reagan wanted Zia to exercise greater control over his tribal frontier areas by restricting the Mujahideen supply routes across his territory. He also wanted Zia to destroy the drug factories in Pakistan's tribal areas, and to put a stop to drug-smuggling activities. The truth was that President Reagan was in no hurry for a settlement to be reached in Afghanistan; he just wanted to cool the situation a little, and to stop the flames blazing beyond control.

At first American aid, financial and material, for the Mujahideen, had been timid and covert, and it was not until July 1984 that the US Congress openly approved $50 million for this purpose, opening a small door, but not a flood-gate. The following month Congress was complaining that the CIA was not doing enough to help the Mujahideen, that insufficient weapons had been sent to them, and that such as were supplied were of poor quality, it being said that 60 per cent were faulty. US financial aid to the Mujahideen for 1985 rose to $250 million (*Washington Post*), being a major part of the CIA covert operational budget; and another $250 million was secretly approved in the following September.

The China Card

China, the Asian superpower, traditionally hostile to the USSR, was glad to see Soviet aggression being directed towards Afghanistan. Some of the money obtained by the Mujahideen was spent on Chinese-manufactured arms, whose quality was not of the best, but which were obtainable and commensurate with the capabilities of the

Afghan guerrillas. Chinese weapons arrived by way of the Karakorum Highway, as the Soviets were blocking the Wakhan Strip, which otherwise might have developed into an Afghan mini-Ho Chi Minh Trail.

China and Pakistan had always been unlikely bed-fellows, thrown together by Indian hostility towards them both. China had become the only main source of major items of weaponry for Pakistan when Western powers generally refused to supply any, partly because in their eyes Pakistan was a rigid military dictatorship that had suspended the democratic process, and partly because it was suspected that President Zia was secretly working to produce a nuclear warhead. President Zia endeavoured to control all in-coming weaponry for the Mujahideen through his Inter-Service Intelligence Branch.

The Soviets claimed (*Pravda*) they were finding large caches of Chinese-manufactured arms in Afghanistan, that Chinese-made SAM-7s were hitting their aircraft, and that Chinese-made 107mm and 122mm rockets were bombarding Kabul and other locations. The Kremlin protested, but the Chinese, as was their custom, denied all knowledge of the matter. Additionally, the Soviets accused the Chinese not only of arming the Mujahideen, but also of training them in Sinkiang province; this was also falsely denied. The few Chinese training camps were for the smaller, secular groups, which the Chinese hoped to influence, but they also trained a sprinkling from other Mujahideen groups who were expediently sent to obtain expertise, and to further the flow of arms.

The Kabul Government

Since the installation of President Karmal in December 1979, the Soviets had been trying to persuade him to 'slow down the Revolution', to make it more acceptable to the people, to unite both factions within the Afghan armed forces, and to obtain more popular support; but they had little success. The Soviets wanted the 'revolution', virtually a Communist one, to survive, and were anxious lest Karmal's methods and unpopularity might provoke a counter-revolutionary backlash. The Soviets had been preparing for Communist stability in Afghanistan, and already had hundreds of political, military and government personnel in the USSR for combined doctrinal-technical training in the Soviet mould, to be ready on their return to take up key positions. Whether there would be a place for them depended on the survival of the Kabul government.

In November 1984, new identity cards were issued in Afghanistan, which brought the whole population within the government's net. Freedom of movement ceased, and people could not even travel from one city, town or village to another, or indeed leave their homes, without express permission. Also, the Soviet system of 'internal exile' was introduced, allowing the government to banish troublesome individuals to remote areas either as a punishment, or for official convenience.

Thwarted in so many ways, President Karmal revived the traditional system of the Afghan Loya Jirga, to bring leaders, both major and minor, together and show them to be in apparent agreement with Kabul policies. One Loya Jirga was held in April 1985, at Kabul, attended by 1,786 delegates (*Kabul Radio*), where it was agreed that the Soviet military presence should continue, that all Afghan refugees should be called upon to return home, and that the Mujahideen lay down their arms.

Another Loya Jirga was held in September 1985, attended by 3,700 delegates, according to Kabul Radio. Karmal was encouraged by increased attendance numbers, and he called upon tribal chiefs loyal to the Kabul government to recruit their own paid, armed militias to keep the Mujahideen out of their respective areas—in other words buying their loyalty. Also, it was agreed that 'armed militias' should be formed in Pakistan's Pushtun tribal areas to disrupt supplies reaching the Mujahideen, something rather beyond his fiefdom. The following month, President Karmal decided, though without giving a date, to hold local elections, none having been held since the Saur Revolution.

In October 1985, an anti-Karmal plot was discovered, led by a senior member of the KHAD, and involving senior officials from other PDPA elements; and the only reputedly qualified Afghan nuclear scientist, Dr Mohammed Akhari, was sentenced to death for allegedly channelling funds from China, designated for nuclear research, to the Mujahideen (*Kabul Radio*). Shootings and explosions had become commonplace in Kabul. Two explosions occurred at Kabul International Airport: the first, in August 1984, killed 13 people and injured another 20, and the other, in September, killed 14 people and injured over 50 (*Kabul Radio*). The latter happened on the same day a car-bomb in the city caused over 50 caasualties. Later, Abdul Haq, the military commander of Khalis' HI group, admitted he had ordered the planting of bombs at the airport.

Pakistan's Problems

Pakistan's price for supporting and supplying the Mujahideen on behalf of the USA was the rearming with modern equipment of its armed forces, now almost 500,000-strong, and compromising 18 divisions and 28 independent brigades (*IISS*), but which was ill-equipped. President Zia was able to persuade President Reagan to promise to provide him with some $3 billion worth of military material, a promise reluctantly given, and fulfilled tardily. Zia also demanded full control of the distribution of all military aid arriving in Pakistan for the Mujahideen, despite the presence of some 200 CIA agents, who had been sent there for that very purpose.

Some of the military material received for the Mujahideen was more modern and sophisticated than any possessed by the Pakistan armed forces, and the suspicion was that certain items were syphoned off by the ISI for their use. Zia complained to Reagan about modern weapons being dispatched to the Mujahideen while as yet none had been sent to him, and this had the desired effect. It was reported (*New York Times*) that the US administration had promised a quick delivery of 100 Stinger and Sidewinder missiles, to help Pakistan defend itself against Soviet and Afghan aerial incursions. This was the first delivery to Pakistan of such weaponry.

President Zia carefully hoarded and guarded arms brought in by the CIA for the Mujahideen, being reluctant to dole them out in any quantity. His first reason was that if the 'traditional' groups received too many arms they would become too strong and independent, and be tempted to come to some agreement with the Kabul government. Zia suspected they would try to reach a compromise, as they did not particularly want to overturn the 'revolution'. Zia's other reason was that if the Mujahideen opposition in the field became too well armed and too strong, the Soviets might be provoked to raid into Pakistan to destroy Mujahideen HQs, bases and stores, or even occupy certain sections of frontier territory. Such an international incident might quickly escalate, to the detriment of Pakistan.

The Kabul government continually accused President Zia of allowing the Mujahideen to cross, and re-cross, into Afghanistan, and of helping them to establish 'liberated zones' in its eastern provinces. Zia had already deployed anti-aircraft units along his border with Afghanistan, even in the tribal areas, but had given them orders not to fire at any Soviet or Afghan combat aircraft straying into Pakistan air space. A few deeper incursion incidents did occur but, although there were some near-encounters, international clashes were avoided for the time being.

To accusations that he allowed the Mujahideen freely to cross the border into Afghanistan, Zia replied that he could not be responsible for the 1,500-mile frontier, and that if President Karmal wanted it sealed, he was welcome to seal it; adding, as always, that he was only affording Afghan refugees humanitarian aid.

In 1984, the number of Afghan refugees in Pakistan exceeded three million, and continued to rise, forming the largest concentration of refugees in the world. Friction between refugees and the local inhabitants did occur, particularly as some Afghans became involved in commercial ventures in competition with local traders. Also, there were continuing quarrels between the various Mujahideen groups over prestige, the poaching of each other's members, and the distribution of arms and money, and these led to violence, explosions and shootings.

It was alleged that KHAD personnel were operating among Afghan refugees, stirring up trouble between groups, and also 'taking out' key personalities. During 1985, according to Pakistan sources, at least 99 Afghan refugees, including six prominent leaders, were killed. After a bomb explosion outside the HQ of the Khalis HI in Peshawar in August 1984, which caused several casualties, the Pakistan government moved more RTVs away from that city. One incident of interest occurred at Peshawar on 27 April 1985, when '24 Soviet and Afghan POWs' (*Pakistan sources*) held in a detention camp, broke out and occupied an ammunition store belonging to a Mujahideen group, demanding their freedom. All were killed when the Mujahideen detonated their own store.

Mujahideen Unity Attempts

The political leaderships of the Mujahideen in Peshawar, remained convinced of their ultimate victory, pointing to the American experience in Vietnam. They also remained bitterly divided among themselves, although attempts to weld them into a workable coalition were periodically made. In March 1985, 10 major groups, mostly coalitions of smaller groups, identified as the Seven Fundamentalist and three Traditionalist groups, formed the 'United Military Command', but this soon foundered over inter-group differences. In May, the 'Peshawar Seven' became known as the 'Islamic Unity of Afghanistan'.

This attempt at Mujahideen unity, especially as it included several Shia groups, some of them under Iranian influence, caused the Soviets to move into the Helmand Valley and surrounding area, which they had so far ignored because the Mujahideen there had been so busy fighting each other. If a semblance of Mujahideen unity was in fact emerging, the Soviets wanted to destroy all small groups before they merged to become larger and more dangerous.

This operation was preceded by high-altitude carpet bombing in which it is thought several hundred people died, as they were taken by surprise in open flat terrain. This Soviet-Afghan air raid caused the Mujahideen in Pakistan to press the USA to supply them with American Stinger anti-aircraft missiles, as their Chinese and Egyptian SAM-7s were inadequate to cope with high-flying bomber aircraft.

In 'active areas' in the field, the Mujahideen were now often operating in groups of 30-40 men, with some semblance of order, using guerrilla tactics such as setting ambushes near bridges or défiles, disrupting roads and destroying bridges, opening fire when possible from a higher level of ground to take advantage of the limited elevation of some Soviet weapons. In certain areas local leaders managed to combine briefly to muster enough men to besiege and assault isolated Afghan-held forts, on occasions successfully. However, when they tried to hold on to these positions they were usually driven out by heavy air attacks.

A major Mujahideen weakness was that the best use was not made of weapons received, such as SAM-7s. RPG-7s and rocket-launchers, because they did not train, and retain, selected personnel to man these weapons but in accordance with their open discussion policy, allowed those who wanted to fire these weapons to do so regardless of their lack of expertise. There were, however, exceptions in a few of the better organised Mujahideen military contingents, a notable one being that of Masoud, in the Panjshir Valley, who organised 'specialist platoons'.

Efforts were still periodically made to form a 'government-in-exile', but they all failed. In 1984, the Saudis again advocated such a course, promising financial support, international recognition and a temporary base in Saudi Arabia from which to challenge the Afghan 'revolution'. Mildly interested, the Americans sounded out pro-Western Muslim states to see what backing could be obtained, but the response was lukewarm. In any case, this attempt was doomed from the start, as a Saudi condition was that the government-in-exile should be headed by ex-King Zahir Shah (aged

70), alive and well, and living in Rome, but not very willing; he had some support among Traditionalist groups, but none at all among the Fundamentalists.

Soviet Military Reassessment

The Limited Contingent of Soviet Forces in Afghanistan also prepared for the anticipated 'long haul' and reassessed the situation, defining new priorities and modifying and changing strategy and tactics accordingly. The first priority was to secure their firm bases and garrisons, and the strategic roads. A large part of the Soviet contingent, mainly young conscripts, was assigned to this task, more than originally intended, due to the Afghan army failure to expand as fast as anticipated.

Another priority was to eliminate Mujahideen groups in valleys and side valleys in the interior, and for this purpose field formations were to become more flexible and to consist of smaller all-arms units, spearheaded by Spetsnaz and airborne troops. Spetsnaz formations, technically part of the Main Intelligence Directorate (GRU) of the Soviet General Staff, had an aggressive commando method of operating, often being lifted by helicopter deep into Mujahideen-dominated territory to search out and attack bases and hide-outs.

Motorised formations, also in smaller units, were to attack the Mujahideen wherever they would stand and fight. Soviet motorised formations, conditioned to riding and fighting in their armoured vehicles, must start to get out and fight on their feet. They were to be given mountain warfare training, something the Soviets, relying so far on massive fire-power and domination of the air, had put off as long as possible. Valleys and areas in which Mujahideen groups were fighting each other were to be left alone, and government garrisons were withdrawn from wild, remote, sparsely-populated regions. The Helmand region seemed to be an exception, perhaps because it was so close to Iran.

Another priority was to restore government control over the eastern provinces and to eliminate the 'liberated zones', as well as to relieve the several besieged Afghan-held garrisons. Strong columns of all arms, with full air support, were to be used for this purpose, and they were to be fully supported by the Spetsnaz and airborne troops, mobile in helicopters. Combined with this priority was that of blocking the maze of Mujahideen supply trails in from Pakistan.

The struggle in Afghanistan had given a new lease of life to the old, almost forgotten tracks that had been in use for centuries before the modern motor-road system was developed. These tracks were saturated with small anti-personnel mines, dropped from aircraft, and the Mujahideen using them were harassed by helicopter-gunships. At night, small Spetsnaz units were put down to ambush Mujahideen supply trains and, using night-sights and silenced sniper rifles, they confused the Mujahideen, who could not identify where the shots were coming from, nor where the ambushers were. The other major Soviet aim was to extend their hold on the main cities, and in this they were less successful.

Soviet arms were arriving in Afghanistan in some quantity, and included the BM-27, multiple rocket launching system (MRLS), the 'Katyushas' (salvoes of which were used to counter Mujahideen 107mm rockets that fell on to cities and government positions), and the new BTR-70 and BTR-80, light armoured vehicles which had extremely good mobility over difficult terrain. During 1984 and 1985, although the Soviets had their failures and disappointments, generally the Mujahideen were pushed slightly further back into their valleys, and it seemed as though the tide might be turning against them.

The Afghan Army

The Karmal government also prepared for the anticipated 'long haul' and decided to make the Afghan army more combat-worthy. In January 1985, some 40 senior Generals and Party officials with military responsibilities were either dismissed, or reshuffled. Generals who had just returned from senior officer training in the USSR took over key commands and appointments.

Morale began to improve and Afghan soldiers successfully withstood several sieges and fought well in certain actions. Small assault groups were formed on the lines of the Soviet Spetsnaz, and new Soviet equipment was received. Desertion remained a problem, and conscripts still avoided military service if they could, so that the strength of the Afghan army seemed to hover around the 40,000 mark. During 1985, it was noted that some elderly Afghan refugees were returning to their homes, but were outnumbered by young men passing the other way to avoid conscription.

Air Attacks

The Mujahideen made several attacks on Soviet-Afghan air bases, using 107mm and 122mm rockets and RPG-7s, with the intention of destroying as many aircraft and helicopters as possible. In June 1984, for example, the Khalis HI group claimed (*Pakistan sources*) that its Mujahideen had attacked the Bagram air base 'destroying 25 aircraft'; it was suggested that this attack was a reprisal for the alleged execution of three Afghan pilots earlier in the year for dropping bombs over desert terrain instead of on an Afghan village.

The Shindand air base also came under Mujahideen attack. On 12 June 1985 (*Pakistan sources*) 20 jets were destroyed on the ground. It was later reported that several AAF officers and personnel were executed in August for complicity in this incident. Soviet ELINT and long-range bomber aircraft stationed at Shindand were withdrawn to air bases north of the Amu Darya, to operate from Soviet territory. However, the Soviet squadron of SU-25 support aircraft remained at Bagram air base.

As improved models of SAM-7s, with an increased range, were received in some number by the Mujahideen in the field, Soviet and Afghan aircraft simply flew a little higher and began to indulge more frequently in carpet-bombing; they were, however, still in danger when landing and taking-off. Kabul airport was vulnerable in this respect, being surrounded by low hills, which made excellent sites for Mujahideen SAM-7s. For example, on 14 October 1984, a Soviet transport aircraft, carrying 240 military personnel, crashed just after take-off from Kabul, and all on board were killed. It had been hit by a SAM-7 missile. The Khalis HI group claimed responsibility.

The previous month, a Mujahideen missile had struck an Ariana Airlines passenger aircraft near Kabul, causing it to make an emergency landing; and in the same month an aircraft of Bakhtar Airlines (the internal Afghan service), was hit by a Mujahideen-fired missile just after take-off from Kandahar airport and all 52 people on board were killed. In November 1985 a MiG-21 was hit and brought down by a missile in the same area. Several helicopters were lost to Mujahideen missiles; precise details were vague, but certainly Soviet and Afghan helicopters tended to fly at low altitudes to avoid missile fire.

Despite seeming loyalty of AAF officers, there were a few defections. On 22 September 1984, an AAF Colonel landed his An-22 transport aircraft at the Pakistan airfield at Miranshah, and sought political asylum; seven AFF personnel in two Mi-24 helicopters did the same on 13 July 1985.

Ground Activity: 1984-85

Ground activity in Aghanistan during 1984-85 was concentrated mainly in the eastern provinces, and the Paghman, Logar, Shomali and Panjshir areas. While generally the Circular Road and the Northern Route were better guarded, they were by no means immune from Mujahideen attention. During this period it did seem that for the first time the Soviets were having more success in ground fighting, often forcing Mujahideen groups to break off the fight, and pressing them further back into their valleys. Liberal use of newly-arrived Spetsnaz rapid reaction groups deterred guerrilla activity, and the Mujahideen became somewhat reluctant to mount their previously-damaging dawn or dusk ambushes on strategic roads, quickly disappearing into the mountains when helicopter-borne Spetsnaz troops were rapidly put down on their escape routes—to ambush the ambushers.

Soviet-Afghan military action concentrated against the Mujahideen in the Panjshir Valley where Masoud sought, and failed, to obtain an extension of his 1983 cease-fire arrangement. Having advance warning of an impending government offensive, Masoud evacuated almost the entire population of his valley, and moved his Mujahideen into the side valleys. After heavy preliminary carpet-bombing, Soviet-Afghan troops moved into the Panjshir Valley in force on 21 April, to find it almost empty; two days later a Kabul spokesman announced they were in complete control. The handful of government-held, helicopter-supplied positions in the valley, had remained throughout the period of the cease-fire.

Government forces soon ran into stiff Mujahideen resistance from the side valleys, and it was not until 16 May that Kabul announced that they had 'secured the floor of the valley ... established 45 positions in it ... and were blocking the exits' (*Kabul Radio*). This was the first operation in which high-altitude carpet-bombing was carried out entirely by aircraft flown from Soviet territory. Government troops remained in the Panjshir Valley, Masoud claiming they comprised '7,000 Soviet and 7,000 Afghan soldiers' (*Pakistan sources*). Some of the original inhabitants were brought back to the valley from the DPCs to be settled near the various government positions, themselves surrounded by protective rings of

146

minefields, as an insurance against Mujahideen ground attacks.

During the Winter (1984-85), Masoud's men were starved of supplies and ammunition. These normally arrived on heavily-laden pack-animal trains from Pakistan, through the Nuristan region mountain passes into the 100-mile-long Panjshir Valley, each such train taking up to two weeks to arrive. In Winter the Nuristan passes were blocked. Government forces remained in occupation of the Panjshir Valley throughout 1985, during the first part of which Mujahideen from the side valleys raided their positions, though with little success. This caused Masoud's Mujahideen to turn away and extend their activities instead towards the Shomali and Kohistan areas, but Masoud himself did not have so much influence away from his home valley.

Large areas in the eastern province of Kunar, criss-crossed with supply trails, were virtually given over to the Mujahideen, but the main government garrison at Baricot, situated at a crossroads, although continually besieged, successfully held out. In May 1984, heavy and frequent air strikes were made to ease Mujahideen pressure on Baricot, held by an all-Afghan garrison, which had to be supplied by helicopter. A Soviet-Afghan column reached Baricot on 21 May, thus breaking an eight-month blockade.

Although soon again besieged, Baricot managed to hold out throughout the Winter of 1984-85, to be again relieved in the Spring by a Soviet-Afghan column. On this occasion there was heavy fighting and heavy losses, causing government troops to withdraw completely from that area. This defeat upset the Kremlin, which transferred operational control of its Limited Contingent of Soviet Forces in Afghanistan from Tashkent to Moscow. Later Soviet figures (*Pravda*) indicated that Soviet fatalities for 1984-85 were 4,211.

The other eastern Afghan province, also flooded with Mujahideen was Paktia, where there were several Afghan army-held garrisons. The three main ones were Khost (some 15 miles from the Pakistan border), Urgun and Jaji. The first to fall to the Mujahideen was Jaji. In January 1985, a large, disjointed Mujahideen attack was made against Khost, which failed; and in the same month a Soviet-Afghan column marched to break the seven-month siege of Urgan. In May, the Mujahideen massed to attack the smaller garrison at Ali Khal, only five miles from the Pakistan border and held by Afghan forces, but with indecisive results. During the summer months sometimes the fighting in this border region spilled over into Pakistan, causing many protests from Islamabad, and many denials from Kabul.

During the final weeks of 1985, the Mujahideen massed in Paktia with the intention of seizing Khost, which had become a prestige target. Consignments of weapons had been received, including 107mm and 112mm rockets, RPG-7s and SAM-7s, giving greater accuracy and range. But the leaderships could not agree on a joint battle plan, and so the project hung-fire. Khost, with its Afghan garrison and with Soviet and Afghan air support, was able to hold out against much stronger forces. The new Afghan army was proving itself, but was still underrated by the Western media which, reluctant to give it credit, concentrated on its weaknesses.

Kabul remained a troubled city, plagued with rocket attacks and, as the Mujahideen progressively received improved, longer-range rockets, another defensive ring was constructed beyond the first one, to keep them at a safer distance. Rockets struck the Presidential Palace, the bazaar, the Soviet Embassy, government buildings and private houses. In September 1984, penetrating Mujahideen became involved in protracted fighting around the Bala Hissar.

In Kandahar, where the Afghan garrison still faced a hostile population, there was a large attack in April 1984, causing heavy losses on both sides. Punitive bombing sorties were carried out on surrounding villages, causing another exodus of refugees into Pakistan. The situation was somewhat similar in Herat, with the Afghan garrison also facing a hostile population. In May 1984, the Mujahideen launched a large, but unsuccessful attack, the government claiming that it 'was repulsed, and 215 rebels were killed' (*Kabul Radio*). In September, the Governor of Herat was assassinated.

The city of Ghazni was almost continually under siege, the Mujahideen being kept at a distance by aerial bombing, and in one such operation, in January 1984, 'over 100 villagers were killed' (*Pakistan sources*). Mazar-i-Sharif was also subjected to spasmodic rocket attacks, and in one, in June 1984, the Mujahideen claimed they had 'killed 140 collaborators' (*Pakistan sources*), the victims believed to be PDPA activists. There was also some sabotage along the Shibargham-Mazar-i-Sharif natural gas pipeline.

Prisoners held by either side were a silent subject, all being reluctant to provide information about their numbers, their fate or their future. Soviet personnel still fell into Mujahideen hands and, for example, in January 1984, 18 Soviet soldiers were captured in fighting near Mazar-i-Sharif. As the Kabul government still refused to give Geneva Protocol status to captured Mujahideen, negotiations for their exchange, release or even humane treatment simply did not materialise.

One of the few exceptions occurred on 24 August 1985, when two Soviet captives were exchanged for six Mujahideen in the Logar Valley, but this was a local arrangement that did not seem to have the authority of the Mujahideen leadership in Pakistan. A UN Resolution in March 1984, had called for an investigation of human rights abuses in Afghanistan, it being alleged the Kabul government held over 50,000 political prisoners.

8

The Soviets Change Horses: 1986

In 1986, the Soviet government, led by Mikhail Gorbachev, took a long look at its Afghan policy, being dissatisfied with President Karmal's record of failure to unite the PDPA, and to broaden his popular support amongst the Afghan people. Moreover, there was a personality clash between Karmal and President Zia, which was not to Gorbachev's liking as it made Pakistan appear to the West to be an anti-Soviet, anti-Communist bulwark that must be supported. Because of this, Zia was making difficulties at the Proximity Talks, which militated against any Pakistan softening of hostility towards the Kabul government. The Soviets decided to change horses in Afghanistan and, accordingly, President Karmal was gradually eased out, and the new Soviet candidate, General Najibullah, eased in.

Mohammed Najibullah

Mohammed Najibullah, a founder-member of the Parcham faction of the PDPA, was from the Ahmadzai Pushtun tribe in Paktia province, and was unusual in that he was one of the comparatively few Pathans in that faction. After the Saur Revolution, Najibullah had been a member of the ruling Revolutionary Council for a short while, and then became Afghan Ambassador to Iran, only to be dismissed from that post, and expelled from the PDPA, for allegedly plotting against the (then dominant) Khalk faction.

Najibullah took refuge in the USSR, but was allowed to return to Afghanistan after the Amin coup in September 1979. When Karmal became President, Najibullah was given the task of forming KHAD, which he headed until December 1985, when he was appointed a secretary to the Central Committee of the Party, with responsibility for security affairs. During his tenure at KHAD he gained a reputation as a hard man, but the Soviets were more impressed by his achievement in gaining tribal support for the Kabul government. It seems that Najibullah was not the Soviets' first choice; this was probably Sultan Ali Keshtmand, the Prime Minister, but they realised that, as a member of the Hazara minority, he would not have been acceptable in a country in which there was still a Pushtun grip on national life (*Urban*). The same authority expressed surprise at the choice of Najibullah who would seem 'to be unacceptable as a former chief of KHAD to senior guerrilla leaders and most Afghans'; but on his record Najibullah was a firm pro-Moscow man.

The PDPA

A meeting of the Revolutionary Council in February 1986, approved the formation of a 74-member National Reconciliation Commission, to consist of 'all nationalities, tribes and clans, and all classes of social strata from the various provinces', to draft a Constitution for Afghanistan. This Commission was headed by President Karmal. For some time, efforts had been made to bring all political groupings into the PDPA, and previously (in July 1984) the 'Organisation of Fedayeen and Workers of Afghanistan' had merged into it.

During the course of 1986, three more organisations similarly merged; the 'Revolutionary Society of Afghan Workers' (July); the 'Vanguard Organisation of Young Workers of Afghanistan' (September); and the 'Vanguard Organisation of Workers of Afghanistan' (October). [The designations of these four groups suffered slightly in translation from the original Daru or Pushtu names.]

In May 1986, Najibullah became General Secretary of the PDPA, a most powerful appointment, but President Karmal retained the Chairmanship of the Revolutionary Council. Immediately, Najibullah announced the 'Collective Leadership' of Afghanistan, consisting of President Karmal, Prime Minister Sultan Ali Keshtmand, and himself. As this announcement, which virtually pushed Karmal to one side, was being made a large show of Soviet military force was organised in Kabul with tanks and troops on the streets; Soviet guns were trained on Afghan army camps with Soviet armoured vehicles blocking their exits; and Soviet road-blocks appeared on all routes leading into the city. The Afghan army was confined to barracks, and the AAF was grounded.

Najibullah made his next move in November 1986 when, at a meeting of the Revolutionary Council, Karmal was formally relieved of the Presidency on the grounds of 'ill health'. Mohammed Chamkani, a compromise candidate, not a member of the PDPA, was appointed acting President to carry out Head of State functions until the Constitution was completed and accepted.

Proximity Talks

Meanwhile, the Proximity Talks at Geneva had dragged on intermittently, the sixth session taking place in December 1985, when a Four Point Agenda for discussion was produced. The Four Points were; non-intervention and non-interference in Afghan affairs; an international monitoring agreement; the return of Afghan refugees; and the withdrawal of Soviet troops. This was a ray of hope, thought to herald a breakthrough, and President Reagan promised US support provided that any agreement included the withdrawal of the Limited Contingent of Soviet Forces in Afghanistan. In March, the Afghan government complained that the Americans were putting pressure on Pakistan to discontinue with the Proximity Talks.

At the following session of the Proximity Talks in May, the time-table for the withdrawal of Soviet troops, presented by the USSR, produced sharply divided views. At the August session no headway was made on this subject. In November, the UN again approved a Resolution calling for the withdrawal of Soviet troops from Afghanistan. During the negotiations preceding the Resolution, on one occasion Afghan government delegates were physically assaulted by Mujahideen representatives while attempting to hold a Press Conference in the UN building in New York.

Gorbachev's Vladivostok Speech

In June 1986, President Gorbachev made his famous 'Vladivostok Speech', emphasising the urgent need for the USSR to make radical changes in its foreign policy. As a token gesture, he had decided to withdraw six regiments from Afghanistan, and all Soviet troops would be withdrawn from that country as soon as a satisfactory settlement was reached; but he hinted that if armed intervention against Afghanistan continued, Soviet troops would remain. Previous announcements of 'Soviet troops withdrawals' had turned out to be simply troop rotations. A Soviet spokesman later stated that owing to the 'step-by-step stabilisation' of the situation in Afghanistan, withdrawals had now become possible.

The six regiments comprised three anti-aircraft, two motorised and a tank regiment (the Soviets had no armoured formations as such in Afghanistan), about 7,000 men in all, and they were withdrawn between 15-31 October. Caspar Weinberger. US Secretary of Defence, accused the Soviet Union of preparing to cheat, claiming that this number of soldiers would have little effect on the overall strategic situation as it did not include any Spetsnaz or airborne units. An Afghan spokesman stated that Soviet military advisers would remain after the total Soviet withdrawal. CIA sources alleged that other Soviet units were brought into Afghanistan to compensate for this withdrawal, and that Gorbachev's policy in this case, in fact, was thwarted by the Soviet military, especially as, according to its calculations, the Limited Contingent of Soviet Forces in Afghanistan was in total only reduced by 2,000 men during 1986.

Soviet Muslim Soldiers

In July, the Soviet military journal, *Krasnaya Zvezda*, commented on the fact that leaders in the Soviet Muslim Republics were using their influence to discourage their conscripts from serving in Afghanistan, and this had especially become a problem in Uzbekistan. As these were early days of Gorbachev's *perestroika*, the discussion of such an issue so openly must have meant it was considered extremely serious. Although the initial contingent of Soviet Muslim troops in Afghanistan had been hastily recalled in 1980 because of their fraternisation and collaboration with their co-religionist Mujahideen, it seemed there had been a continuing, though small, element in the Limited Contingent of Soviet Forces in Afghanistan all the time, necessitated, no doubt, by a shortage of manpower, the European theatre then still having strategic priority.

In August, there was a general tightening up of conscription regulations in the Soviet armed forces caused, it is believed, by suspected low morale in Afghanistan. In October, there were reports (*Pakistan sources*) of a mutiny in northern Kunduz province of Soviet Muslim troops, in which 80 were said to have been killed while it was being put down. At first it was thought the report probably referred to Afghan troops, but this was denied in Kabul, so the assumption must be that Muslim soldiers serving with the Limited Contingent of Soviet Forces in Afghanistan occasionally mutinied. The Soviets were silent on this issue.

The Turning Tide

Despite Western assessments of the struggle in Afghanistan, it was becoming obvious that the tide was beginning to turn against the Mujahideen. Soviet strategy and tactics had been consistently hard and unyielding, with large sectors of land adjacent to strategic roads, and surrounding garrisons, cities and some towns being deliberately depopulated, rural inhabitants either fleeing into Pakistan, or being pushed into the DPCs. The Soviets were reversing conditions conducive to the operation of Mao Tse-tung's theory of guerrilla warfare, based on the 'guerrilla fish' swimming and hiding in the 'sea of the people'. The Soviets were draining away the 'sea' by removing the inhabitants, and so making it harder for the Mujahideen, either long-range penetration groups, or local ones, to operate, as they were being deprived of shelter, food and information.

For example, in September 1986, the Kabul government began moving some 300,000 people from the eastern provinces of Paktia, Kunar and Paghman, to the barren wastes of Farah, Helmand and Nimroz provinces. The ostensible reason was to take people from overcrowded areas to develop the economy in south-western parts of the country by bringing virgin land under cultivation. The real reason was to drain off people from some of the Mujahideen 'liberated zones'.

Additionally, the Soviets and the Afghan government were making progress in arranging local cease-fires with certain Mujahideen groups, to enable them to plant and harvest crops, and prevent their valleys being subjected to scorched-earth, starvation and depopulation measures. This was extended to many tribal chiefs who simply wanted to live and let live.

Also, progress was being made in persuading tribal and local leaders to form their own private militias, which were paid and armed by the Kabul government, to 'protect themselves from the Mujahideen'; in other words to keep the Mujahideen away from their valleys. These arrangements, not well publicised by Western media at the time, disrupted Mujahideen supply trails across the country, trails that were already saturated with anti-personnel mines dropped from aircraft, which caused many casualties to both men and their valuable pack-animals. One tribal leader, for example, took on the task of virtually guarding the important Shomali power station, near Kabul. Keeping the Mujahideen at bay often resulted in inter-tribal clashes, which was to the government's advantage.

Another distracting factor, which was little mentioned, was the degree to which banditry and extortion rackets developed and flourished in the interior where central government authority rested only lightly, or not at all. Armed caravan trains from Pakistan, destined for distant Mujahideen groups in Afghanistan, and having to pass through territory controlled by other Mujahideen groups, hostile or friendly, had to pay a levy in kind for their safe passage. Shortage of arms may have excused this expedient practice, but did not excuse the progression, to open seizure of Mujahideen provision trains, for the purpose of selling the goods on the black market, a practice which became prevalent.

Aerial Activity

A significant factor in 1986 was the receipt by the Mujahideen of modern Western shoulder-held anti-aircraft missiles. By this time most of the Soviet helicopters were equipped with infra-red decoy flares and jamming equipment that more-or-less neutralised the SAM-7s. The Mujahideen cry now was for the latest version of the US Stinger anti-aircraft missile, which the CIA was reluctant to provide in case they fell into hostile hands. Co-operation between the CIA and the British MI-6 (intelligence organisation) resulted in the supply of 300 British Blowpipe anti-aircraft missiles (*Urban*), for the Mujahideen, which reached Pakistan, were taken over by the ISI, and doled out sparingly.

Another significant factor that year was that the KGB, in co-operation with KHAD (reputedly now about 30,000-strong) began to obtain and use information from Soviet satellite surveillance sources which, together with other sophisticated apparatus including night-vision and infra-red detectors, enabled them more easily to detect and track Mujahideen movements across Afghanistan. Spetsnaz units were able to mount night ambushes and attacks, which often surprised and dismayed the Mujahideen. It was estimated that in 1986, seven Soviet Spetsnaz and seven airborne regiments were almost constantly in action in Afghanistan, and that four newly-formed Afghan special forces groups were also engaged in operations.

During 1986, Afghan-piloted aircraft increasingly came into conflict with Pakistani combat aircraft and anti-aircraft weapons over alleged infringements of Pakistani air space. For example, on 15 January, Pakistani gunners shot down an Afghan-piloted MiG-21, which had allegedly crossed into Pakistan air space. In May, Pakistani MiG-19s brought down an Afghan-piloted aircraft, and damaged another, in a confrontation over the Pakistan city of Parachinar. The Mujahideen still made occasional attacks on air bases, notably one in June, at Shindand, when it was claimed (*Pakistan sources*) that they 'destroyed eight aircraft, and killed 24 Soviet personnel'.

Afghan Army

In March 1986, the Afghan Revolutionary Council approved certain measures designed to tighten the conscription net and at the same time offered another amnesty to deserters, which by the end of the year, according to Najibullah, had brought in over 15,000 rebels (*Kabul Radio*). However, he still complained that conscription was not working well. On the anniversary of the Saur Revolution on 27 April, Afghan armed forces put on a fairly smart and imposing ceremonial March-Past and Fly-Past in Kabul, which impressed Western journalists, who reported it fairly and accurately, though most added that the conduct of the Afghan troops on parade belied their performance in the field; this was rather unfair as some were successfully holding out in remote garrisons against considerable odds.

Mujahideen in Pakistan

In June 1986, Burhanuddin Rabbani, leader of the Fundamentalist IA, and spokesman for the Mujahideen's Islamic Unity of Afghanistan, visited President Reagan in Washington, urging him to sever diplomatic relations with Afghanistan and transfer them to his coalition; but Reagan was not convinced of its 'unity'. Afghan leaders in Pakistan were again beginning to converge on Peshawar from their RTVs, bringing their quarrels, arguments and inter-faction violence with them. On 23 January, an explosion at the Peshawar office of Pakistan Airlines killed three people; and in June, there was a rash of explosions in the city, causing the police to round-up over 7,000 Afghan refugees, who were sent back to their

RTVs. Mujahideen leaders alleged that most of the explosions and assassinations were the covert work of KHAD.

They also alleged that KHAD agents were giving weapons and ammunition to Pathan tribesmen living on the eastern side of the Afghan frontier, to persuade them to block Mujahideen supply trails through their territory. This was an indirect admission that the Kabul-sponsored Pushtu tribal militias were having some success.

Fighting in 1986

The year began with heavy Soviet-Afghan bombing of the town of Charikar, on the Northern Route, followed by bombing sorties in Free Fire Zones in the Paghman Valley, the Shomali Plateau and in the Kohistan area, all designed to protect the Northern Route, and especially the Salang Tunnel. After this, the Northern Route was comparatively quiet throughout the rest of the year, the main exception being a Mujahideen attack, on 23 October on withdrawing Soviet columns, near the Salang Tunnel, after which the Mujahideen claimed to have killed 35 Russian soldiers (*Pakistan sources*). The remoter western provinces were largely left to their own devices, as many of the tribes, factions and groups were content to live and let live.

A large Spring offensive was launched against the remnants of Ahmad Shah Masoud's Mujahideen group in the upper reaches of the Panjshir Valley. By mid-June, he had withdrawn all his forces, said to number about 3,000, from his now devastated and largely depopulated valley, moving northwards over the Hindu Kush into Badakhshan province.

The previous year, Masoud had been primarily involved in grouping together Mujahideen forces in the north-eastern provinces of Kunduz, Takhar, Baghlan, Kapisa and Parwan into what became known as the 'Council of the North', and by 1986, had successfully combined most of them into what became known as the 'Central Forces'. In June, the Central Forces were involved in fighting against government troops in Badakhshan, in which both sides stood off after suffering heavy casualties. However, in November, Masoud's Central Forces succeeded in seizing the garrison town of Nahrin (Baghlan province), which one authority (*Urban*) regarded as the most important victory for Rabbani's Fundamentalist IA since 1979, an operation which enhanced its almost nationwide spread of influence across Afghanistan.

Much of the real fighting was confined to the eastern provinces, parts of which were 'liberated zones', where a few Afghan-held garrisons were usually besieged. Soviet-Afghan operations began early in January, with the intention of preventing armed Mujahideen, who had wintered comfortably in RTVs in Pakistan, from returning refreshed to their battle areas. A number of 'search-and-destroy' and 'relief columns' were launched, while Spetsnaz units hit at Mujahideen bases, staging camps and villages known to be part of the supply-communication chain.

The main fighting in the early part of the year centred around the Mujahideen base of Zhawar, a strong position built on a series of caves in a hillside actually resting on the Pakistan border, and defended by about 8,000 Mujahideen. The dominant leader was the competent Jalalabuddin Haqqani, of the Khalis HI, who had persuaded a number of groups to operate with him in this defence complex. After bombing sorties in April, a large Soviet-Afghan force, under the Afghan Brigadier Abdul Gafur, attacked Zhawar, and a hard three-week struggle ensued.

Eventually, the defending Mujahideen escaped through subterranean cave passages into Pakistan, leaving government troops in triumphant possession of Zhawar. Mujahideen spokesmen in Peshawar admitted this defeat. British Blowpipe anti-aircraft missiles were used by the Mujahideen for the first time in action at the Battle for Zhawar, but it was claimed that if they had been more abundant the Mujahideen would have been able to hold out longer, even perhaps indefinitely.

There was also intense fighting in April, in the provinces of Kunar, Nangrahar and Ghazni, which resulted in fairly heavy casualties on both sides. By this time the Mujahideen were conceding that the Afghan army had improved and was fighting effectively. In May, the Soviet-Afghan force that had seized Zhawar was largely dispersed, some elements being diverted to Paktia province. Zhawar was evacuated, to be immediately reoccupied by the Mujahideen, but this did not unduly worry the Soviets, whose policy was not to stand and hold ground gained at all costs, but for its field force elements to remain mobile.

Most of the action in Paktia province was centred around Jiji, still held by the Mujahideen: a rare example of prolonged defence, but as government forces in the area were suffering fairly heavy casualties, they were withdrawn, leaving the Mujahideen in possession. In July, the Mujahideen in Logar province launched a series of attacks against government-held garrisons, but these soon ran out of steam, rather indicating that while the Afghan army seemed to be improving, Mujahideen battlefield discipline was not. Jalalabad came in for occasional Mujahideen attacks, one occurring on 11 August, when it was claimed (*Pakistan sources*) that 110 Afghan troops were killed.

The city of Herat remained divided. The fort, government buildings, the old city and the air base remained in government hands, protected by wide belts of mine-fields. On the other side were the Mujahideen, mostly dominated by Ismael Khan, of Rabbani's Fundamentalist IA, occupying most of the new city, which was frequently bombed. It is believed that only about 20,000 Afghan inhabitants remained in Herat.

Burhanuddin Rabbani, leader of the IA, speaking in Peshawar, claimed that his Mujahideen had launched an offensive which, by 20 June, had made considerable local gains, and killed 200 Afghan soldiers (*Pakistan sources*). Certainly, fighting in and around Herat dragged on through June and into July, to subside during the hot month of August. Despite IA claims, and sympathetic Western media support, it seems the fighting had slightly gone against Ismael Khan in Herat.

As in the two previous years, during 1986 fighting continued in and around the city of Kandahar, with government forces holding government buildings, the administrative centre and the detached airport. Street fighting was not uncommon. Again, it seemed that Afghan troops, who bore the brunt of the ground actions in the Kandahar area, might be gaining a slight edge over the Mujahideen.

During 1986, Kabul remained a troubled city which, despite being saturated with military, both Soviet and Afghan, suffered periodic rocket attacks from the surrounding hills, several direct Mujahideen break-through assaults, sabotage, in-fighting between Khalk and Parcham factions, and—a new dimension—violence between rival Parcham groups, between those who supported Najibullah and those who favoured Karmal. This new development made the Soviets wonder whether they had underrated Karmal's popularity. A bomb explosion occurring outside the Soviet Embassy on one occasion, killing three people, was believed to have been intended for Najibullah, who had been due to attend a reception there.

Three rings of defences surrounding Kabul had been constructed progressively outwards as the range and accuracy of Mujahideen weapons had improved, and a fourth was being built. Aircraft and helicopters, with Spetsnaz personnel, were ever ready to react rapidly against any Mujahideen aggression. The diplomatic corps and their families had been moved from their southern residences to the northern side of the city, which was more sheltered from rocket fire from the surrounding hills.

Explosions and car-bombs became a familiar hazard in Kabul. On one day, (16 July), there were six in the area inhabited by Soviet personnel; and in the following two days there were running battles in the streets, when at times it was difficult to determine who exactly was fighting whom. On 26 and 27 August, a series of explosions occurred in the vicinity of Qargha airport, just to the east of Kabul, in which the Mujahideen claimed to have killed '50 collaborators' (*Pakistan sources*). Barrages of rockets followed, causing casualties and damage in various areas. In September, the Mujahideen were pushed further away from Kabul, their aggression being diverted to adjacent areas of Paghman and Qarabagh; this spasmodically continued until October, but eventually subsided because the Mujahideen had expended most of their rockets. Government aircraft, also bombed suspected Mujahideen hideouts on the Shomali Plateau.

Prisoners and Human Rights

The lot of prisoners on both sides remained sad and uncertain. The Kabul government still refused to comply with the Geneva Convention, and continued to treat captured Mujahideen as political criminals. Soviets taken prisoner by the Mujahideen still fared badly. It was thought the number of Soviet personnel 'missing in action' (MIAs) exceeded 400, but no one knew exactly as neither side disclosed how many prisoners they held; nor did they know whether their MIAs were alive or dead.

Under arrangements made by the ICRC in 1982, a total of 11 Soviet prisoners had been allowed to spend a two-year period of release-parole in Switzerland, and the last of these was released in March 1986. Two had been allowed to stay in Switzerland, one was granted political asylum in West Germany, and the remainder returned home safely to the USSR. In November, five Soviet deserters were smuggled out of Afghanistan into Pakistan and thence, by arrangement with the Canadian government, to Canada. Impromptu exchange of prisoners in the field was rare, but did happen occasionally; on 24 February, a Mujahideen leader, Mohammed

Ishaq, captured near Kandahar in 1984, was exchanged for a captured Soviet soldier.

None of the combatants published their own casualty figures, but only made claims of 'enemy' dead and wounded. These were invariably grossly inflated so analysts had to make their own 'guesstimates', which in hindsight were also invariably inflated. None seemed too concerned with civilian casualties, which included women and children.

Lack of basic human rights in the Afghan conflict did become a deep concern of the West, though the Soviets alleged that the motivation was political bias. A UN Human Rights Report on 26 February 1986 alleged that both Afghan armed forces and 'foreign troops' (the Soviets) were waging a campaign of systematic brutality against the rural population, as part of what amounted to a deliberate scorched earth policy; that they used both napalm and phosphorous bombs; and that there was widespread torture in prisons. These allegations were denied by both Soviet and Afghan governments, which pointed out that this Report had been compiled solely from uncorroborated evidence obtained from refugees. It was notable, however, that the UN Commission for Refugees was refused entry to Afghanistan.

9

The Year of the Stinger: 1987

During 1987 probably over 900 US Stinger anti-aircraft systems, and probably three times that number of missiles, reached Pakistan for distribution to the Mujahideen for use in Afghanistan. Only a proportion of them reached their destination. Those that did arrive did not cause the Soviets to change their basic Afghan strategy or priorities, but certainly had a profound and dramatic effect on both Soviet and AAF tactics and air transportation.

On 22 November 1987, the US State Department estimated that since Stingers had begun to reach Afghanistan, on average one Soviet or Afghan aircraft a day had been brought down. This was an exaggeration but, as the Soviets did not issue details of their losses or comment on such statements, this estimate was widely believed, especially as it was known that the CIA had direct access to US satellite surveillance data, which could locate and identify aircraft wrecks in Afghanistan, although it too was reluctant to categorise and quantify. Without doubt, 1987 was the Year of the Stinger, in Afghanistan.

Stingers in Mujahideen hands deprived the Soviets of complete air domination, which so far they had enjoyed, and had two main repercussions. One was that while previously personnel and some stores were usually transported quickly by air, mainly for security reasons as the roads and countryside were 'Mujahideen-ridden', they now had to revert to road transport. The other was that the Mujahideen were given considerable freedom of movement by day which enabled them to concentrate more on disrupting roads and attacking convoys, and also allowed their pack-animal supply trains, which previously had had cautiously to pick their way over hazardous mountain trails by night, to move in daytime.

The US Stinger (FIM-92) is optically-aimed and infra-red guided, which means that, being 'heat-seeking', a missile had only to be launched in the general direction of the aircraft and found its own way to the target. It had a range of about three miles and, weighing only about 30lbs, was easily transportable. The Stinger, developed for the US Army Missile Command, had gained a combat reputation for lethality in the Falkland Islands campaign (1982), its manufacturers (General Dynamics of California) claiming that it had an 80 per cent 'strike-rate' on any aircraft from helicopters to jets. By this time a consortium in Europe was building Stingers for NATO and in September 1987 another secondary source (Raytheon) also began to build them for the US army. In short, there were plenty of Stingers available.

The British-built Blowpipe anti-aircraft missile systems, already received in Pakistan for the Mujahideen, were also significant but as these were initially sent secretly, and their presence officially denied by the British for many months, they attracted much less publicity than the Stingers. The Blowpipe was similar in most respects to the Stinger, also having been blooded in the Falkland Islands campaign, although Afghans said they found it to be more complicated to operate.

Once they had Stingers in their hands, the Mujahideen in Afghanistan turned them against the internal Bakhtar Airlines, which had about a dozen ageing Antonov-26 transport aircraft running scheduled and special services between the major cities. In an eight-month period commencing in February 1987, five of these aircraft were hit by Stinger missiles, and brought down, respectively on 9 February, 30 March, 11 June, 13 August and 14 September. On 16 September, *Pravda* condemned such attacks on 'civilian airliners', and claimed that over 100 lives had been lost due to this hostile activity since the beginning of the year.

The Antonov-26 losses had a profound effect on the morale of civilian pilots, and there were instances of refusal to fly on certain routes considered to be too dangerous for reasonable safety. This reluctance also spread to some AAF pilots and there was at least one mutiny at the Bagram air base because of the 'Stinger factor' (*Pakistan sources*). In July, Najibullah had to cancel a planned airborne tour of the country, accompanied by Western journalists, for this reason.

Aircraft were at their most vulnerable to Stinger missiles when taking-off and landing, and several had been lost this way. Protective measures were evolved to cover this vulnerability and, for example, helicopters circled a plane when it was landing and taking-off, ejecting flares at two-second intervals to divert heat-seeking missiles away from their target.

The success of Stingers in Afghanistan made them prestige weapons much in demand by insurgent and terrorist groups worldwide, and by neighbouring Iran, still at war with Iraq. This alarmed the US administration which sought to curb their proliferation. In November 1987, the House of Representatives banned the sale of Stingers to all except NATO and certain Middle East countries, and accordingly certain US promises had to be modified.

One report (*Sunday Times*) stated that the CIA had halted supplies of Stinger missiles to the Fundamental Khalis HI group after it had been discovered that it had sold '32 Stinger systems to Iran for $1 million'. On 21 September, Stinger cases were found on Iranian naval vessels captured in the Gulf by the US Navy. Caspar Weinberger said the missile systems had been stolen by the Iranian Revolutionary Guards. At first the Khalis HI denied the allegation of collusion with the Iranians, but later indirectly admitted the charge.

In Pakistan, President Zia still retained a firm grip on all modern weapons coming into his country for the Mujahideen, including Stingers and Blowpipes (not yet on his own military inventory), and his ISI continued to dole them out sparingly and selectively, or withhold them. But there was corruption somewhere in the ISI distribution chain as these weapons were finding their way both into the arms bazaars of Peshawar, and into the tribal areas. A lion's share of incoming weaponry went to the Khalis HI group, but as individualism began to surface, and its discipline, and even cohesion, seemed to deteriorate, fingers of suspicion were pointed at it.

The Stinger factor further divided the political leaderships of the Mujahideen in Pakistan and their military leaders in the field, between the 'haves' and the 'have nots', causing friction that frequently led to inter-group clashes. In Kunar province, for example, the Traditionalist Mohammadi-led IRM (a 'have not') spent much of its time fighting Hekmaytar's HIA and the Khalis HI, both Fundamentalist 'haves'. In Peshawar all groups and factions seemed to quarrel over the distribution of Stingers, whether they had any or not, and use threats, bribery, theft or force to obtain them, or to obtain more. Some thoughtful Mujahideen politicians expressed the opinion that it would perhaps have been better if no Stingers had arrived, as before their appearance there had always been hope that Mujahideen unity would be achieved one day, but the Stinger factor seemed to have dissolved that dream.

A Cease-Fire

At a meeting of the PDPA on 30 December 1986, the new General Secretary, Mohammed Najibullah, dropped his KHAD rank of General, and his short-lived diminutive of 'Najib', to become known as Dr Najibullah. He had just returned from a visit to the USSR, where Shevardnadze, the Soviet Foreign Minister, had told him that the Kremlin leadership was in favour of a political settlement to the Afghan problem. Dr Najibullah announced that all Afghan armed forces (and by implication Soviet forces too) would observe a cease-fire from 15 January 1987, for a period of six months and, subject to a positive response from the Mujahideen, would be withdrawn back into barracks.

At the same time, he announced his 'National Reconciliation Policy', calling upon Mujahideen groups to join a Government of National Unity. He stated there would be an amnesty for all Mujahideen and that all Islamic and Afghan national and cultural traditions would be respected, and he urged Afghan refugees to return home, promising them rehabilitation benefits.

The Mujahideen Islamic Unity of Afghanistan coalition, in Pakistan, rejected Najibullah's cease-fire offer, its spokesman, Mohammed Nabi Mohammadi, stating that it would have nothing to do with the Kabul government but would be prepared to enter into direct negotiations with the Soviet Union. The London-based Islamic Council of Europe also called for direct talks to be held between the USSR and the Mujahideen.

The cease-fire was a fiction, as neither the Soviets, the Kabul government nor the Mujahideen observed it, and the insurrection continued. The farce was maintained however, and on 14 July the Kabul government formally extended it for another six months. This coincided with the Second Congress of the National Fatherland Front, which was slowly extending into a nationwide organisation. Najibullah suspected there was a plot being hatched against him on that occasion and in the evening (14 July) Kabul was packed with Soviet armoured vehicles and soldiers, all Afghan troops were confined to camp and Soviet armoured vehicles blocked the exits of

Afghan military camps, with Soviet guns trained on them.

National Reconciliation

In May 1987, Karmal was arrested, some reports indicating that he was held for a while in the notorious Poli Charki prison, before being sent to the USSR for 'medical treatment'; he was thus removed from the Afghan scene. Previously, in April and May, there had been a series of explosions in Kabul, which were attributed to Karmal supporters. During May, Najibullah released a number of Khalk members, some of whom had been in detention since December 1979, in an effort to unite the PDPA; one of them, Mohammed Ghilabzai, was appointed Minister of Internal Affairs. Also in May, Najibullah announced further relaxations in the almost moribund Land Reform Programme, so unpopular with landlords and peasants alike, allowing individual holdings to be increased to 45 acres, and also permitting land to be bought, leased or sold.

On 6 July, Najibullah announced that political parties could be formed under certain conditions, explaining his views on 'power-sharing'. Those permitted to become engaged in this new democratic political activity were listed, and included Traditionalists (but not Fundamentalists), social and political personalities from previous regimes (including ex-King Zahir Shah), leaders of armed groups and tribes, and democratic Left-wing organisations. During 1987, ex-King Zahir Shah became a talking point, hovering on the edge of Afghan politics, favoured by Traditionalists but rejected by Fundamentalists.

Najibullah visited Gorbachev in Moscow, who emphasised that a political settlement must be reached very soon, but when the Proximity Talks resumed at Geneva in September they remained at stalemate. Three of the Four Points of the agenda had been settled by this time, but the fourth, the Soviet time-table for withdrawal, remained controversial and unsolved. Behind the scenes there were continuing disagreements on several other issues, especially over continued aid by both superpowers to their respective clients. President Reagan, for example, insisted on continuing to send aid to the Mujahideen up to the moment the last Soviet soldier left Afghan soil.

At a meeting of the Revolutionary Council on 30 September, Najibullah was elected Chairman, and the following month claimed (*Kabul Radio*) that his National Reconciliation Policy was working and that already 'some 1,500 villages had joined', that '90,000 refugees had returned from Pakistan', and that '30,000 rebels from 174 armed groups had surrendered'. However, during the year Najibullah had less success in persuading the Parcham and Khalk factions to forget their differences and work together. Occasional scuffles, explosions and even gun-battles erupted on the streets between the two factions. Also, some explosions were attributed to Karmal supporters, again causing the Soviets to wonder if they had misjudged him, although they came to accept the Afghan view that Najibullah's failures were due to his comparative youth as, traditionally, peacemaking in Afghanistan was an elderly man's role.

At a Loya Jirga held on 29-30 November 1987, the new Afghan Constitution was adopted for an 'Afghan Republic', with a bicameral National Assembly, and an Executive President, in which the PDPA was to lose its monopoly of political power. Najibullah was elected President of the Revolutionary Council Presidium, and appointed C-in-C of the Afghan Armed Forces. Since April 1980, the country had been guided by a provisional document, the 'Basic Principles of the Democratic Republic'. Najibullah's satisfaction was slightly marred by the defection of his brother, Sidiqillah, to Rabbani's Fundamentalist IA group.

Mujahideen Unity

Although Najibullah's National Reconciliation Policy offer and the cease-fire had been sharply rejected by the Mujahideen political leaderships in Pakistan, they did arouse considerable anxiety as, if these offers attracted a sufficient number of Mujahideen in the field, the back of the armed struggle could be broken, or at least severely weakened. On 7 January 1987, it had been announced (*Kabul Radio*) that a Mujahideen commander in the Herat area 'with 1,000 armed men' had defected to the government. This report was exaggerated, as were other periodic reports of a similar nature put out over Kabul Radio for psychological effect; but nevertheless there was a steady stream of Mujahideen defectors to the government side throughout the year.

In May, yet another attempt was made to achieve Mujahideen unity in Pakistan, when the main groups in the Islamic Unity of Afghanistan coalition agreed to establish a 230-seat Council (*Shura*), which would consist of 20 per cent representation from Afghan refugees in both Pakistan and Iran, with the remaining seats going to political leaders and military commanders of the main groups. Some Mujahideen field commanders in Afghanistan were critical of this allocation, feeling the politicians, who had lived in comfortable security in Pakistan throughout the struggle, would seize a large majority of seats for themselves, to the detriment of those who had borne the brunt and hardships of battle.

The Tehran Eight

In the meantime, the Iranian government had been giving some attention to the Afghan problem, and had long been attempting to persuade the myriad of small Shia Mujahideen groups in western Afghanistan to stop fighting each other and join together in a coalition under Iranian influence. It had a degree of success in June 1987, when it was able to announce that eight of the Shia Mujahideen groups had come together to form the 'Alliance of Eight' (to counter the Sunni Peshawar Seven perhaps), led by Mohammed Karim Khaladi.

The four major groups within this alliance were [given in English translation for simplicity]: the Islamic Movement, The Word, Revolutionary Guards Corps and the Party of God. The four minor groups were: Invitation, Progress, Islamic Strength and the United Front. The larger Council of the Union group, the original resistance movement of the Hazara Jat region, still stood aloof (*Urban*).

These Shia groups had been largely ignored by the Kabul government, with the exception of occasional bombing sorties, as they seemed more concerned with fighting one another than Kabul government authority. Realising that the Soviets would soon be pulling out of Afghanistan, the Iranians had made this effort to gain influence within western Afghanistan to give them muscle when it came to peace negotiations.

Reaction came quickly when on 12-13 July, about '1,200 representatives' (Urban) of Sunni Mujahideen groups from the Badghis, Farah, Faryab, Jawzjan and Herat provinces met at Saghar (Jawzjan province), at the instigation of Ishmael Khan, leader of the military contingent at Herat of Rabanni's Fundamentalist IA group. At this gathering the 'Supreme *Jihad* Council' was formed to co-ordinate Mujahideen operations against the Tehran Eight and also to put forward their views on the political future of the country. Mujahideen field commanders and their exiled political leaderships were invariably out of touch, and often at odds with each other, but this was the largest united expression of their discontent so far.

In Pakistan, on 16 September, an explosion at the office of Hekmatyar's Fundamentalist HIA group killed eight people, and injured 36 (*Pakistan sources*). The Afghan KHAD was blamed, but not everyone accepted this, the general suspicion being that a rival Mujahideen group had been responsible. In October, Younis Khalis, of the Fundamentalist HI group, after an acrimonious all-night sitting, was elected Chairman of the Islamic Unity of Afghanistan coalition, with limited powers. It was a compromise nomination.

Mujahideen Activities in the USSR

Gorbachev's policy of *glasnost* gradually brought more open and factual coverage of events in Afghanistan to the Soviet people, as Soviet journalists and TV teams were allowed more latitude and were able to obtain on-the-spot stories. In March and April 1987 *Pravda* ran a series of articles exposing Afghan activities against Soviet territory. In response to a Tadjik petition from Badakhshan province in 1985, the Kabul government had constructed a second bridge over the Amu Darya near Shignan, to facilitate people crossing the river to visit friends and relatives, and to help local trade. This had been in keeping with the Kabul government's policy of gaining tribal support.

According to *Pravda* in early 1987, and even before, Gulbuddin Hekmatyar, the Fundamentalist leader of the HIA, had been crossing the Shignan bridge on political missions, trying to rouse the local Tadjiks into open rebellion to 'liberate their republic' from the Soviet grip. This source also stated that Hekmatyar's Mujahideen attacked Soviet territory three times. The first attack was on 7-8 March, coinciding with the trial in the Tadjikstan SSR of Abdulo Saydov, a Mullah, accused of being the spiritual leader of the underground *Vakhabist* organisation of the Fundamentalist Ishmaeli sect. Rockets were fired at the small Soviet border town of Pyandzh, one person being killed and others injured.

The next Afghan Mujahideen attack against Soviet territory was on 8-9 April, when a similar rocket assault was made on a small Soviet border post in the same area, but this time Soviet Border Guards fired back at the attackers, causing casualties. The third attack took place on 17 May, when the Afghan Mujahideen actually crossed the river, penetrating a short distance into Soviet territory until they ran up against Border Guards and, becoming involved in a gun-battle, had to withdraw hastily, again suffering casualties.

These Afghan frontier incidents brought General Viktor Cherbrikov, Head of the KGB and responsible for the Border Guards and frontier security, hot-foot to the spot to assess the situation. Border Guard units in the area were reinforced, and other troops moved into supporting positions, while extensive Soviet reprisals took place in that part of Badakhshan, in the form of carpet-bombing, razing crops, destruction of houses and the depopulation of villages. This heavy-handed counteraction deterred Hekmatyar from further rabble-rousing 'liberation' incitement on Soviet soil.

Afghan-Pakistan Frontier Friction

Despite Pakistan's reluctance to take military action against Afghan combat aircraft straying into its air space, the position along the joint frontier remained abrasive and touchy; incidents were not infrequent as both Afghan pilots and Mujahideen pushed their luck as far as they could. Long sections of the frontier were completely unmarked, and it needed only the slightest error in map-reading for Afghan pilots to find themselves in Pakistan air space; or for Afghan troops to find themselves on the wrong side of the border. For example, the Pakistan government claimed (26-27 February 1987) that AAF planes deliberately flew over and dropped bombs on villages in Waziristan and the Kurram Agency, though this was denied in Kabul.

In response, the Pakistan government decided to move more anti-aircraft units, some now armed with Stinger and Blowpipe missiles, right forward along the frontier; and the Pakistan air force was allowed to react more aggressively. On 30 March 1987, two Pakistan F-16s shot down an Afghan MiG-21, which allegedly entered Pakistan air space; the Kabul government, however, while admitting the incident, claimed it was not a MiG-21 but an Antonov-26 passenger plane of Bakhtar Airlines carrying civilians. On 18 April, Karachi Radio admitted that one of its F-16 aircraft had been brought down over the border town of Miranshah in an engagement with two Afghan MiG-21s.

Later, *Tass* on 7 August, stated that 'thousands of deaths had occurred in the Kurram Agency' when two tribes, the Turi and the Bangasha, resisted the Pakistan 'depopulation policy'. The allegation was that these two tribes were being forcibly removed from their traditional lands adjacent to the Afghan frontier so that Peshawar-based 'rebels' could have operational freedom of movement in that area.

Insurgent Activity: 1987

During 1987 as had become customary, hundreds of incidents, large and small, and some very small indeed, occurred in Afghanistan, but all were meticulously logged and publicised by Mujahideen HQs in Pakistan, though their records lacked credibility as confirmation was invariably lacking. Moreover, the suspicion was that not only were some magnified but that many were fictitious. Only a few significant examples of Mujahideen action and government counteraction will be quoted here to illustrate trends and tactics, in what, despite talk of possible future Soviet withdrawal, most of the antagonists still regarded as part of the 'long haul'.

Again, generally speaking Soviet and Afghan armed forces managed to keep the Northern Route and the Salang Tunnel open, despite occasional Mujahideen attacks. One major Mujahideen ambush of a government road convoy occurred on 21 February, near Puli Khumari (Baghlan province), when it was claimed that over 50 Afghan soldiers were killed (*Pakistan sources*).

The Shomali Valley and Plateau were the scene of several clashes between government forces and Mujahideen, it being reported that the 'rebels' had held positions in the Shomali area since the beginning of the year, and during operations in August '290 villages had been liberated' (*Izvestia*). This area attracted a flow of refugees from Kabul and its environs, escaping from Mujahideen rocket-fire and raids, government counter-reprisals within the perimeter defences, and its depopulation policy outside to clear Free Fire Zones. These refugees tended to huddle together near the Northern Route, and were soon infiltrated by active Mujahideen. Government bombing and other harassing tactics were employed to drive the refugees away from the Northern Route.

To the north-west, on the Circular Road, the Mujahideen claimed in August, to have overrun the Afghan garrison at Maimana, mid-way between Herat and Mazar-i-Sharif, close to the Soviet border, breaking through its defences and 'capturing 28 posts' (*Pakistan sources*). In the North-east region all was comparatively quiet after KGB reprisals in Badakhshan.

Later Masoud's Central Forces carried out several attacks against government garrisons, obtaining success at Kalafghan (blocking a route into the Panjshir Valley) in July, and at Kirano Monjan (another blocking position) in October (*Urban*); he was, however, rather unjustly criticised by other Mujahideen leaders for inactivity against Soviet forces. Masoud's position was improved when the government garrison at Pechgur, in the Valley, was withdrawn in September. Masoud seemed to have reached a degree of efficient cohesion in combat, using radio communications within his formations, something as yet rare in most Mujahideen combat groups, and he had also accumulated a quantity of infantry weapons and missiles.

Much of the fighting took place in the eastern Kunar, Laghman, Nangrahar, Logar and Paktia provinces, where the Mujahideen were thickest on the ground and closest to their sources of arms, supplies and political sanctuary. Elsewhere, despite claims by Mujahideen leaderships in Pakistan that their men in the field were ignoring the cease-fire, lack of activity tended to belie that claim. However, in the eastern provinces the Mujahideen did make several attempts to seize small Afghan-held garrisons, quick reaction by combat aircraft and helicopter-borne commando troops breaking up Mujahideen musterings.

Mujahideen activities flared up in Paktia province in May and June, as Afghan columns, with Soviet and Afghan air support, and occasionally also Spetsnaz units, tried to break the siege of the Afghan-held border garrison of Jiji, culminating in a 24-hour pitched battle, said by some to be the largest since Soviet military intervention in the country, but ending in stalemate. Extravagant claims were made by the Mujahideen of casualties caused.

In Nangrahar province, government forces suffered set-backs as their road convoys were ambushed, and in one such action in April, the Mujahideen claimed to have 'killed 50 Soviet troops and captured 28' (*Pakistan sources*). In Kunar province government-held garrisons and towns were usually under siege by night. Several raids were made on Jalalabad, and in a rocket attack on its airport on 18 May, the Mujahideen claimed there were 13 Soviets amongst the dead. There was also internal dissidence at Jalalabad, provoked by the PDPA feud, and on 8 February a car-bomb explosion killed a number of people.

Kabul remained an unstable city, plagued with car-bomb explosions. On 1 February, one exploded outside the Indian Embassy, killing four people and injuring others; in July, Mujahideen

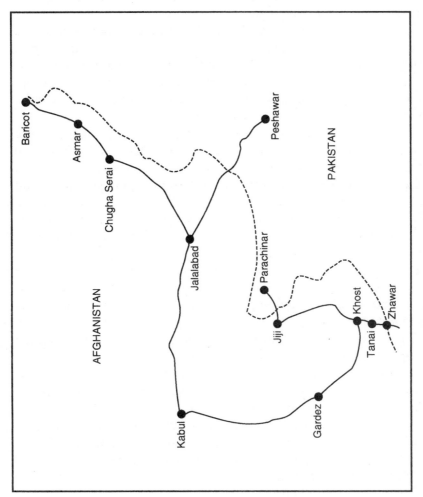

Kabul – Khost – Baricot

173

ground attacks broke through the outer defences to seize and briefly hold six military posts in the western suburbs, which resulted in heavy casualties; in October, an explosion at the Grand Mosque at Sherpur killed 27 people; on the morning of Najibullah's speech to the November Loya Jirga a rain of rockets hit the city; and in December there were heavy rocket attacks on both the Bala Hissar and the military residential area (*Pakistan sources*).

Spasmodic fighting occurred in and around Kandahar during the year without any significant gain by either side. In March, Mujahideen groups attacked the nearby airport-air base, and in May, there was a three-week bout of fighting when a Mujahideen group, calling itself the 'Mercenaries of Reaction', entered the Kharka Mosque and killed the Imam of Kandahar.

In June, the Kabul government responded by launching a series of small operations designed to seal off Kandahar city from the Mujahideen-controlled suburbs. In July, government troops launched an offensive against Mujahideen positions in and around the small town of Panjana, just east of Kandahar, and this fighting did not slacken off until mid-August, the Mujahideen retaining their hold on the small adjacent towns of Arghandab and Mahlajat. In September, the Mujahideen mustered '35 rebel groups, belonging to six rebel organisations' to launch a co-ordinated attack on government positions on the 50-mile road between Kandahar and Spin Baldak, all held by Afghan troops, blocking communications (*Kabul Radio*).

There was a strange stillness in Herat during 1987, as government troops and Mujahideen seemed to agree to 'live and let live'; such incidents as occurred were spontaneous minor combustions and opportunity brawls or shootings. However, there was considerable friction and some fighting between the Tehran Eight groups and those of the Supreme *Jihad* Council. In July, a Mujahideen military commander in the Herat area, named as Safillah Afzali, was killed in an ambush on the road from Herat leading to Iran, and while overtly the Tehran Eight was blamed, a finger of suspicion pointed at the Rabbani's Fundamentalist IA.

The Battle for Khost

Khost remained a prestigious prize both to the Mujahideen and to the Afghan army which had held it since before the arrival of the Soviets. In fact, although situated at a junction of several routes,

Khost had little real tactical value, as the surrounding terrain was such that it could be easily bypassed. The Soviet and Afghan military had one major difference in their strategic view: the Afghan army was in favour of seizing and holding on to cities and territory gained, while the Soviets, apart from holding firmly on to their main bases, were reluctant to tie down troops in static positions, which deprived them of mobility, and absorbed huge numbers of men.

In November 1987, a combined force of Mujahideen mounted an operation to seize Khost, and closed the approach road from Gardez. This was unexpected as Winter was almost upon them, the time when most Mujahideen headed for their home villages or for the RTVs in the sanctuary of Pakistan, but Mujahideen leaderships badly wanted to occupy the city, both for prestige and to provide a valuable pawn in any negotiations that might arise. Mujahideen rocket fire on the Khost airfield stopped airborne supplies. On 25 November, an Afghan column moved out from Gardez to reopen the road to Khost, but by 9 December had been beaten back.

Led personally by General Boris Gromov, commander of the Limited Contingent of Soviet Forces in Afghanistan, with General Shah Nawaz Tanai commanding the Afghan element, a column of about 10,000 Soviet and Afghan troops, supported by bomber aircraft, helicopter-borne Spetsnaz and artillery, moved out from Gardez towards Khost on 27 December, in extreme winter conditions. Afghan troops, weapons and equipment had been drawn from several formations to make up this task force.

There was hard fighting along the winding Gardez-Khost road, part of which ran through the Kanay Valley, where the twisting ravines were ideal for ambush tactics. As the column advanced, the heights on either side of the road were picketed by Afghan troops while helicopters continually flew overhead, the 'path-finders' weaving between the flanking mountain crests to draw Mujahideen fire, and Mi-24 gunships followed ready to eliminate any Mujahideen they found. Afghan commandos were progressively put down ahead of the column to trap Mujahideen detachments, and to attack ambush parties in the rear.

It was not until 3 January 1988, that victory was announced (*Kabul Radio*), and claims made that '1,603 counter-revolutionary elements had been eliminated, for the loss of seven Afghan soldiers'. Probably three helicopters were also lost. The siege of Khost had indeed been lifted and the road from Gardez reopened. This operation was the only one launched in 1987 involving more than

175

one regiment of Soviet ground troops, and it was the last major one before Soviet withdrawal (Urban). Military commentators generally remarked upon how well Soviet troops had conducted themselves, and how improved their morale and discipline were in this operation.

10

Soviet Military Withdrawal: 1988-89

By the beginning of 1988 the talking point on Afghanistan was of Soviet military withdrawal. Very few people doubted this would happen sooner or later; it was simply a matter of when, and on what terms. Antagonists believed the 'long haul' period was over, but all agreed that much remained to be done to be ready to take full advantage of any vacuum created by the eventual Soviet departure. Both the Kabul government and the Mujahideen remained equally confident that they would eventually be victorious. None doubted that Gorbachev, who had described Soviet involvement in Afghanistan as a 'bleeding wound', for which he laid the blame at Brezhnev's door, was determined to withdraw his troops as soon as possible, but that he wanted to leave behind in Kabul a friendly government strong enough to be able to resist an anticipated Mujahideen offensive against it.

The Mujahideen leaderships thought Gorbachev was dragging his feet to give President Najibullah time to improve his military strength. Despite increasing doubts about the Mujahideen's continued lack of unity, the Americans still had faith in their ultimate victory against the Soviet-supported Kabul government. The United States was now strongly supporting President Zia of Pakistan, who was rigidly anti-Soviet, hostile to the Kabul government, and in favour of a Fundamentalist Islamic government for Afghanistan, preferably headed by Gulbuddin Hekmatyar, the extremist leader of the HIA group; it was not apparently realised that if this happened there would be an anti-American Islamic bloc of Iran, Afghanistan and Pakistan in southern Asia. The Soviets, on the other hand, were fully aware of the danger of such an Islamic bloc materialising on their southern frontier, which would tend to destabilise the some 60 million Muslims in their southern Asian Republics.

Much of the ice of the Cold War in Europe was melting and although neither the USA nor the USSR anticipated such a rapidly approaching thaw, relations between them were improving. President Reagan, casting aside his former 'evil empire' image of the Soviet Union, was coming to realise that Gorbachev, struggling to implement his *glasnost* and *perestroika* policies, was really a serious reformer. On 1 January 1988, President Reagan and Gorbachev televised New Year greetings to each other for the whole world to see. A similar, but lower key, televised exchange of greetings had occurred in 1986, but a proposal to repeat this in 1987 had been rejected by Gorbachev.

The Afghan question had featured at the Reagan-Gorbachev Summit held in Washington in December 1987, and the Fourth Point of the Proximity Talks agenda, the time-table for the withdrawal of Soviet troops and the only outstanding issue, was being seriously negotiated. Indeed, on 8 February, Gorbachev announced that this withdrawal would take place over a 10-month period. Omens for 1988 seemed to be good.

The Afghan Interim Government

Immediately Gorbachev announced the timing for the withdrawal of Soviet troops, Pakistan began pushing for the formation of 'a friendly transitional government' for Afghanistan (which meant one dominated by the Fundamentalist Mujahideen) to cover the period of the Soviet withdrawal. This became known as the Fifth Point or 'Instrument'.

The leadership of the Islamic Unity of Afghanistan (Peshawar Seven) set about forming such a government, which they announced on 23 February. There was to be a Supreme Council, consisting of the seven leaders, and a 28-member government made up of 14 representatives of the Mujahideen leaderships-in-exile, seven from the Afghan refugees, and seven 'good Muslims' (that is non-PDPA ones) living in Kabul. This impromptu Afghan Interim Government (AIG) demanded to be signatory to any agreement produced by the Proximity Talks.

On 25 February, Ahmad Shah, deputy leader of the HIA, and

Hekmatyar's nominee, who was supported by Saudis working to obtain influence on the Afghan scene, was elected President of this AIG. He was a compromise candidate intended to reconcile the continuing leadership squabbles, especially over the role ex-King Zahir Shah might, or might not, play in future. The Director of the Afghan Information Centre, Bhaeddin Majrooj, a Traditionalist favouring the return of the ex-King, had been shot dead on 11 February. Sibghatullah Mujadidi of the Traditionalist NLF, and rotation chairman of the Islamic Unity of Afghanistan, resigned on 8 March in protest against Pakistan's unfair distribution of arms and money to non-Traditional groups, but rescinded his decision a couple of days later to 'preserve unity'.

More Proximity Talks

It had become difficult to remember that the Proximity Talks were officially between only Afghanistan and Pakistan (Iran having declined the invitation to become involved), as the presence of the USA and the USSR was so heavy as to make it appear that the two principals were reduced to the status of delegates. When the issue of the 'interim government' first began to dominate discussion, Edvard Shevardnadze visited President Zia in Pakistan, the first such visit to that country by a Soviet Foreign Minister for many years, and reputedly offered him $1 billion in economic aid if he would open negotiations with President Najibullah on this issue. Zia refused point-blank. He had other visions for the future Afghanistan, and wanted a Mujahideen 'interim government' of his own choosing.

When the Proximity Talks resumed on 2 March 1988, they became bogged down over Pakistan's insistence that a coalition government be formed to cover the period of the Soviet military withdrawal from Afghanistan. Also, the USA and the USSR each demanded that the other cease sending military aid to their clients after agreement had been reached, and this demand, in the jargon, became known as 'negative symmetry'.

On 30 March, George Shultz, US Secretary of State, came up with a compromise offer: that the United States would reserve the right to supply the Mujahideen with military aid as long as the Soviet Union was doing the same to the Najibullah regime. This, in the jargon, became known as 'positive symmetry'. Just previously, General Dmitri Yasov, the Soviet Defence Minister, had visited Kabul and promised Najibullah a huge consignment of arms.

The Geneva Accords

At last, at the 12th Session of the Proximity Talks in Geneva, on 14 April 1988, the Geneva Accords were signed by Abdul Wakil, Afghan Foreign Minister, and Zain Nooranj, the Pakistan Foreign Minister, and countersigned as Guarantors by George Shultz and Edvard Shevardnadze; they were to come into force the following day. Soviet military withdrawal from Afghanistan was to commence on 5 May and be completed within nine months, that is by 15 February 1989. This withdrawal was to be 'front-loaded', meaning that the majority of Soviet troops would depart within the first months.

There were differences of interpretation on some aspects of the Geneva Accords; for example, both Pakistan and the USA insisted that their signing did not mean recognition of the Najibullah government. President Zia had been taken aback by the casual way the Soviets had shrugged off the Fifth Instrument, brushing it aside with the comment that it was 'a purely Afghan affair'; this in the jargon became known as 'de-linking'. Pakistan had signed under American pressure.

Previously, on 9 April, Gulbuddin Hekmatyar, probably the most influential personality in the contending Mujahideen leaderships-in-exile, had issued a statement rejecting the Geneva agreement and, after the Accords had been signed he called a mass protest rally in Peshawar and repeated his rejection. The Geneva Accords left unsolved the nature of the Afghan 'interim' government as well as the issue of continuing supplies of military aid by the two superpowers to their respective clients.

Earlier, on 28 March, the United States had shown its first real sign of a cooler attitude towards the Mujahideen when it decided to stop the supply of Stinger missiles to them. In Washington a 'general administrative nervousness' had developed at the thought of leaving such weapons, so desirable to terrorists, insurgent groups and Third World countries, in Mujahideen hands, once American control over them, however tenuous, was removed. Stingers in the supply pipeline were delivered, the last reaching Pakistan in October. But, prior to signing the Accords, the United States had dispatched some $300 million worth of arms, including 120mm mortars and mine-clearing equipment, to Pakistan, destined for the Mujahideen.

UNGOMAP

The Geneva Accords provided for the formation of a UN Good Offices Mission in Afghanistan and Pakistan (UNGOMAP), which soon comprised 50 personnel from 10 countries, commanded by a Finnish General. One UNGOMAP detachment was positioned in Afghanistan, and another in Pakistan, and both rapidly became 'complaint-logging' functionaries of alleged violations of the Geneva Accords by both sides. The Afghans complained that Pakistan was supplying the Mujahideen with arms and was providing 'foreign advisers' (meaning Pakistanis); while Pakistan complained of border violations by the Afghan armed forces.

The 'Mine Factor'

During the course of the Soviet occupation, Afghanistan had become 'mine-ridden', and this is thought by some authorities to have been a main factor, on a par with the Stinger factor, in influencing the Soviet decision to withdraw from that country. It had become unacceptably dangerous to remain, as Soviet casualties from Mujahideen mines were mounting alarmingly. At first the Soviets themselves had relied upon mines as defensive and hampering measures against the Mujahideen, and one authority (*Urban*) states they had laid 2,131 minefields, which presumably they charted. It was the 'uncharted mines' that were the problem, and presumably the Soviets could not have charted the thousands of anti-personnel mines dropped by aircraft over Mujahideen trails.

In 1987 and even before, the Mujahideen began to receive mines of various types in increasing quantity from both the USA and the Chinese, which they tended to use in an aggressive manner. As they gained expertise in mine-laying, they began to place them along strategic roads, which due to the Stinger factor, Soviet convoys had been forced to use again. Soviet supply road convoys now moved slowly and cautiously, virtually 'sweeping' for mines ahead, taking days rather than hours to reach their destinations. Soviet military engineers lifted thousands of mines from roads, but as fast as they did so, more were planted by the Mujahideen, who did not seem to bother to chart their own mines. 'Guesstimates' were that there were over three million mines of various sorts scattered across the length and breadth of Afghanistan. The factor of uncharted mines deterred would-be Afghan returnees, as well as those working on rehabilitation schemes in the country.

181

A New Afghan Constitution

In Afghanistan, President Najibullah began to implement the new Constitution, calling general elections for the new National Assembly (*Meli Shura*), which were held between 5-14 April 1988. He invited the Mujahideen to take part, reserving an unspecified number of seats for them, but they refused. The PDPA, although winning only 46 seats, dominated the new National Assembly because of its built-in support from the National Fatherland Front, and other allied groups. Mohammed Hassan Sharq, who was not a member of the PDPA but reputed to be sympathetic towards the Parcham faction, was appointed Prime Minister (Chairman of the Council of Ministers), and he announced his government on 7 June.

In his speech at the opening of the new National Assembly, President Najibullah called for national reconciliation, inviting the Traditional Mujahideen groups-in-exile to talks, and also saying that ex-King Zahir Shah would be welcome in Kabul. On the anniversary of the Saur Revolution, Najibullah granted amnesties to a number of political prisoners, and also released a French and an Italian journalist, both of whom had been convicted of 'espionage'.

In furtherance of his 'multi-party policy', Najibullah authorised the formation of two new political parties, the Union of *Ansarollah* and the *Fada-e Yan Afghanistan*, both to be officially independent. Also, a new province was created taking in parts of Balkh and Jawzjan provinces north of Kabul and called Sar-e Pol province. This was because of apprehension that the Soviets might create a demilitarised zone (DMZ) across the northern part of Afghanistan to try to retain a toe-hold. Sar-e Pol province embraced part of the Hindu Kush, and was visualised as a more natural forward defence in such a contingency.

Soviet Statistics Revealed

So far the Soviets had never issued any official statistics about their Limited Contingent of Soviet Forces in Afghanistan, or its casualties; nor had they commented on Western, or other 'guesstimates'. The day after the Geneva Accords were signed, Marshal Akhromeyev, Chief of the General Staff of the Soviet Armed Forces, stated that Soviet 'military strength in Afghanistan was 103,300 all ranks'—less, much less in some cases, than most foreign estimates.

This was followed, on 25 April, by General Lizichev, head of the

Soviet Armed Forces Political Directorate, announcing (*Tass*) that since December 1979 Soviet casualties in Afghanistan were '13,310 killed in action; 35,478 wounded; and 311 missing in action'. These figures were also much lower than most 'guesstimates' by Western analysts, who invariably equated the Afghan situation with that of the Americans in Vietnam. (US casualties in Vietnam, for the period 1962-73, were 58,135 killed in action—including 2,414 MIAs—and 153,303 wounded). No explanation or analysis of these Soviet figures was given, nor was any mention made of Afghan armed forces or civilian casualties.

Western estimates for the period from December 1979 to July 1988, generally suggested that probably one million people had been killed in Afghanistan (out of a population that had probably risen to about 16.3-million: *IISS*), including military, Mujahideen and civilians; and in addition to that there were over five million refugees in exile in Pakistan and Iran, and another one and a half million internal refugees and displaced persons. Lizichev had thrown in a few more statistics to gain credit, saying that during their stay in Afghanistan, the Soviets had built or repaired '168 schools, 35 mosques, 352 blocks of apartments, 570 miles of road, and 239 bridges' (*Tass*), and adding the snide comment that the Mujahideen had 'sold 33 US Stinger missiles to Iran, and 10 to drug traffickers'.

First Soviet Column Departs

The first Soviet land column, some 3,000 vehicles and 12,000 men, moved out from Jalalabad on 15 May, leaving the defence of that city and its environs entirely to the Afghan armed forces. Groups of Mujahideen crept forward to ring Jalalabad at a distance, but did not attack, this hesitation being ascribed to differences between Mujahideen field commanders, and their inability to form a battle plan that would suit all involved. On 18 May, the Soviet convoy moved virtually unhindered into Soviet territory, by way of Friendship Bridge, the only incident being two rockets fired at it near the Salang Tunnel.

Mujahideen Reaction

As might be expected, Mujahideen reaction to the Soviet withdrawal differed: some leaders, anxious not to provoke the Soviets into extending their stay any longer than necessary, felt that attacks on the departing Soviet troops would simply invite massive aerial and artillery retaliation, causing heavy casualties to both the Mujahideen and the civilian population. Somewhat belatedly, Mujahideen leaders had begun to angle for popular support to help them achieve power in Kabul.

Other Mujahideen leaders of similar mind were in favour of making local cease-fires or truces with the Soviets, to enable them to have a speedy safe passage home, in the belief that once they had all gone, the Afghan armed forces would disintegrate and present no obstacle. Yet others, such as the poorly-armed Traditionalist groups, saw attacks on departing Soviet columns as their main source for obtaining weapons and ammunition. And still others, more 'gung ho', favoured attacking whenever possible, motivated by revenge, and the wish to forge legends of driving out the Soviets by armed force, for international and domestic consumption.

However, the consensus of the Mujahideen leaders was that the Soviets should be allowed a hazard-free, smooth departure. Mujahideen energy and vindictiveness was to be directed against the Afghan armed forces, who were to be attacked whenever possible, and who were less likely to respond with such heavy volumes of fire-power. But there were exceptions, some Mujahideen attacks on departing Soviets being due to greed, vengeance and opportunity targets that could not be resisted. During the period of the Soviet withdrawal, there was considerable in-fighting between Mujahideen groups in the field, much of it unrecorded, in the struggle for dominance, territory and arms. For example, Masoud's Central Forces coalition tended to fall apart, mainly perhaps because, as a Tadjik in the IA group, which was itself undergoing disintegration problems, he had little real influence outside his own valley.

The advent of Spring brought hordes of Mujahideen, refreshed from their winter sojourn in Pakistan, flooding into the eastern provinces, where there were an abrasive, angry patchwork pattern of besieged government garrisons, to tighten up the sieges and attempt to capture them. In mid-March, the government garrison at Sumankat, near Khost, fell to the Mujahideen, who managed to retain possession.

After the Geneva Accords had been signed and Soviet troops were preparing to pull out, it was announced in Kabul that the eastern provinces of Kunar, Ningrahar and Paktia were to become a Demilitarised Zone (DMZ), from which all government garrisons would be withdrawn 'to assist the return of refugees'. This DMZ was to be extended gradually southwards to include Ghazni, Zabul and Kandahar provinces and eventually both Helmand and Nimroz. Some garrisons were withdrawn, vulnerability and viability being key factors in deciding which would be abandoned, and in what sequence. Those abandoned early included Baricot (Kunar) and Maruf (Kandahar). This policy enabled the Mujahideen to make several hollow claims of victory.

In April 1988, Ahmad Shah Masoud, with some 5,000 Mujahideen, mostly his own following, began to move back from north-east Afghanistan towards the Panjshir Valley, slowly advancing down its 100-mile length on the heels of withdrawing Soviets, taking over abandoned Afghan posts and inching ever closer to the Northern Route. Masoud had led the way in introducing field radio communications within, and between, his military detachments, which greatly assisted control and co-ordination of operations; a few other field commanders had followed this example. But this did have the disadvantage of enabling the Soviets, using electronic means, to listen-in to Mujahideen radio traffic, and so have foreknowledge of many of their plans.

On 15 May, Masoud claimed (*Pakistan sources*) to have captured Tabana, in the Valley, after a stiff fight in which his men killed 50 Afghan soldiers. Two days later, he claimed that during a three-week campaign, he had 'taken control of 13 districts and 50 military posts'; but Masoud was simply reoccupying his abandoned valley. The truth was that, anticipating that the Soviets would quit the Panjshir Valley by July, Masoud had made an agreement with them to observe a cease-fire and not to harass their departure. Masoud was a realist; friction with the Soviets would simply have meant more casualties and even more devastation in his home valley.

Throughout the period of the Soviet withdrawal, Kabul became the focus of Mujahideen rocket attacks, which caused considerable damage, loss of life and injuries. Although the rockets more recently received by the Mujahideen were more accurate than the earlier ones, they were never really able to pin-point targets, and remained weapons of indiscriminate destruction. Defensive rings around Kabul kept the Mujahideen at the extreme end of their rocket range, but as the Soviets thinned out and Afghan military manpower became a problem, the outer defence rings were abandoned, enabling the Mujahideen to get much nearer their targets.

The worst month for Kabul in this respect was July, when there were at least five separate heavy spates of rocket firings, and in one week alone some 170 rockets struck the capital and its environs. Explosions in Kabul continued to be a hazard: one in March killed four Soviet soldiers, on 26 April, a truck-bomb killed seven people, and on 20 May, a car-bomb killed over 20 people.

Meanwhile, the Soviet military withdrawal was going according to plan and almost without harassment. When the last Soviet troops left Kandahar on 5 August, the authorities confirmed that, apart from the Shindand air base, all Soviet military personnel had been withdrawn from southern Afghanistan. It was also reported that arrangements had been made between the Soviets and local Mujahideen leaders for a trouble-free exit from Shindand and Herat, northwards along the road to the Soviet border at Kushka (*Tass*). It was confirmed on 5 August, that over half the Limited Contingent of Soviet Forces in Afghanistan had left the country on schedule (*Pravda*). It was now an open secret that the Soviets were collaborating with local Mujahideen groups to ensure a relatively safe road exit through hostile territory.

The Kalagay Explosion

Rocket fire was the greatest hazard to both Soviet and Afghan armed forces as the Mujahideen seemed to have ample stocks of rockets, and were anxious to fire them off while there were still opportunities. While many rockets hit their targets, the majority missed, some by wide margins, but a few made lucky strikes. For example, in June, eight Soviet SU-25 combat aircraft were standing on the runway at Bagram air base when one was hit by a Mujahideen rocket and exploded, causing the remaining seven to be destroyed by fire in the chain reaction.

Another Mujahideen 'lucky strike' occurred on 11 August, causing a terrific explosion, adjacent to the Northern Route at the Kalagay (Baghlan province), the largest Soviet munition store in the country, which was thought to contain, in a maze of concrete bunkers and underground tunnels, sufficient arms, ammunition, shells, explosives and fuel supplies to last the Afghan government for two years. Soviet trucks were unloading ammunition and fuel when a rocket struck a fuel-bowser which exploded, causing a chain reaction of other explosions that continued underground.

This massive disaster was not reported by either the Soviet or Afghan media, but partially confirmed by Pakistan sources and by a CIA assessment that '598 Soviet troops, 112 Soviet civilians and 180

Afghans were killed; and 284 people badly injured'. Material loss was incalculable. The Northern Route was closed for three days. the Kalagay explosion was the worst of its kind so far in Afghanistan, the previous worst having been in August 1986, when the Kharga munition depot, near Kabul, was hit, also by a 'lucky strike' Mujahideen rocket. In September 1988, a rocket struck an aircraft loaded with ammunition at Kabul airport, and the explosion caused many casualties.

Battle for Kunduz

On 12 August, only six days after the last Soviet soldier had been withdrawn from it, the Afghan garrison at Kunduz (capital of the northern Kunduz province) was overrun by the Mujahideen who, in their over-enthusiasm, sacked and looted the city, which then had about 20,000 inhabitants. This affected antagonists in different ways. The Soviet reaction was that this hole in the dyke must be quickly plugged in case the whole dyke caved in. A combined Soviet-Afghan force, with air support, mounted an attack on Kunduz, which was retaken by 15 August, with '173 rebels were killed for the loss of seven Afghan soldiers' (*Kabul Radio*)—a considerable understatement of Mujahideen casualties, with no mention at all of civilian dead and injured.

According to strong rumours, many Afghan soldiers were killed when Kunduz was overrun, some being taken prisoner, tortured and then executed. This had the effect of stiffening Afghan army morale and determination, a fact that the Soviets did not appear to appreciate. The Kunduz massacre and atrocities exacerbated the type of 'blood-feud' hatred and aggressive antagonism towards the Mujahideen that had been developing in the Afghan army for some time.

President Najibullah, who blamed the initial loss of Kunduz on Pakistan's (unspecified) direct involvement, and also indirectly on the garrison for not putting up stronger resistance (hinting that there had been secret collaboration with the Mujahideen). He, therefore, decided to shake up the command structure of the army, certain elements of which were less than whole-heartedly in the struggle against the Mujahideen, partly due to the internal feud within the officer corps, where Khalkis at times felt themselves disadvantaged by the dominant Parchamis.

General Shah Nawaz Tanai, Chief-of-Staff, of the Relief of Khost fame, was promoted to Defence Minister, and General Mohammed Asef Delawar, Commander of the 1st Army Corps, who had a good combat record, became Chief-of-Staff; and another 15 active Generals were given key combat appointments. The Afghan army had been slowly improving and expanding, its strength by this time exceeding 50,000 men, a large proportion of whom were campaign-hardened, although problems of reluctant conscripts and desertion remained.

Afghan army morale was not helped by the government's policy of abandoning remote garrisons in the face of Mujahideen advances. One Afghan garrison at Taliqan, in the north-east, had been overrun about the same time as Kunduz, and no attempt was made to recapture it. As the Afghan army adopted its new defensive posture, it began to concentrate its strength at key points and, in the two months following the signing of the Accords, over 100 garrisons and outlying posts were evacuated.

At first the Mujahideen political leaderships were delighted with their success at Kunduz and that, at last, their guerrilla fighters had fought and won a real battle; but dismay quickly followed exhilaration, as both Soviet and Afghan troops took deadly punitive action, in which aerial bombardment on Mujahideen camps and gatherings brought a heavy toll of casualties. More important and detrimental to the political leaderships, however, were the Mujahideen rampage excesses in Kunduz, which were carried out in true medieval style suggesting that this would be how they would behave as they fought their way towards Kabul, and accordingly alienated popular support.

The Soviets were also dismayed at the initial loss of Kunduz, mistakenly putting it down to poor morale and incompetence. After some hesitation they slowed down their withdrawal, feeling that before pulling out they must first rearm the Afghan army with more modern weaponry, and re-motivate it, otherwise the Najibullah government would be swept aside as soon as they left. More Soviet arms poured into Afghanistan.

Activities Resumed: July-October 1988

During July Masoud, back in his Panjshir Valley and with a live-and-let-live agreement with the Soviets, realised that he had been mistaken about the date of their withdrawal, and so began attacks against the Northern Route and the Salang Tunnel. That month there was a three-week battle in the south-east for the fortress at Qalat-e-Ghilzai (Zabul province) during which the Mujahideen launched several large attacks, repulsed by the Afghan defenders with difficulty, and only with the support of heavy aerial bombing.

In August, the Afghan army base at Bab Wali, in the Arghandab mountain range, near Kandahar, was overrun by the Mujahideen; and on 14 September, they also seized the Takht bridge, overlooking Kandahar airport. During September, Asadabad fell to the Mujahideen, giving them full control of Kunar province. Rumours abounded at this time that the Soviets were about to ditch Najibullah.

On 6 October, the three Traditionalist Mujahideen groups (IRM, NIFA and NLF) in the Islamic Unity of Afghanistan (Peshawar Seven) coalition began negotiations with the Governor of Kandahar to persuade him to allow the city to fall into their hands rather than be taken by storm by the Fundamentalists, reminding him of the Kunduz massacre; but Gulbuddin Hekmatyar of the HIA, speaking for the four Fundamentalist groups, threatened an all-out war against the Traditionalists, unless they ceased negotiations. In the 'interests of unity', the Traditionalists withdrew from their project.

The pace of the Soviet military withdrawal slowed still further and, on 4 November, ceased entirely, the Soviets openly admitting that this was due to Mujahideen attacks on their departing convoys. They then brought in certain sophisticated weapon systems including the advanced MiG-27 combat aircraft, and the SCUD-B (SSC-1) surface-to-surface ballistic missile, with a range of about 180 miles.

Soviet SCUD-Bs had been used in quantity by both protagonists in the Iran-Iraq War, especially in the 'War of the Cities' phases, which had terminated in July 1988 with a cease-fire. The Soviet General Staff had become concerned and anxious to avoid a repetition of the disastrous British withdrawal from Kabul in January 1842, realising the effect it would have on the reputation of Soviet arms worldwide. There is no doubt the presence of SCUD-Bs on Afghan soil restrained the Mujahideen's over-enthusiasm. Although the Soviets insisted that no SCUD-Bs were fired by them, they caused the Mujahideen leaders, with perhaps the exception of Masoud, to back away from confrontation. The Soviets did however, admit using their MiG-27s to harass Mujahideen positions.

The Pakistan Factor

Meanwhile, momentous events were occurring in Pakistan, the

sanctuary for over three million Afghan refugees. A terrific explosion took place at the Pakistan Munition and Ordnance Depot at Orji, near Islamabad, on 10 April 1988, causing considerable loss of life and great devastation, live shells, ammunition and items of weaponry being showered over nearby residential areas. American weapons destined for the Mujahideen, including Stinger missiles, were stored at this depot, and a fully-loaded truck convoy was about to drive out of the camp at the time the explosion occurred. The official Pakistan casualty figures were 93 killed and over 1,100 injured. Sabotage was immediately suspected, with KHAD being the main suspect, but subsequently the official government enquiry found the cause to be 'accidental' which satisfied few people.

The next major event in Pakistan occurred on 17 August 1988, when President Zia, together with the US Ambassador, Arnold Rafael, an American General, and at least 17 Senior Pakistani military officers were killed when the C-130 aircraft in which they were travelling exploded in mid-air. Again, first thoughts were that sabotage was the cause, and again the finger of suspicion pointed at KHAD; but Zia had other enemies too. Zia had no obvious successor, and Ghulam Ishaq Khan, Chairman of the Pakistan Senate, became acting President. American aid for Pakistan, and also for the Mujahideen, continued to arrive, weapons for the Mujahideen still being doled out selectively to certain Fundamentalist groups by the ISI.

Both America and the Afghan Mujahideen lost a good friend and helper in Zia. Initially, the Americans had not favoured him, partly because of his military dictatorship, and partly because he was suspected of working to produce a nuclear warhead; but they had been forced into his company by Cold War strategic necessity. The Americans liked Zia's 'no compromise' stance against the Soviets and the Kabul government, and he became their main bulwark against Soviet expansion in southern Asia, especially after the Shah of Iran was removed from power.

After initial hesitation, the USA lavished military and economic aid on him, and a $4.1 billion package had been agreed in 1988, making Pakistan the third largest recipient of US foreign aid, after Israel and Egypt. Zia meanwhile had been working hard to install a Fundamentalist government in Afghanistan, with Gulbuddin Hekmatyar as its President, a course strongly favoured by the US administration and the CIA, who obviously still did not realise just what this solution could eventually mean.

In November 1988, a general election was held in Pakistan, the first since March 1977, and on 2 December, Benazir Bhutto, leader of the Pakistan People's Party (PPP), became Prime Minister of a coalition government. On 12 December, Ghulam Ishaq Khan became the Constitutional President. Ms Bhutto's appointment was popular with the West, and the United States promised continued military and economic aid.

'Ambassador' Vorontsov

To counter the adverse situation in Afghanistan, Yuli Vorontsov, Soviet First Deputy Foreign Minister, was appointed Ambassador to Kabul, retaining his Kremlin status as it was thought this would assist his negotiations with both Pakistan and the Mujahideen. His task was to arrange for a smooth, incident-free withdrawal of the remaining Soviet troops in Afghanistan.

The situation looked ominous to the Soviets, with some 30,000 Mujahideen sitting around Kabul, and another 15,000 squatting around Jalalabad, daily becoming more arrogant and impatient; rocket barrages were still hitting Kabul and other cities and Stinger missiles were still bringing down aircraft. In August, a Soviet MiG-21 was brought down by a missile over Parachinar (Pakistan), and in November an Afghan Antonov-26 crashed in the same area as a result of Mujahideen missile fire, with the loss of all 30 people on board. There were several other Mujahideen anti-aircraft missile successes.

On 28 November, Vorontsov, as Ambassador, visited Pakistan, and arranged talks at the Soviet Embassy at Islamabad with Mujahideen representatives. The Mujahideen had long been calling for direct negotiations with the Soviets, but had always been refused. Now, with *glasnost* giving the Soviet people a thirst for news of what was going on in Afghanistan, Vorontsov sought information about the 311 Soviet MIAs. Mujahideen representatives countered by saying that they too sought information about the 30,000-40,000 Mujahideen MIAs who, if not dead, were thought to be in Afghan jails. Najibullah still refused Geneva POW status to captured Mujahideen.

Arrangements were made through the Saudis to hold talks at Taif, Saudi Arabia, between Vorontsov and Rabbani of the IA, then Chairman of the Islamic Unity of Afghanistan. At this meeting, on 3-4 December 1988, it was agreed that the Mujahideen would give

Soviet armed forces a safe passage out of Afghanistan if they kept to the withdrawal date. Nothing was said about Soviet SCUD-Bs being in Afghanistan, which was the real spur for these talks; but ballistic missiles were certainly a talking point in the region.

On 7 December, Gorbachev addressed the UN General Assembly, and stated that a comprehensive settlement of the Afghan question could only be achieved by the formation of a broadly-based government in Kabul, meaning the inclusion of some Mujahideen element. He called for the cessation of military supplies to both sides, the dispatch of a UN Peace-keeping contingent to oversee the situation while the Kabul government and the 'insurgents' negotiated a political settlement, and the convening of an international conference under UN auspices to guarantee the neutrality and demilitarisation of Afghanistan.

Vorontsov also shuttled to see ex-King Zahir Shah, to ask him to return to Kabul, or at least to take part in negotiations; but he had no success. He also visited Iran to try to bring the Alliance of Eight (Tehran Eight) resistance coalition into the equation. There had been practically no contact between the Alliance of Eight, still led by Mohammed Karim Khaladi, and the Islamic Unity of Afghanistan.

Afghan Shia refugees in Iran were well regimented and controlled, most being grouped in three areas, virtually concentration camps, in the interior, where they had to work to earn their keep, and were allowed no political freedom of expression at all. About 20,000-30,000 Afghan refugees were retained in 'vetting' camps near the Afghan frontier, mainly as a show-case for UN and other international bodies interested in refugee problems. According to one source (*Bakhtar News Service, Kabul*), on 29-30 June 1988, Iranian Revolutionary Guards responsible for Afghan refugees fired on them in their camps near the Iranian city of Zaheden, killing 30 people, including some children, while trying to prevent their returning home. Afghan refugee unrest had broken out, as on previous occasions, when they made demands for the appropriate documents to cross the Iran-Afghan frontier.

Peshawar *Shura*

Gorbachev declared there would be a cease-fire with effect from 1 January 1989 but, despite Vorontsov's pleading, the Mujahideen refused to accept it. On 3 January, under Vorontsov's urging, the Islamic Unity of Afghanistan announced at a *Shura* its plan for an interim non-elected government to be formed until a general election could be held. Vorontsov persuaded Mohammed Karim Khaladi, leader of the Alliance of Eight, to visit Peshawar in the hope he would co-operate and take part in this *Shura*, but the Shia leader was dissatisfied with the proposed allocation of 60 seats (out of 240) offered to his coalition and, although this number was raised to 100 seats, he could not be persuaded, and returned to Iran. On 22 January 1989, the Shia Alliance of Eight boycotted the Sunni Islamic Unity of Afghanistan.

Withdrawal Reaction

In January 1989, Soviet troops had resumed their halted withdrawal, and their departure was soon in full flow, hundreds leaving almost daily in road convoys and from air bases. Having withdrawn their troops from the east and south of Afghanistan, the Soviets concentrated on holding two road routes open for their final evacuation; the Northern Route from Kabul northwards; and the Shindand-Herat-Kushka section of the Circular Road. Watching them depart, the Mujahideen somehow felt they had missed a trick by accepting their own political leaderships' order not to attack the Soviet troops when they were most vulnerable. During the months the Soviet withdrawal had been in progress they had seen the Afghan armed forces acquiring modern weaponry, that included new Soviet BTR-70 armoured vehicles, fitted with 30mm guns, and the BM-27 Multiple Rocket Launching System.

As they withdrew from their garrisons, the Soviets handed over to the Afghan army their military stores and ammunition, and indeed almost everything except the vehicles they rode out in and their personal weapons. Also, Soviet transport aircraft ferrying Soviet personnel home, invariably returned loaded with modern weaponry and military stores for the Afghan armed forces. A Moscow spokesman (*Tass*) later stated that military material, valued in excess of $1 million had been handed over. The watching Mujahideen were painfully conscious of their shortage of weapons and, especially, ammunition.

The Soviets had regained a degree of aerial dominance, which they had lost in 1987 due to the appearance of US Stingers in Mujahideen hands. This American supply had ceased in October 1988, since when the Mujahideen had almost expended their stock of these missiles. One of the last Stinger missiles fired by the Mujahideen in

January 1989, was near Kandahar, which forced the Afghan pilot to fly higher, and inadvertently drop his bombs on his own garrison.

Foreign embassies in Kabul had been apprehensive for their own safety for some time and from August 1988 onwards they began to reduce their staffs. Then, in January 1989, one by one they began to close down as the capital became surrounded, with the Mujahideen blocking roads into Kabul, causing a severe food shortage that began to verge on famine. By the end of the month all Western embassies had closed, much to Najibullah's chagrin and disgust, and only a small ICRC contingent remained.

During January, the Soviets organised a huge air-lift to bring food into Kabul. Whenever the Northern Route was closed by the Mujahideen, as it was for brief periods, the Soviets used bomber aircraft based in the USSR to drive them away, as they had been doing for some time to assist the Afghan army to hold or reoccupy Kunar, Kunduz and Spin Baldak earlier that month. In early January, Masoud moved out in strength from his Panjshir Valley to block the Northern Route in the vicinity of the Salang Tunnel, and this intensified food shortages in Kabul.

The Final Weeks

Bottled up in Kabul, the Soviets wanted to keep as low a profile as possible in the final weeks of their military evacuation, but found themselves with no option but to take very drastic action to break the Mujahideen encirclement. A four-day joint Soviet-Afghan military offensive was launched on 23 January to reopen the Salang Tunnel, which was momentarily successful, allowing food convoys again to reach the capital. Soviet bomber aircraft, including TU-22s, carried out carpet-bombing raids around the Tunnel area, and for stretches along the Northern Route on either side of it. On 29 January, General Yasov, the Soviet Defence Minister, hurried to Kabul to assess the situation, as the Soviet General Staff dreaded a repeat of the American panicky Saigon evacuation. It is believed that Yasov authorised the use of SCUD-Bs if necessary (*CIA report*).

Shevardnadze tried to strike a bargain with the Mujahideen to keep the Northern Route open for the Soviet evacuation, and to enable food convoys to reach Kabul. It is believed (*CIA reports*) that Gulbuddin Hekmaytar of the Fundamentalist HIA demanded in return the removal of Najibullah, and his own installation as temporary incumbent at Kabul; but this was more than the Soviets were prepared to give. They continued to rely upon carpet-bombing to keep the roads open, in the course of which 'hundreds of civilians died or were injured' (*Pakistan sources*), causing the Americans to allege the Soviets were using scorched-earth tactics. The threat to use SCUD-Bs, if necessary, also remained.

The last Soviet military road convoy left Kabul on 3 February, moving northwards under strong air cover, leaving behind about 1,500 personnel to guard certain vital installations and the airport at Kabul. Responsibility for the security of the Northern Route was handed over to the Afghan army. On 8 February, Masoud launched another operation, managing to block the Salang Tunnel, but his Mujahideen were again driven back by Soviet bombing. The Soviets now no longer had any need of this route for their own evacuation, but it was vital to enable food supplies to continue to reach Kabul; and almost until the last day of the Soviet occupation bomber aircraft, operating from USSR territory, were active in the area.

During the first 10 days of February, some 20,000 Soviet military personnel were safely evacuated from Shindand and Herat, the majority by road to the Soviet border at Kushka. The local Mujahideen had kept their secret agreements. On 12-14 February, all remaining Soviet personnel were flown out from Shindand, Kabul and Bagram, while a 'token Soviet road column' formed up near Mazar-i-Sharif. There had been speculation as to whether the Soviets would remain in the Wakhan Strip, a traditional route into Afghanistan from China, which they had 'annexed' in 1981, and where they had reputedly installed intermediate range ballistic missiles and surveillance apparatus; but this territory, too, was completely evacuated by the beginning of February.

Soviet and Western assessments of 30,000 Mujahideen waiting to rush into Kabul and 15,000 Mujahideen waiting to charge into Jalalabad, had remained constant and uncontradicted for weeks. When interviewed after the event, General Serebrov, Head of the Soviet Politburo in Afghanistan, praised Vorontsov for the comparatively uninterrupted final stages of the evacuation, saying it had been due to his diplomatic skill in negotiating with the Mujahideen political leaderships in Peshawar. There seems to have been no liaison at this stage between the Soviets and the Alliance of Eight, which was probably being kept quite busy in confrontation with the Supreme *Jihad* Council coalition in western Afghanistan, now secretly in league with the Soviets. Serebrov did not mention the almost continuous carpet-bombing, or the presence of SCUD-B ballistic missiles, about which, despite *glasnost*, the Soviet media had neglected to tell their readers and viewers.

On 11 February, President Najibullah broadcast to his nation, alleging that Pakistan, in conjunction with the Mujahideen leaderships in Peshawar, was preparing to mount an invasion of Afghanistan the moment the last Soviet soldier had left. Soviet representatives in Kabul confirmed this; and later Pakistan 'leaks' indicated that this was indeed the secret 'Zia Plan'. But Zia was no longer around to implement it, although Pakistan troops did mass near the Afghan border at the time. Najibullah also alleged that 'Pakistani irregulars' were already fighting side-by-side with the Mujahideen in Nangrahar province.

Friendship Bridge Exit

On the night of 14 February 1989, the token 'last Soviet column' to leave Afghanistan, consisting of 450 armoured vehicles and 1,400 troops, under the personal command of General Boris Gromov, Commander of the Limited Contingent of Soviet Forces in Afghanistan, moved from its staging camp near Mazar-i-Sharif, halting at dawn the following day on the south bank of the Amu Darya to prepare for its crossing over Friendship Bridge, heralded as a historic publicity event which the world media had been invited to witness. When all TV cameras and journalists were in position the Soviet 'last' column began crossing on to Soviet soil, which was completed just before noon on the date promised by the Soviets.

The last Soviet soldier to leave Afghan territory was General Gromov, who grandiosely told assembled journalists: 'We have fulfilled our international duty to the end', adding that Soviet troops 'have shown the greatness of the Soviet soldier's intellectual and political maturity and devotion to Socialism'. The gilt of the occasion tended to be slightly tarnished later that day when an article appeared in the Soviet *Literary Gazette*, admitting for the first time that Soviet soldiers serving in Afghanistan had been brutalised and had committed atrocities against civilians, quoting instances.

After nine years and nearly two months, the Limited Contingent of Soviet Forces in Afghanistan left that country in a far worse state than it had found it. Few gave President Najibullah more than a few weeks at the most in office before victorious Mujahideen swept him aside. The Soviet General's gesture in being the last Soviet soldier to leave Afghanistan was likened by the watching media to that of a naval captain abandoning his sinking ship.

11

Civil War

As the last Soviet soldier crossed northwards over Friendship Bridge on 15 February 1989, both the Kabul regime and the Mujahideen braced themselves for the coming clash, which both were sure would be a prelude to their victory. That day, the Soviet Union proclaimed its strict adherence to the Geneva Accords, and reiterated Gorbachev's appeal to the United Nations (in December 1988) for a cease-fire in Afghanistan. The following day, the new American President, George Bush, declared that the USA would continue to support the Mujahideen 'as long as the resistance struggle for self-determination continues'; and he accused the Soviets of leaving vast stocks of weaponry and ammunition behind for the Afghan armed forces. The few Soviet military advisers left behind in Kabul were attached to the Afghan government instead of to the armed forces, so that they could be seen to have no combat function.

President Najibullah began to strengthen his position. On 18 February, he dismissed seven non-PDPA Ministers, replacing them with PDPA members, all believed to belong to the Parcham faction. The following day he declared a nationwide State of Emergency, claiming as the reason the discovery of a large arms cache, hidden ready for Mujahideen-use in their anticipated attack on the capital. He also announced the formation of a 20-man Supreme Council for the Defence of the Homeland (SCDH), to be the 'Supreme military and political organ, with the aim of implementing central leadership under conditions of the State of Emergency'. Four Vice Presidents were appointed, including General Tanai (Defence Minister) and General Delawar (Chief-of-staff). Mohammed Hassan Sharq was replaced as Prime Minister by Sultan Ali Keshtmand, the only Shia in the SCDH.

Preparations had been made for the defence of Kabul. A 5,000-strong detachment of the Presidential Guard had been trained in street fighting; a special guard had been formed of two Afghan commando brigades; within the city, local civil defence groups were formed and co-ordinated; and the 30,000-strong PDPA youth organisation was mustered. These formations and militias were given the pick of the Soviet arms left behind. A number of Soviet SCUD-B ballistic missiles had been secretly left behind too, with trained Afghan crews.

Mujahideen Leadership

Voting for the President of the AIG took place at Islamabad on 23 February, by 240 Mujahideen delegates, each having two votes to cast for one of the leaders of the Islamic Unity of Afghanistan groups. Sibghatullah Mujadidi, leader of the Traditionalist NLF, received 174 votes, and Abdur Rasaul Sayaf, leader of the Fundamentalist IULA, received 173 votes; so, by a single vote, Mujadidi won and was appointed President of the AIG.

Other leaders in descending order of popularity, according to the number of votes gained, were:

> Mohammed Nabi Mohammedi, of the Traditionalist IRM,
> Gulbuddin Hekmatyar, of the Fundamentalist HIA,˙
> Younis Khalis, of the Fundamentalist HI,
> Burhanuddin Rabbani, of the Fundamentalist IA,
> Mohammed Gilani, of the Traditionalist NIFA.

A 'Cabinet' was formed with Abdur Rasaul Sayaf as Prime Minister, and Gulbuddin Hekmatyar as Foreign Minister.

On 24 February, 'President' Mujadidi called on all countries, especially those in the Islamic Conference Organisation (ICO), to recognise the new 'Islamic Afghan Government'. Mujadidi announced a general amnesty for all Afghans working for the Kabul government, providing 'there was no Afghan blood on their hands'. In Pakistan, Prime Minister Bhutto was cautious and, while welcoming this new government-in-exile, said recognition was premature.

President Bush was more specific, saying he would only recognise the Mujadidi government when it controlled a substantial part of Afghan territory, had a functioning civil administration, and broad popular support. At the ICO meeting at Riyadh, Saudi Arabia, on 13

March, the AIG was invited to occupy the Afghan seat, vacant since January 1980. This was accepted by Hekmatyar, speaking as the AIF Foreign Minister. The first international recognition of the AIG had been by Saudi Arabia, followed quickly by Sudan and Bahrain. Najibullah condemned this ICO decision.

Siege of Jalalabad

The Mujadidi government-in-exile had hoped to be able to announce its existence and manifesto on Afghan soil, preferably in Jalalabad. But as this had not been possible, the impatient *Shura* had gone ahead on foreign (Pakistan) soil. After, the Soviet military presence had been withdrawn, the Mujahideen surrounding Kabul, Jalalabad, Khost and other garrison cities shuffled their feet uneasily but expectantly, as though waiting for a Saladin or a Nasser to rise up and lead them to victory. As such a leader did not appear, Mujahideen activity for three weeks or so was limited, restricted mainly to rocket-firing and sabre-rattling.

Eventually, on 6 March, the Mujahideen mustered about 10,000 men and began to attack Jalalabad, which was garrisoned by about 4,500 Afghan troops. This operation was master-minded and directed by the Pakistan ISI. Initially, the outlying defences were compressed, including part of the adjacent ruined airport, while rockets rained down on the city and its environs. Both the ISI and the Mujahideen had anticipated an easy and speedy victory, and both were rudely surprised by the stubborn resistance put up by the Afghan army garrison. Strong defensive positions had been constructed, ammunition reserves had been built up, and air support was given by MiG-21s and other Afghan aircraft.

The Soviets had been generous and, according to the *IISS*, the Afghan air force, with a strength of about 5,000 men had '193 combat aircraft and 74 armed helicopters', including 60 SU-7Bs, 30 SU-22s, 15 MiG-23s, 30 MiG-21Fs, and 40 MiG-17s, with ample pilots, and an adequate technical staff. The army had 1,788 armoured vehicles, over 1,000 guns, 1,000 mortars and over 600 anti-aircraft guns.

Lack of leadership cohesion and battle discipline among the Mujahideen soon caused the fighting to become bogged down in stalemate. The road from Kabul was blocked by Mujahideen (later government claims that it was never closed during this period must be discounted), and the besieged garrison, with its citizens and refugees, had to be supplied by air for a time, usually by helicopters, but also by transport aircraft making parachute and free-fall drops. The AAF had 13 transport aircraft (*IISS*).

After government troops had recovered some of the overrun outer positions, and gained full control of the airport, during April, the Mujahideen began to run short of ammunition, and there was a slackening of determination and intensity. Thwarted of an anticipated quick victory, the Mujahideen tended to regard the war somewhat casually, with groups moving towards the Jalalabad outer perimeter in the morning to fire a few shots, and then returning to a secure area in the evening; on some days they might not even make the effort to adopt an attack posture. Operational structure gradually began to disintegrate with individual groups fighting their own little battles, often amongst themselves, in their own sector, in their own way.

On 10 May, the Kabul government was confident enough to fly a media party, including Western journalists, in to Jalalabad by helicopter. The journalists reported that the airport was completely in government hands, that many buildings in the city had been destroyed or badly damaged by rocket fire, and that civilians were trying to carry on normal life as far as possible. Urgent supplies were still brought in by helicopter, but truck-convoys with armoured escorts and helicopter-gunships flying overhead, were becoming more frequent. Trees had been cut down in Jalalabad to facilitate helicopter landings, impromptu ammunition parks were scattered along side-roads, more defensive positions were being constructed, and Afghan troops were constantly moving artillery and rockets to alternative positions to confuse the Mujahideen.

The journalists were taken in vehicles to the Nangar Power Station, on the junction of the Kabul and Kunar rivers, about eight miles from the city; this was seen to be in government hands, and was functioning. Journalists noted that people were working in the fields, but that houses in the villages were empty and usually boarded up.

General Delawar, Chief-of-staff, had been additionally appointed GOC Eastern Front, and was in Jalalabad. He briefed the journalists, saying that activity had generally been reduced to long-range (10-15 miles) rocket exchanges, which were becoming less frequent as the Mujahideen was running short of rockets. He was confident he could hold out indefinitely, and stated that the local Mujahideen military commanders had indicated they would like cease-fire agreements, but that the Pakistan ISI had firmly blocked any such approaches.

200

The GOC praised the AAF MiG-21 pilots, who gave the defenders close air support, bombed and rocketed Mujahideen concentrations, especially when they were marching to and from the 'front', and also hit their bases and sanctuaries. The GOC could have added that SCUD-Bs (with 1,700lb warheads), aimed with some accuracy at suspected Mujahideen positions around Jalalabad, and Afghan aircraft flying just above Stinger range to drop cluster bombs on Mujahideen forward positions with even greater accuracy, played a significant part in this successful defence of Jalalabad.

Squabbling between Mujahideen leaders, both political and military, intensified as each blamed the other for lack of success, and this continually detracted from the main operation, until the Pakistan ISI gradually lost control of the situation. The siege of Jalalabad was relaxed by mid-May 1989, by which time the road from Kabul was open again, and remained so for a period. Few Mujahideen could be persuaded to stay in forward battle positions, and many were drifting from the battle area. As a face-saver, there was boastful talk of changing direction, and mounting an all-out assault on Kandahar, part of which was in Mujahideen hands, but this was hardly feasible since it stood in an open plain and attacking Mujahideen would have been decimated by the AAF.

The successful defence of Jalalabad by the Afghan army and AAF was both a prestigious boost and a vital material success for Najibullah. Had it failed, hordes of Mujahideen would have rapidly converged on the capital. On the other hand, it was a tremendous prestige loss and set-back for both the Mujahideen cause and the Pakistan ISI. Afghan armed forces referred to it as their 'Stalingrad' and with good reason, as it was a vital turning point in the Afghan civil war. Consensus 'guesstimates' put the casualties for the 10-week siege of Jalalabad at about 5,000, probably fairly equally divided between government troops and the Mujahideen, but including civilians in the city and adjacent villages. The attrition rate of weaponry, ammunition and material damage was thought to be considerable.

It was admitted in the UN Security Council that the Mujahideen performance on the battlefield had been disappointing, and that their attack on Jalalabad had been a disaster. It was not mentioned, but perhaps should have been for a true perspective, that the effectiveness of the new Afghan armed forces had been established. In May, General Varennikov, Commander of the Soviet Ground Forces, visited Afghanistan to assess the military situation, touring both

Jalalabad and Kandahar. His report was assumed to be favourable, and soon large quantities of munitions were again coming into the country.

The Pakistan ISI

General Hamed Gul, Director General of Pakistan's Directorate of Inter-Service Intelligence (ISI), was widely blamed for the Mujahideen failure at Jalalabad, and he was criticised by the Americans for improperly boasting (given his official status and position) that it was his intention to replace the Najibullah regime in Kabul with an Islamic one headed by Gulbuddin Hekmatyar.

When Benazir Bhutto became Prime Minister in December 1987, she had to walk softly in the face of the powerful, suspicious and unfriendly armed forces, moulded in the Zia image, with its ISI continuing to implement Zia's plans and policies. By 25 May 1989, she felt strong enough to move General Gul sideways into another post, and to appoint in his stead a retired army General, who became a civil servant, thus removing the ISI from direct army control, and bringing it into the administrative body.

Although this was taken as a mark of reprobation for General Gul, the unfortunate General had, in fact, advised against attacking Jalalabad, owing to the well-known Mujahideen military weaknesses, as well as their lack of combat aircraft, helicopters, armoured vehicles, anti-aircraft guns and artillery. He had recommended that, instead, the Mujahideen should wage a war of retribution, and concentrate upon enlarging, and then merging, their several small Liberated Zones, until they were able to put a stranglehold on internal communications, and really isolate all government garrisons. Had this course been followed the Mujahideen could have immobilised and starved out many Afghan army garrisons.

Loya Jirga: May 1989

The successful defence of Jalalabad gave Najibullah confidence to further his policy of reconciliation, and on 21 May, he assembled another Loya Jirga at Kabul, calling for active political involvement by Mujahideen military leaders in the field, and offering them appointments in the Afghan armed forces, provided they would observe a cease-fire. Furthermore, if they would 'consolidate' their own localities, he would give them arms to fight off any encroaching

Fundamentalists. This was an extension of the existing scheme for 'government militias', which had been successful in some areas, whereby the local Mujahideen leader was paid and armed to keep everyone else away from his own particular valley, especially Fundamentalists. Previously, Najibullah had always referred to the Mujahideen in his speeches as 'bandits', but now he began calling them 'brother compatriots'.

American Involvement

Although extremely disappointed by the Mujahideen failure at Jalalabad, the US administration did not give up and, after the transfer of General Gul from the ISI, President Bush appointed a Special Envoy for Afghan Affairs, Peter Tomson. His brief was to liaise directly with the Mujahideen leaderships in Pakistan, and he was given an exclusive channel of communication back to the White House.

With undoubted help from the now low-profile ISI, and grudging support from Prime Minister Bhutto, who was under some American pressure, Tomson made direct contact with the AIG, and virtually took over where General Gul had left off, encouraging the Mujahideen to take the military option, and distributing arms to them. There was just one change in US policy: Tomson steered away from Hekmatyar, who by this time had aroused American suspicion and distrust. The flow of arms and ammunition, especially Stingers and rockets, to Mujahideen in the field was resumed in greater volume. Tomson began planning another operation to seize Jalalabad.

Suddenly, on 4 July, Afghan ground troops, supported by the AAF, launched a surprise attack against Mujahideen dug in around Jalalabad and, after three days of heavy fighting, regained control of a considerable amount of territory to the south and south-east of the city. Afghan soldiers also recovered the adjacent garrison position at Samarkhel, one of the first Afghan outposts to fall the previous March. This left the Mujahideen generally in unfavourable defensive positions, and indeed a majority retired to the mountain ranges overlooking the city and the surrounding locality. Stalemate again set in around Jalalabad, as Tomson's operational plan had been scuppered.

Continued Mujahideen Disunity

Mujahideen pressure against Afghan army-held cities and garrisons increased in July as fresh supplies of rockets and missiles were received. Kabul remained a special Mujahideen target. Najibullah complained that the USA was breaking the Geneva Accords by continuing to supply munitions to the Mujahideen, but it was six of one and half-a-dozen of the other, as the Soviets, too, were pouring in weaponry and ammunition for the Afghan forces at a great rate. Najibullah offered a four-day cease-fire on 12 July, on the occasion of the Feast of Eid al-Adcha, which followed the fasting month of Ramadan, while this was officially rejected by the Mujahideen leaderships, in places it was unofficially observed by some local Mujahideen military leaders.

Disunity between Mujahideen groups in the field steadily increased, and in particular a violent feud developed between Hekmatyar's HIA, and its Fundamentalist rival, Rabbani's IA. On 9 July 'seven military commanders and 23 Mujahideen of Rabbani's group were ambushed in a valley in Takhar province and killed' by Hekmatyar's men (*Pakistan sources*). There had been other fatal clashes between these two groups, but of those reported, this seemed to be the most serious so far. Many inter-group incidents were not reported at all, or deliberately played down by tacit consent by the Mujahideen leaders 'in the interests of unity'. This particular inter-group feud extended to a tussle between them for possession of the strategically important Panjshir Valley, in which the IA element was led by Ahmad Shah Masoud.

Disunity continued to reign between the Islamic Unity of Afghanistan groups in Pakistan, and on 20 August 1989, Hekmatyar said he would not attend any more meetings of the *Shura* until elections were held in Afghanistan; meanwhile, he called for elections in the several Liberated Zones and in the Afghan refugee camps (meaning only those in Pakistan) to broaden support for the AIG. Anxiety was felt in Peshawar that the superpowers might come to some compromise agreement over the Afghan problem that would freeze out Fundamentalists; the cooler attitude of Prime Minister Bhutto towards a Mujahideen option also caused concern.

Tomson and Jalalabad

Meanwhile, Peter Tomson had continued working on a plan to seize

Jalalabad, to make it the temporary seat and capital of the AIG, as the first major step on the road to Kabul. News of his intention was given by President Najibullah, on 13 November, in a nationwide broadcast, when he claimed that Tomson, 'a CIA agent', was planning an assault on Jalalabad, and had mustered a force of some 10,000 Mujahideen, including 1,000 foreign mercenaries, Arabs, Pakistanis and Westerners (*Kabul Radio*). Najibullah said this was to be a CIA operation and, therefore, must have the backing of President Bush.

Najibullah's prediction was correct. The Mujahideen attacked Jalalabad on 15 November, just as Winter was approaching. The Mujahideen force probably only numbered about 2,500, but by this time was formed into smaller units, which were in radio contact with each other and their HQs, and which had some semblance of cohesion and discipline. By using 'fire and movement' tactics, two small Afghan army outposts were overrun. Discipline then tended to waver, and although the Mujahideen held on to their gains, they made no further progress. Soon Tomson was unable to control them and another stalemate ensued. Counteraction by artillery, rockets and AAF aircraft caused heavy Mujahideen casualties. The Mujahideen had made a small but pyrrhic gain.

Meanwhile, Kabul remained the main target for Mujahideen rockets, and seldom a day passed without one or more falling on the city and its environs, as well as on other government-held cities. Twice in October, rocket fire closed the Kabul airport; on one day in November over 50 rockets fell on the city; and on 26 December, the anniversary of the Soviet military invasion, 63 rockets struck Kabul (*Pakistan sources*). As had the War of Resistance, the civil war was now causing thousands of displaced people to flood into Kabul, whose suburbs expanded to encompass much of the 15-mile wide flat plain on which the capital stands, and its population reached an estimated two million.

International Sea Change

On 9 November 1989, the Berlin Wall was breached, heralding the demise of the Cold War between the two superpowers, which was followed by the progressive loosening of the Communist grip on Eastern Europe, and eventually far-reaching reforms in the USSR, and culminating in the London Declaration on the 6 July 1990. The Cold War was formally at an end. Afghanistan was no longer a pawn in the modern Great Game, but rather an embarrassment to both superpowers.

A two-day conference (31 July-1 August) between American and Soviet officials had been held in Stockholm, where the Afghan problem had been discussed and this had alarmed Mujahideen leaders as to their future. Further alarm was occasioned by improved Soviet-Iranian relations, which could mean that the Iranian-backed Shia Alliance of Eight could be forced upon the AIG. From November 1989 onwards there was a steady decline in Western, and in particular American, interest, aid and donor support for the Mujahideen.

Sensing the mood of the moment, Hekmatyar called a Press Conference in Islamabad on 19 November, and declared that he would support the cessation of arms supplies by both the USA and the USSR. In short, he was suddenly supporting the 'negative symmetry'. He reasoned that as his group was by far the best armed and as he was becoming isolated within the Mujahideen movement, if American arms supplies ceased altogether his group would remain the strongest militarily and so continue to have an advantage over others. The surprise visit of the Soviet Foreign Minister, Shevardnadze, to see ex-King Zahir Shah in Italy, also dismayed the Mujahideen Fundamentalists.

One small spin-off in the new international atmosphere was that on 29 November, two Soviet POWs were handed over by the Mujahideen to the ICRC in Peshawar, the first occasion that such an exchange been made so openly. In return the Kabul regime released eight Afghan and 25 Pakistani prisoners.

January 1990 brought an American fact-finding team to Pakistan, led by the US Under Secretary of State for Political Affairs, Robert Kimmett; this was a forerunner of the impending meeting of American and Soviet foreign ministers. The team came to the conclusion—which had long been obvious—that the Afghan Resistance had failed to overthrow the Najibullah regime, and privately thought they were unlikely to be able to do so.

The New AIG Formula

The Mujahideen did, however, have a realistic element within its leadership, and on 17 January 1990, the 'Prime Minister' of the AIG, Abdur Rasaul Sayaf of the Fundamentalist IULA, stated that instead of promised elections in the forthcoming April, there would be a

'16-Point Formula' to find a new Mujahideen leadership to wage the fight against the Najibullah regime. This provided for a Loya Jirga of over 2,000 delegates, 10 from each of the '216 Districts' of Afghanistan, plus 15 from each of the seven major groups in Pakistan, to elect first a government and eventually a parliament. On 19 January, the Islamic Unity of Afghanistan agreed to this formula, although Hekmatyar claimed it was simply an expedient to extend the life of the *Shura*, due to expire the following month.

Plots in Kabul

Meanwhile all was not well with Najibullah in Kabul, and it was reputed that plots against him were being hatched. Two were pre-empted in December 1989, which resulted in '127 army and air force officers' being arrested (*Far Eastern Economic Review*). The first plot, it was alleged, was engineered by a group of dissident officers linked to Hekmatyar's Fundamentalist HIA group; in the second one, General Tanai, the Defence Minister, demanded the release of arrested officers, and staged a three-day 'sit-in' in his GHQ, until some were freed.

For some time differences had been festering between Najibullah, a Parchami, and his Defence Minister, a Khalki, over policy. Najibullah was now pursuing a total reconciliation policy, which involved the armed forces abstaining from aggressive operations; Tanai, on the other hand, wanted to pursue the military option actively and vigorously, as he felt the Mujahideen were at their weakest in the military sense. This major difference of opinion had exacerbated the continuing Parchami-Khalki feud within the PDPA and the armed forces.

The Khalki faction had remained strong within the armed forces, despite action taken by Najibullah to weaken it, while the Parchami power-base still rested mainly within government administration and PDPA circles. This difference caused several clashes in Kabul between the two factions, resulting on one occasion, in early January 1990, in Najibullah confining the Afghan armed forces in Kabul, including all officers, to barracks for two weeks. Also during January, the inter-Parcham friction between those who favoured Najibullah and those who did not, broke into open scuffles, mainly on the issue of reconciliation versus the military option. Prime Minister Sultan Ali Keshtmand, the only Shia in the SCDH, tried desperately to calm the situation down.

The Tanai Revolt

Matters came to a head on 5 March 1990, when the trial opened in Kabul of a number of officers alleged to have been involved in the projected December plots, and evidence was produced that implicated General Tanai and other senior officers. Anticipating trouble, Najibullah had placed some 'loyal' units on the alert, and confined all others to barracks. General Tanai struck the following morning and, basing himself initially on the Defence Ministry building, launched a coup to topple Najibullah. First, his supporters took control of the Bagram air base north of Kabul, and just before noon three combat planes bombed the Presidential Palace, the radio and TV transmission stations and other government buildings. The first government broadcast (*Kabul Radio*), a few minutes after noon, gave news of the Tanai revolt, but few details.

'Loyal units', meaning mainly the Presidential Guard and the Special Guard, began an assault on the Defence Ministry building, and in the course of some three hours or so of hard room-to-room fighting, succeeded in crushing all 'rebel' resistance. It took a little longer to bring rebellious officers and servicemen at the Bagram air base to heel. The two or three other Tanai resistance centres in Kabul were also soon eliminated. Confined to barracks, most other Afghan army units did not realise what was happening, though they could hear the firing and see the bombing; in any case the exits from their camps were blocked by armoured vehicles and guns manned by 'loyal' personnel.

Suddenly and surprisingly, General Tanai gave up the struggle, abandoned what seemed to be a poorly-organised operation, and decamped with his family and a few close supporters in three military aircraft and a helicopter from Bagram air base, arriving at Parachinar in Pakistan, between 1330 hours and 1430 hours (*Pakistan sources*). The aircraft were impounded by the Pakistani authorities.

At 1600 hours, Najibullah broadcast to the nation (*Kabul Radio*), announcing that General Tanai was stripped of his rank and appointments, and dismissed from the Afghan army. In his stead, he appointed General Mohammed Asla Watanjar, a prominent Khalki officer, to be Minister of Defence, with the task of cooling the situation and minimising the damage done to the armed forces by the Tanai revolt. On the afternoon of 6 March, Gulbuddin Hekmatyar of the HIA broadcast from Pakistan stating that he supported General Tanai, and had been working with him to remove

Najibullah from power for some time.

Najibullah made another nationwide broadcast by radio and TV at 2200 hours, declaring that the revolt had been crushed, claiming it had been supported by Hekmatyar, and revealing that Tanai had fled the country. Five prominent Khalkis were dismissed from the SCDH, as were two overseas ambassadors, one a former Head of KHAD. Media sources in Kabul quoted casualties incurred during the Tanai revolt as 'about 200', but Pakistan sources were more precise, stating that they were '56 dead and 300 injured'.

Rumours abounded, and there are other versions of the Tanai revolt, most extending its duration, but this is believed to be the most probable account: it was virtually all over in four hours, with the exception of some mopping up in parts of Kabul and at the Bagram air base, and the instigator fled to Pakistan. On 7 March, the AIG spokesman denied it had any 'solidarity' with the Tanai revolt; the Islamic Unity of Afghanistan leaders (except Hekmatyar) denied any knowledge or involvement in it, and the Pakistan government insisted that the ISI was in no way involved. However, few believed it was as simple as that.

One version is that Najibullah knew about the Tanai plot as much as six months before it was activated, and was simply giving Tanai enough rope to hang himself; and that if he had arrested him sooner he would have had a Khalk martyr on his hands, when any prolonged detention or a show trial would have provoked the armed forces into open mutiny. At the best, this could only be partially true. It is most probable that Najibullah first knew of the plot when evidence was being collected for the trial of the 'December plotters', and it may be that he then set a trap for Tanai, into which the Defence Minister walked.

Obviously expecting trouble at the trial of the 'December plotters', which had begun the previous day, Najibullah had mustered his 'loyal' troops, and confined all others to camp, and so was ready when Tanai was provoked into showing his hand. Tanai's intelligence sources seem to have been poor, and he seems to have been outsmarted by Najibullah, an ex-Director of KHAD, and an old intelligence hand.

Another story was that Hekmatyar and Tanai had actually been plotting together for some considerable time, and that Hekmatyar had given considerable support and help and had foreknowledge of the date and time of the projected coup. There seems to be little evidence, if any, to support this theory, and it is probable that the quick-witted Hekmatyar simply jumped on the band-wagon, making an impromptu opportunistic decision. Tanai had probably landed in Pakistan before Hekmatyar first announced his involvement. Hekmatyar's intelligence too was weak. Had he been fully informed, he should have been able to orchestrate diversionary and supporting Mujahideen activity.

On 16 March, General Tanai in full uniform, accompanied by General Abdul Wadir Agha (dismissed Chief of the Afghan air force) appeared in a Liberated Zone in Logar province, to hold a Press conference, where he stated he had joined Hekmatyar's Fundamentalist HIA group. Tanai insisted that he and his companions were still 'good members of the PDPA', and that his sole purpose had been to remove Najibullah, and install Hekmatyar in his stead.

At first the Tanai-Hekmatyar relationship seemed unbelievable—a die-hard Soviet-trained Communist General, strongly against reconciliation, who had long fought the Mujahideen, personally commanding troops in the field on some operations, joining hands with a Mujahideen Fundamentalist leader who hated all things Soviet and Communist and was unswerving in his determination to establish an Islamic state in Afghanistan. It seemed to be a sudden, spur-of-the-moment expediency partnership, a shot-gun marriage, with each partner holding a shot-gun.

Tanai had bungled his coup attempt and also underestimated Najibullah, and Hekmatyar was becoming isolated within the Mujahideen movement. Generally, in Afghanistan, failed or discredited national and political leaders could usually fall back on their tribal roots for support and sanctuary, but these two personalities had both cut themselves off from, and considered themselves to be well above, tribal level, and so had nowhere to go in a dire emergency. The Tanai (Pathan) tribe had a Kabul-subsidised militia, but none deserted the government side of this occasion to support their fellow tribesman; indeed, they continued the fight against the Mujahideen.

The Tanai-Hekmatyar partnership was a big blow to the Mujahideen cause, showing it to be not so much a part of a *Jihad* against a godless government, but merely an uncertain ally in a civil war, in which Afghans were squabbling amongst themselves for power and influence, with tribal, ethnic and religious affiliations to be used or discarded as might be expedient. If two such hard-liners, complete opposites, could collaborate, why then should not other groups and factions enter into agreement with the Kabul government or the Afghan armed forces? On the government side, Tanai now symbolised failure and desertion, a war hero with feet of clay, who had changed sides. Hekmatyar, too, was regarded with distaste by the Mujahideen movement as a heretic and a turncoat.

Herat Failure

Najibullah was considerably encouraged by the outcome of the Tanai affair, which had given his reconciliation programme such a boost, so he arranged a widely publicised ceremony at Herat, where some 3,000 Mujahideen indicated that they would hand in their arms and declare loyalty to the Kabul government. The date was to be 6 April (*Defence Journal*, Pakistan). There had been on-off agreements between local Mujahideen groups around Herat and the Kabul government for years. This planned ceremony back-fired badly. When the Mujahideen parade was assembled, at a given signal, the Mujahideen fired at the official reception party, killing the Governor of Herat and some senior military officers and officials, and in the subsequent mêlée others were killed or wounded. The Mujahideen target had been Najibullah, who had been due to preside at this mass parade, but he had backed out at the last minute and did not attend. Perhaps he had received a whisper from some old KHAD contact, or perhaps his luck was still holding out.

Interim Entity

Conciliation and settlement seemed to be the watchwords whenever the Afghan problem was considered internationally. During the first week of April 1990, Soviet Foreign Minister Shevardnadze and US Secretary of State Baker met to consider the Afghan situation, and both talked of the 'negative symmetry', giving the impression that they might adopt it. Previously, in January, the French had said they would reopen their embassy in Kabul. They were the first Western diplomats to return, and others began to follow.

The major remaining difference between the two superpowers over Afghanistan seemed to be the 'interim entity', a new jargon expression, meaning an interim government in Kabul until a general election could be held. The Soviets insisted that Najibullah should stay in power during this period, while the Americans insisted that Najibullah should be removed so that he would not gain any residential advantage, and that any interim government should be formed by all parties, including the Mujahideen.

Refugee Problem in Pakistan

In Pakistan, Prime Minister Bhutto and her government became increasingly concerned about the behaviour of the three million or so Afghan refugees, who were tending to become a law unto themselves, considering themselves in some respects as a 'state within a state'. It was estimated that 1.3 million of them were armed (*Official Pakistan government figures*) and unrest, divisions and violence amongst them were rampant. Killing rivals was a common crime, and assassinations became so numerous that they were not even reported in the Pakistan media unless the victim was a prominent leader.

Factions had their own 'prisons' in which kidnapped victims were held, sometimes as an insurance against attacks from rivals but often simply so that they were available to be executed in reprisals. Also each of the major Mujahideen groups had their own intelligence service. Fears began to be openly expressed in Pakistan that the Afghan refugee population was fast becoming as lawless as that existing in Lebanon.

Loya Jirga: May 1990

Najibullah lifted the State of Emergency on 4 May 1990, although a night curfew remained in Kabul. The following day, Sultan Ali Keshtmand became the First Vice President; and on 6 May, Fazl Haq Khaleqiar (a former Governor of the North West Military District) became Prime Minister. On 27 May, he announced his government, which for the first time in that country included two women.

A Loya Jirga quickly followed (28-29 May), attended by 722 delegates (*Kabul Radio*), at which Najibullah announced his plan for ending the civil war. First a referendum was to be held both in government-controlled areas and Mujahideen Liberated Zones, to determine whether a cease-fire should be implemented. If this was approved, as expected, a 'cooling off period' would follow, leading to an international conference to deal with foreign aspects of the Afghan civil war. Certain amendments were made to the 1982 Constitution to allow for 'plurality of political parties', and to delete all reference to 'the leading role of the PDPA'. This Najibullah peace plan was rejected out-of-hand by the AIG the following day.

Military Activity

Meanwhile, Afghanistan devolved into a patchwork pattern of 'part-war and part-cease-fire', as some Mujahideen leaders in the field retained private arrangements with the Afghan army, and some did not; of pockets of small Liberated Zones, especially in the eastern provinces, interspersed with government-held cities and garrisons and (mainly) government-controlled strategic roads. Liberated Zones were usually left alone under Najibullah's reconciliation policy, but periodically small punitive operations were launched against them to deter Mujahideen expansionist ambitions.

The Afghan army was far too small even to attempt to hold territory on this scale. Rockets continued to fall on Kabul, and other cities and garrisons, and in reply the Afghan army fired off a few SCUD-Bs to show its teeth. On 14 March, the Afghan government had confirmed that it had received more Soviet SCUD-Bs, and that in the three previous days 10 had been fired from the area of the capital, to bolster the defence of Khost (*Kabul Radio*).

Several Mujahideen rocket bases were within a radius of 20 miles or so of Kabul, and the Afghan air force and the army occasionally tried to eliminate them. For example, on 17 May, it was announced (*Kabul Radio*) that after a month's fighting in the Laghman area, government forces had 'destroyed 15 rocket bases', which was probably true; but invariably the Mujahideen returned to the locality when Afghan troops were withdrawn.

On 8 July, the Defence Minister, General Watanjar, at a Press conference in Kabul, claimed that 'after a 25-day operation in the Paghman mountains … over 400 rebels were killed' (*Kabul Radio*). This, and other similar announcements, were designed to give the inhabitants of Kabul confidence that something was being done, but they may not have had much validity. It is true that the incidence of rockets falling on government targets was slowly declining, but this was mainly due to the reduced volume of arms the Americans were sending to Pakistan for the Mujahideen.

The Hizb-i-Watan Party

The Second PDPA Congress, which ended on 28 June, was also its last, as the PDPA dissolved its Politburo and Central Committee, and changed its name to the *Hizb-i-Watan* (Homeland Party), and amended the constitution to have a 33-member Executive Council and a 144-member Central Council. (The First PDPA Congress had been held in secret in 1965). This change was part of Najibullah's plan to gain wider support. The Watan Party stressed Islamic values instead of Marxist ones. Najibullah was striving to remove the old hard-line Communist image from his old party.

Divide-and-Rule Tactics

Throughout the summer of 1990, Najibullah continued to work on his reconciliation campaign, trying to persuade diverse factions to support him. For example, he promised the Hazaras and Uzbeks, peoples regarded by the dominant Pushtunis as somewhat inferior and who were often discriminated against, a degree of autonomy which attracted them. Also, his divide-and-rule tactics were paying some dividends, and especially his 'government militias' programme had some success in the more remote regions and those away from the main road network, as many local Mujahideen groups succumbed to offers of arms and cash to 'protect' their own localities.

These measures tended to have an unsettling effect on the main Mujahideen body, which had another disappointment when the fighting for Kandahar was brought to a stop by a *de facto* cease-fire. Generally, during the Summer heat Mujahideen activity throughout Afghanistan was at a low ebb, largely confined to opportunity tactics, which provoked government forces into making aerial counter-attacks. In fact, there was more internecine Mujahideen fighting than action against the Kabul government's armed forces.

In Pakistan, on 5 August, Prime Minister Bhutto was dismissed from government, thus removing a curb on the ISI, which began planning for an Autumn frontal attack on Kabul, to be led by Hekmatyar and General Tanai—a swing back to the Fundamentalist solution. Truck loads of weaponry and ammunition were rushed to the Fundamentalist HIA. Using arms and ammunition as bribes, the ISI tried to persuade other Fundamentalist groups in the Islamic Unity of Afghanistan coalition to co-operate in this projected operation, but was met with hesitation and reluctance.

American policy towards Afghanistan was faltering, largely due to improved relations between the two superpowers, and also because of America's preoccupation, after the occupation of Kuwait by the Iraqis (August 1990), with mustering a multi-national force in Saudi Arabia. Now the Cold War was over, the US State Department wanted to pull out from Afghanistan as quickly and quietly as possible, and it indicated that if there were no signs of a swift military solution all aid to the Mujahideen would be suspended. On the other hand, the CIA wanted to continue the war in Afghanistan until a military victory was achieved and the Najibullah regime was toppled, no matter how long it took; and in this resolve it was actively encouraged by the ISI.

12

The Elusive Peace

For sometime, several principal Sunni Mujahideen military commanders in the field in Afghanistan had been meeting to discuss military and political plans and policies, having become disillusioned by their leaderships' sitting passively and comfortable in Pakistan while they were undergoing the rigours of campaigning. They had the feeling that they were being bypassed, that their views were not given sufficient weight; and that the Islamic Unity of Afghanistan leaderships were losing their political edge and deviating from the main task of removing Najibullah from power in Kabul, instead devolving into feuding, struggling for individual power, and sometimes being tempted by riches gained from drug trafficking.

These meetings, impromptu at first, developed and were dubbed by the Afghan media (*Kabul Radio*) as the Mujahideen 'Field Commanders' Conferences', or sometimes as the Mujahideen field commanders' 'Consultative Councils'. Owing to his combat experience, aptitude for war, and the fact that he commanded a body of some 10,000 armed and trained guerrilla fighters, Ahmad Shah Masoud, of the Panjshir Valley, came to dominate these meetings.

Masoud had been generally cold-shouldered by the Pushtun-dominated Islamic Unity of Afghanistan leaderships, mainly perhaps because he was not the leader of his Fundamentalist IA group but simply one of half-a-dozen of its major field commanders, did not visit Pakistan, and perhaps also because he was a Tadjik; also his flair for attracting Western publicity probably rankled. Masoud deliberately stayed away from Pakistan, not wanting to be regarded as a puppet of the ISI, and consequently of the Americans. Also Masoud, who was heavily involved in a bitter blood-letting feud with

216

Hekmatyar, on behalf of the IA, was considered to be an out-spoken, disruptive influence.

At a Mujahideen Field Commanders' Conference (9-12 October), Masoud spoke out against the ISI's projected frontal attack on Kabul, insisting that it could not be successful as the capital's defences were too strong, and the Mujahideen had neither sufficient weapons of the right kind, nor the capability to achieve victory in positional warfare. He declared that such an operation would simply be another disaster, similar to the previous year's battle for Jalalabad. Masoud also pointed out that a disastrous defeat at Kabul could emasculate the Mujahideen movement in the field and leave it easy prey for government reprisals which might set the cause back some years. Finally, any attack on Kabul would cause many civilian casualties and further erode the Mujahideen's popular support in the country.

Masoud's recommended strategy was to conduct a war of attrition, sealing off roads leading to provincial capitals so as to besiege them and force them either to surrender through starvation or defect through persuasion or bribery. He said it would be better to continue to expand the Liberated Zones, and gradually merge them together to make huge sectors of the countryside into 'No-Go' areas for government troops and officials. Masoud pointed out that government armed forces could not be strong everywhere, could only conduct a few limited counter-insurgency operations at a time, and had abandoned the policy of seizing and holding on to cities and terrain at all costs for occasional punitive 'search and destroy' tactics. Therefore, the war of attrition should be as widespread as possible. Tarin Kot, capital of Uruzgan province, had fallen on 3 October to Hekmatyar's Fundamentalist HIA through such tactics, with the garrison of some 500 troops defecting from the government side.

The Attack on Kabul

On 10 October, while the Mujahideen Field Commanders' Conference was still in session, Hekmatyar's HIA, practically alone, launched a two-pronged assault on Kabul, which made no headway at all. On 12 October, the garrison reacted with aircraft strikes, helicopter-gunship attacks, and missile, rocket and artillery barrages, which caused the attackers to fall back and scatter. It is believed that SCUD-Bs were also used by government forces. Being repulsed so fiercely, a majority of the attacking Mujahideen left the combat area either for Winter camps in Pakistan before snows blocked the mountain passes, or to shelter in Liberated Zones. A few bold spirits stayed on for a while, to fire whatever missiles, rockets and ammunition they possessed at Kabul, before also departing.

The onset of Winter precluded major Mujahideen operations, and Kabul settled down to endure spasmodic missile and rocket fire which invariably caused civilian casualties. Any Mujahideen opportunistic attacks, raids, ambushes or missile and rocket firing provoked heavy government combat aircraft and helicopter-gunship activity.

Already on 1 October the USA had suspended the proposed 1991 economic ($564 million) and military ($518 million) aid to Pakistan, ostensibly because it was suspected of working to produce a nuclear warhead, something to which the US administration had turned a blind eye for many months. Funds and arms destined for the Mujahideen through the CIA, were also suspended. A general election in Pakistan on 24 October, brought Nawaz Sharif to power as Prime Minister and in collusion with President Ghulam Ishaq Khan, he continued Zia's policy of trying to install Hekmatyar in Kabul.

Islamabad Agreement

The failure of the Mujahideen attack on Kabul caused the ISI to try to heal the vitally damaging feud between Hekmatyar's HIA, and Rabbani's IA. Masoud, whose stock had suddenly risen due to his haranguing recent Mujahideen Field Commanders' conferences, was persuaded to make his first visit for many years to Islamabad, for talks with the Pakistan leadership. He remained in Islamabad for about two weeks and met and talked with, among others, the President, Chief of Staff and Director of the ISI, the retired General Assad Durrani. He was also instrumental in persuading both Hekmatyar and his own political leader, Rabbani, to end their feud for the good of the common cause. Prominent Mujahideen military leaders in Afghanistan were now having to be treated as semi-independent war lords, which was actually what some of them had become.

On 27 October, what became known as the Islamabad Agreement was announced, which stated that a consensus had been reached on a 'new plan' to remove Najibullah from power, though no details were given. The main essence of the new plan was to reshape and broaden the largely discredited AIG by forming a closer alliance between the Islamic Unity of Afghanistan and its field commanders in Afghanistan, to enable the latter to have more say in policies and plans, and to be kept more fully informed.

The Islamabad Agreement also called for elections in the 13 northern provinces of Afghanistan before 21 March 1991, in which only the HIA and the IA would participate. This covered the region where much of the feuding between these two groups, which were now dictating the campaign against the Kabul regime, had been going on.

Najibullah's Travels

Meanwhile, President Najibullah travelled abroad to seek friends, attract international support and economic aid; at home he tried to cobble together a broad-based coalition government led by himself to administer the country until the promised UN-sponsored general election could be held throughout the country and in the refugee camps. The Americans insisted that Najibullah step down during this interim period, but the Soviets wanted him to remain. The other stumbling block was the 'negative symmetry', to which the Americans would not commit themselves unless the Soviets first openly stated that they would stop sending military aid to the Kabul regime.

At the beginning of August, Najibullah had disappeared for a few days to Moscow, ostensibly for 'medical treatment', causing rumours that the Soviets were planning to replace him. However, he soon returned to Kabul after the Soviets had persuaded the Americans to agree that he should head an interim government, on condition that he handed over to a neutral body control of the armed forces, Ministry of Interior troops, and the media, although this was not announced until later.

On 29 August, Najibullah visited Prime Minister V P Singh of India, a country vaguely sympathetic towards him, and hostile to Pakistan and, of course, the Mujahideen. He was promised Indian support. To gain international standing, Najibullah asked Singh to propose Afghanistan for membership of the South Asia Association for Regional Co-operation (SAARC), and Singh agreed to do this. In return, Najibullah promised to support India internationally on its Kashmir problem, Singh complaining that hostile Kashmiri militants were being armed and trained in Pakistan. On 6 September,

Najibullah flew to Paris, by way of Moscow, to attend the UN Trade and Development Conference, designed to assist the world's poorest nations, which included Afghanistan, to ask for economic aid. Najibullah claimed that since 1980, his country had suffered devastation estimated at $10 billion.

Neutral Transitional Authority

Next, on 19 November, Najibullah flew to Geneva to have a series of consultations with (anonymous) Traditionalist Mujahideen leaders, and other contacts, in an effort to form a broad-based government. He said that the Fundamentalists would automatically exclude themselves from such an interim body. The US Secretary of State, James Baker, and Soviet Foreign Minister Shevardnadze, meeting in Moscow at that time, agreed that Najibullah could head the interim government, causing Najibullah to announce triumphantly that 'certain Western nations have made a 180 degree turn'. This was almost true.

Back home again, Najibullah on 3 December, offered to relinquish certain powers to a 'Neutral Transitional Authority' if Traditional Mujahideen leaders would enter into discussions with him during the run-up to the UN-supervised general election (*Kabul Radio*). As 1990 drew to a close there was still an air of uncertainty in Kabul, as Traditional leaders failed to respond to Najibullah's offer—at least openly.

New Factors

In the first quarter of 1991 the main protagonists, in the Afghan equation, the USA, USSR, Pakistan and increasingly Iran began to reappraise the situation in the light of the changing international political climate. New factors were the imminent collapse of the USSR and the US-led and instigated war in the Gulf to liberate Kuwait from Iraqi occupation. It was now becoming clearer to all involved or interested in Afghanistan that neither the Kabul regime nor the Mujahideen could obtain a quick, decisive military victory, and that the USA and the USSR were seeking ways of ridding themselves of a troublesome burden with the least embarrassment and the most benefit to themselves. They decided to try a 'joint approach', in which there would be negotiations with all parties and factions. American interest in Pakistan diminished which reduced its influence as an ally, while the appearance of Iran on the Afghan scene became an embarrassment to the USSR.

The Soviets decided to talk directly to Mujahideen leaders, which it had avoided doing for so long, and the Soviet Ambassador to Pakistan met Pakistan-based Mujahideen leaders at its embassy in Islamabad. All saw the writing on the wall and seemed more amenable than before to compromise, except that they all stuck on one point—that Najibullah must be removed from power in Kabul. Fearing that a Fundamentalist replacement would have an unsettling effect on their Muslim Asian republics, the Soviets wanted Najibullah to remain in power in the interim government, and afterwards, so that they would have a Soviet-moulded ally on their southern flank.

The Pakistan-based Traditionalist Mujahideen groups were less emphatic on this point: although officially they, too, said they wanted Najibullah removed, unofficially they were not too keen on seeing him replaced by a Fundamentalist leader. In protest Khalis of the Fundamentalist HI later resigned his appointment in the AIG as 'Minister of the Interior', accusing some of the AIG members (meaning the Traditionalists) of collaborating with the Kabul government. The invigorated Iranian-backed nine Shia Mujahideen groups also wanted a say in the composition of the 'interim entity', favouring a Fundamentalist-dominated (Shia, of course) government in Kabul, if possible.

The Fall of Khost

Meanwhile, the Pakistan ISI was working on the military solution for Afghanistan, preparing for an opening Spring campaign to capture the prestigious city of Khost, long isolated in a broad Liberated Zone, which continued to hold out against the Mujahideen. Military detachments of several Mujahideen groups, from both Hekmatyar's HIA and its rival, the Khalis HI, were mustered under the field command of Jalalabuddin Haqqani, who had gained a good combat reputation, and whose HQ was at Miranshah, just inside Pakistan territory. The ISI formulated the operational plan, provided much of the back-up and logistic support, and selectively distributed American munitions, including Stingers. Hekmatyar, and his now chief military advisor, General Tanai, sought to dominate this operation, which caused some friction with other contributors.

For some months, the Pakistan ISI had been distributing US arms and aid destined for the Mujahideen direct to military leaders in Afghanistan, thus bypassing their political leaderships in Pakistan, because so many munitions were going astray, and so few reaching

Mujahideen warriors in the field. Stansfield Turner, a former Director of the CIA, doubted whether 20 per cent of American arms sent to Pakistan got through to the Mujahideen in Afghanistan (*New York Times*).

The Mujahideen operation to capture Khost began in mid-March 1991, against its already partly invested defences, the ground assault meeting stiff resistances for several days and making only small advances. Blatantly magnified reports and rumours of the horror of the Kunduz massacre by Mujahideen caused the defenders to feel they were fighting for their lives, which boosted their determination. The garrison of about 3,000 Afghan soldiers, supported by a few government-paid militias, fired artillery and rocket barrages at the attackers, while the AAF carried out high-level (out of range of the Stingers) bombing raids, and the Afghan army launched several long-distance SCUD-B ballistic missiles.

On 30 March, the small government-held airfield close to Khost fell to the Mujahideen and, suddenly, on the following day the whole Khost garrison surrendered, some 2,500 Afghan soldiers becoming prisoners; another 500 or so, mainly wounded and sick, were found inside the city of Khost. Government militias hastily changed sides, apparently quite willingly, while the apprehensive civilian population remained unmolested. Battle casualties seemed to be comparatively few, although verifiable figures were unobtainable, but casualties amongst other Mujahideen and civilians in the area were fairly heavy.

On 31 March, Jalalabuddin Haqqani triumphantly announced the fall of Khost, to the chagrin of Hekmatyar who had wanted that honour so that he and his group would be paramountly associated with this prestigious gain. Mujahideen forces under Haqqani had showed improved cohesion, co-ordination and battle discipline, although they were on the point of falling apart by the end of March.

The fact is that Khost fell not by military assault but by negotiation, the key negotiator being General Tanai, himself a notable defector, who had successfully persuaded the garrison, government militias and civilian population that there would be no reprisals, no massacre and no atrocities, and that all would be fairly treated. Had Tanai not been successful in his endeavours, it is probable that the fighting at Khost would have simply subsided into stalemate, as already Mujahideen fighters were drifting away from the battlefield: a fortnight was a long time to hold the attention and concentration of Mujahideen in action. Even so, the fall of Khost was considered by the Mujahideen to be their biggest success in the civil war so far, a great morale booster, an ace negotiating card, and important in countering its Kunduz reputation.

Admitting defeat, the Kabul government complained (*Kabul Radio*) that 'Pakistani troops entered the battle at a decisive moment which turned the tide' also mentioning the 'involvement of foreign mercenaries' trained by Pakistan. The latter allegation referred to secret camps in Pakistan where foreign Muslim volunteers were trained and armed under ISI supervision, although this was consistently denied by the Islamabad government. A report (*Sunday Times*) alleged there were 'several hundred members of the Saudi Salafi Wahabi sect', some of them former members of the Saudi armed forces, in one such camp, and many volunteers from other countries in similar camps. Muslim volunteers took part in the battle for Khost, but reliable details are not available.

Shortly afterwards, on 10 May, Haqqani presented 10 captured Afghan senior military officers to the media at his Miranshah HQ. They gave their reasons for surrender as a shortage of supplies and ammunition, the failure of expected reinforcements to arrive, and the absence of signs that a relief column was being mounted: in short they had felt abandoned.

It does seem that the Kabul government was not prepared to dispatch numbers of troops to Khost to hold it 'at all costs', as its prestige value, useful enough while it lasted, was cancelled out by its negative military importance when lost.

The UN Peace Plan

The CIA was looking for an alternative to the ineffectual AIG to form the 'interim entity' and, under American pressure, on 3 May, the Pakistan government decided to open a dialogue with the USSR, formerly regarded as a hostile power. Also in May, 77-year-old ex-King Zahir Shah, long merely regarded as a reluctant background talking point at last began to show an interest in the Afghan situation, putting forward proposals for a national committee to include Mujahideen representatives, free elections, and the establishment of a parliamentary system: rather broad brush, but at least he had made a contribution. The ex-King did have a small following in Afghanistan, mainly among the Traditional Pakistan-based groups, which had long been urging him to participate in Afghan politics. However, Zahir Shah obviously had more enemies than supporters as little notice was taken of his utterances. It was not until September that citizenship was restored to him, and it was November before he declared himself willing to return to his homeland.

Bolstered and encouraged by a degree of prominence and credibility earned during the Gulf War, on 21 May, the UN Secretary General, Peres de Cuellar, encouraged by both the USA and the USSR, stepped boldly on to the Afghan scene, with a Peace Plan. It contained little that was new, being a rehash of various proposals and suggestions that had previously been put forward by one party or another, at one time or another. The five points of the UN Peace Plan, much the same in essence as others, were: sovereign independence for Afghanistan; self-determination; a broad-based interim government; the ending of arms supplies to all Afghan sides; and international help for the return of refugees and reconstruction.

The difference was that the UN Peace Plan was launched in a changed international political atmosphere, when all involved were realising that time was no longer on their side but was, in fact, running out fairly quickly. External support for Afghan hard-liners was falling away so, if compromises were not made, they might lose out altogether.

For example, both Hekmatyar and Khalis, the two main Fundamentalist rivals, had been asked by the Saudis to send token detachments of Mujahideen to support them in the Gulf War, and both had refused. This resulted in a subsequent sharp decrease in Saudi aid. Other Mujahideen groups were more far-sighted and mustered a few volunteers; in all about 300 reached the Gulf region. Also Hekmatyar, Khalis and Abdur Rasaul Sayaf, leader of the Fundamentalist IULA, openly supported Saddam Hussein in his struggle against the 'Americans', overlooking the fact that the Saudis were on the American side.

On 23 May, the UN Peace Plan was rejected by Sayaf, speaking as Prime Minister of the AIG, who declared it was an affront to the 'memory of a million and a half Afghans who had died in the 12 years of civil war' (*Pakistan sources*), and by Hekmatyar, speaking as 'Foreign Minister'. On 27 May, Najibullah provisionally accepted the UN Peace Plan, but the following day it was abruptly dismissed by Sibghatullah Mujadidi, speaking as 'President' of the AIG. Iran hesitated but agreed to consider it, which was an advance as previously the Tehran government had refused to deal with the 'Soviet puppet regime' at Kabul. Despite overt rejections,

224

reservations and hesitations, the unofficial consensus seemed to be that the UN Peace Plan was the only alternative to a further downward slide into chaos.

Economic Woes

The US administration had severely reduced its aid to the Afghan Mujahideen, and in July 1991 let it be known that it would not be seeking funding for this purpose for 1992, confirming that it had already cut its 1991 allocation from $126 million to $105 million (*USA Today*). Another source (*Financial Times*) estimated that American aid to the Mujahideen had been running about $500 million a year, and that similar Soviet aid to the Kabul government had been averaging about $400 million annually. Somewhat surprisingly, on these figures it would seem that the Americans were sending more aid to their surrogate than the Soviets to theirs. However, one should perhaps appreciate that most of the Soviet aid did reach its intended destination, while only a small percentage of American aid actually reached the Mujahideeen in the field.

The economic situation in Afghanistan was of chronic depression, making the Kabul regime extremely anxious over reduced Soviet aid, now virtually confined to food and fuel, and the occasional impromptu arms delivery. Soviet policy was by now to a large degree under the influence of Boris Yeltsin, leader of the Russian Federation, who was far less enthusiastic than Gorbachev about sending supplies to Najibullah, when the Soviet economic situation was in such straightened circumstances; however, he did realise that unless Soviet aid was continued, economic adversity would cause the collapse of the Kabul regime.

Like Gorbachev, Yeltsin wanted a friendly, like-minded government in power in Afghanistan, knowing that the alternative would enflame the southern Soviet Muslim Republics. In August, the Afghan Prime Minister, Faiz Haq Khaleqiar, stated (*Kabul Radio*) that he had urgently requested 200,000 tons of grain from the USSR, and another 50,000 tons from India. The hint of Indian involvement in Afghanistan, even for a humanitarian purpose, raised Pakistani hackles.

There had been some trade friction between Kabul and Moscow for some months before the Soviets pulled out, and when they finally went they closed down the natural gas production centre at Shirbarghan, so terminating Afghanistan's most valuable export to the USSR. Negotiations to resume this export foundered over price, the Afghans demanding that the Soviets pay international rates in hard currency, which they were unable to do. The consequences were that the internal supply of natural gas for domestic use also tailed off, causing hardship. In the hope of a breakthrough in negotiations, both Soviet and Afghan engineers were working to reopen the natural gas production plant and pipelines.

Throughout 1991, the Soviets provided food and fuel, with up to 30 Soviet transport aircraft landing at Kabul airport and dozens of heavily-laden road convoys arriving daily. Without these supplies the Afghan population would have been reduced to starvation level, and many government-held towns and garrisons would not have been able to hold out. Eventually, a trade agreement was signed on 3 November, under which the Soviets agreed to continue to supply food and fuel; but the dispute over the price of Afghan natural gas remained unsolved.

Crime and Drugs

The CIA became concerned that reduced American aid to the Mujahideen would tempt their political leaders in Pakistan and their field commanders in Afghanistan to sell their American munitions, including an unknown number of Stingers, to the highest bidder to obtain money for bare subsistence survival. Rumours abounded that both Iran and Libya had made offers for Stingers in this potential market, as did fears that some of these sensitive weapons might fall into the hands of international terrorist groups or hostile (in the eyes of America) national insurgent organisations.

The year 1991 can be thought of as the 'Year of the Petty War Lord' in Afghanistan, when commanders of Liberated Zones became almost autonomous in their own jealously-guarded localities, leading to inter-group and inter-locality rivalry and blood-letting. Some war lords raided each other simply to obtain loot—weapons, ammunition, food and valuables—while levies were made on supply caravans or convoys passing through their domain, even on those of their parent organisations; protection rackets also flourished. In short, war lords thrived on banditry.

Bitter and bloody political feuding between groups in the field continued for dominance, arms and territory, such as the continuing feud between the HIA and the IA. Larger groups sought to take over, or eliminate, smaller ones, and to seize their weapons and equipment.

For example, in Kunar province in July and August the HIA launched a campaign to eliminate the small Saudi-backed *Ahle Hadith* group of the Wahabi sect outside the Islamic Unity of Afghanistan coalition, and Kabul Radio reported that during July over 200 'rebels' had killed each other in the fighting, and on 3 August had ambushed and killed the leader of the *Ahle Hadith* group.

Away from the Liberated Zones, the rest of Afghanistan was under the notional authority of the Kabul government, but large areas of the countryside, and a few towns, were actually controlled by government-funded militias, (in other words the local war lord), whose remit was to keep the Mujahideen away from his area and keep the roads open for government use. These local war lords were unreliable, but were the best solution the Kabul government could come up with. They tended to become greedy, occasionally looting government convoys, raiding rival war lords to expand territory and obtain loot, and changing allegiances. Plain banditry was becoming big business in Afghanistan, with the central government able to do little about it, apart from the occasional punitive raid when a situation developed that affected strategic necessities.

However, an even larger, and potentially more serious problem was developing—drug trafficking. Afghanistan was becoming a well-trodden route from Pakistan's North-West Frontier Province, where drugs were grown in quantity and processed in small 'factories' beyond the direct writ of the Islamabad government, to the West, the way being smoothed by bribery. Because of the big money in drug trafficking, local war lords began to fight each other for domination over sections of the drug routes to obtain profitable 'concessions', as had been happening in Helmand province. Drug routes became trails of corruption, in which government officials and Mujahideen alike were becoming tainted. Some scenes were reminiscent of gangland fighting between organised drug and crime syndicates in the West as political motivation evaporated, overwhelmed by greed and avarice.

Gardez Invested

Meanwhile, now fully in favour of the UN Peace Plan, the Iranian government was making its presence felt and its views on the Afghan problem known. On 29-30 July Foreign Minister Velayati visited Islamabad to try to persuade the AIG to accept the UN plan. Some hard-line attitudes were softening, but both Fundamentalists and

Traditionalists were dismayed by Velayati's pushing forward the nine Iranian-backed Shia Mujahideen groups, and insisting on their inclusion in any solution. Hekmatyar, Khalis and a few other leaders, remained obstructive over the issue of Najibullah, insisting that first he must be removed from power.

After the Mujahideen victory at Khost in March, due to disunity within the Mujahideen movement, no similar operation was mounted until 18 September, this time against Gardez. Several Mujahideen groups contributed, all under the leadership of Jalala-buddin Haqqani, while the planning, organisation and logistic back-up was carried out by the Pakistan ISI. A four-pronged assault closed on the outer defences of Gardez, penetrating them in several places, but the momentum of the attack was held by the defenders, if tenuously, for some days.

The Afghan armed forces seemed slow to respond, and it was not until 3 October that they counterattacked with a heavy air offensive, and by firing a few SCUD-B ballistic missiles at Mujahideen concentrations around Gardez. The offensive then degenerated into a stalemate as Mujahideen fighters began to drift from the battlefield: nearly three weeks was too long a time to hold the Mujahideen at their battle stations. On 7 October, Najibullah visited Gardez, his home town, to boost morale.

The action at Gardez was notable for being the first one in which the Mujahideen used tanks in battle, allegedly manned by mercenary crews (*Kabul Radio*), though they proved to be of little value being vulnerable to ambush tactics and air attacks, and were of doubtful mechanical reliability, making little difference to the outcome of the fighting. As a reciprocal gesture for certain Mujahideen groups sending a few token volunteers to Saudi Arabia in the Gulf War, the Saudis had shipped about 300 captured Soviet T-62 tanks to them, by way of Pakistan, most of which were unable to go forward into Afghanistan due to lack of maintenance and technical faults. Up to 50 tanks appeared in the Gardez battle area, and a few others were deployed around Jalalabad.

The Soviet 40-ton T-62 tank, with a 125mm gun, in service about 30 years, had its share of shortcomings. The alleged mercenary crews seemed to lack expertise in armoured tactics, while the Mujahideen (or perhaps the ISI) seemed unable to cope with the problem of supplying tank ammunition and fuel to the battle area. The Mujahideen had high, but false, expectations when these tanks arrived, overlooking the fact that the Afghan army had ample anti-tank weapons, and that the terrain is unsuitable for tanks.

Continuing Negotiations

High-level negotiations, based on the UN Peace Plan, continued, and on 13 September, Boris Pankin, Russian Foreign Minister, announced in Moscow that both the USSR and the USA had agreed to 'discontinue weapons deliveries to all Afghan sides' by 1 January 1992; he called upon all other arms suppliers, particularly Pakistan and Saudi Arabia, to follow this example. This was welcomed by both President Najibullah and the Mujahideen leaderships. On 25 September, Najibullah suggested the formation of a 'National Unity Government', to include representatives of the Mujahideen.

The USSR agreed for the first time to talk directly to Mujahideen representatives, and a meeting took place in New York early in October under the auspices of the UN, when Pankin offered to accept a Mujahideen President in an interim government, provided that Fazl Haq Khaleqiar remained as Prime Minister. This was a considerable shift of position, and was welcomed by the leader of the Mujahideen delegation, Sibghatullah Mujadidi, 'President' of the AIG. However, on his return to Pakistan, under pressure from his own NLF group, and the other two Traditionalist groups, who would not accept a Fundamentalist President, he rescinded his support.

More talks took place in Moscow starting on 13 November, but this time the Mujahideen delegation was led by the Fundamentalist leader. Burhanuddin Rabbani of the IA, representing the nine Iranian-backed groups and the four Fundamentalist groups based in Pakistan; the three Traditionalist groups in Pakistan boycotted this meeting. On 15 November, Pankin agreed to end Soviet support for Najibullah, and that his powers should be handed over to an Islamic interim government, to rule for two years before holding a general election under UN and ICO auspices. Najibullah did not comment.

For their part, the Mujahideen agreed to begin releasing Soviet POWs, admitting they held 75-80, which presumably meant that the remaining 311 MIAs that the Soviets were seeking, were dead. The Russian Vice President, Colonel Alexander Rutskoy, himself an Afghan veteran, took a direct interest in POW releases, persuading Iranian and Pakistani ministers to use their influence on this question. The first formal releases began and between 22-26 December four Soviet POWs were handed over by the AIG in Pakistan. In Kabul, on 29 December, Najibullah released 100 political detainees.

Refugees or Hostages?

The problem of the five million Afghan refugees, some of whom had been in exile for ten years or more, and their return and resettlement, was proving to be more intractable than anticipated. The 3.5 million in Pakistan, left much to their own devices by the host country, had developed a sense of permanency as their original tents in the official Refugee Tented Villages had in many cases been replaced by mud-and-stone or similar dwellings. Some indulged in commerce in competition with local traders, to the latter's annoyance, and a few had drifted from the camps, but the overwhelming majority passively remained, relying upon UN and charitable organisations for food and amenities. The Pakistan government had long wanted to be rid of a problem which was potentially dangerous to internal security, especially as so many refugees were armed, but had to resign itself philosophically to the fact that for the time being the Afghan refugees were immovable.

Charitable organisations involved in the Afghan refugee problem in Pakistan mushroomed and at one stage numbered over 60, each having different aims, programmes and tasks to achieve; occasionally differences flared up between them. After the Soviet troops departed in February 1988, in anticipation of floods of refugees rushing home again, the UN Organisation for Co-ordinating Afghan Relief (UNOCAR) was formed and internationally funded to control the various relief agencies, and was especially charged with the repatriation of Afghan families.

It was found that generally Afghan refugees were reluctant to be repatriated, and UNOCAR hardly became effective. The refugees had little incentive to return to devastated villages, bereft of all livestock, and with shattered irrigation systems, to work land that was dangerous because unexploded mines littered fields and valleys. Trying to overcome this reluctance, UNOCAR offered food and money as incentives, but the amounts were pitifully tiny, being $150 and 660lbs of wheat for each family, in return for which all members of a family had to surrender their UN Identity Cards, meal tickets which entitled them to UN-provided rations. Very few Afghan families accepted these conditions.

The very tiny majority of Afghan families who did accept these UN conditions, on their return home invariably faced hostility from their fellow villagers and the local Mujahideen, both of whom criticised them for remaining in safety and comfort in Pakistan, while they were enduring the hazards and hardships of war. 'Fines' were imposed on them, meaning that their 'dollars and wheat' were confiscated, and generally they were discriminated against. Donor-nations to the UNOCAR project were disappointed and one, Japan, which had contributed some $45 million, froze the money until some positive progress was made. Allegations surfaced that funds were being misapplied, or even that they had gone missing.

Another major deterrent to repatriation was the opposition of the Mujahideen leaderships in Pakistan. The Afghan refugee population was their power base and they did not want it to diminish in size until they had finally achieved their political aims. Dwindling numbers of refugees meant dwindling popular support, so essential to the Pakistan-based Mujahideen leaderships for international credibility, recognition, political sympathy and funds. Bereft of their power base, they would simply degenerate into token, powerless exiles representing no one except themselves: the refugees had become their hostages.

The one and a half million Afghan refugees in Iran were tightly controlled, especially politically; they were regimented into camps, and many were directed into menial jobs. Also fed by UN and other international agencies, they were forbidden to return to Afghanistan, but were largely neglected until the Iran-Iraq cease-fire in August 1988, after which their political value was recognised, as the Iranian government began to look outwards towards Afghanistan and the Soviet southern Muslim Republics. Afghan refugees in Iran became hostages to Iranian strategic ambitions.

Ethnic Factors

Towards the end of 1991, a new factor emerged in the Afghan problem, that of groups with a new-found higher ethnic loyalty appearing within both the Mujahideen movement and amongst the government militias. On 21 December 1991, the USSR ceased to exist as such, and in its place appeared the Commonwealth of Independent States (CIS). Three of the states that opted for complete sovereign independence from the CIS were Turkmenistan, Uzbekistan and Tadjikistan, many of whose inhabitants had fled southwards into northern Afghanistan during the 1920s when the Soviet Red Army was reconquering their homelands.

These exiles and their descendants began to look with some pride towards their roots across the northern Afghan border; and the new sovereign republics began to regard them with increasing interest, especially as it occurred to them that if Afghanistan fell to pieces, they might be able to extend their territory to encompass that inhabited by their ethnic exiles. These tribal exiles, especially those involved in Mujahideen activities, had long been irritated by the smug superior attitude of the dominant Pushtuns towards them. Farseeing Ahmad Shah Masoud (a Tadjik) of the IA, still leading the remnants of his Central Forces, during the Autumn of 1991 had occupied sections of territory in north-eastern Afghanistan adjacent to Uzbekistan and Tadjikistan. This attitude of new-found tribal pride caused a few government militias to reconsider their loyalties.

Iran and Turkey began competing with each other for influence in the erstwhile Soviet Asian Muslim Republics, and Velayati, the Iranian Foreign Minister, was quick to visit them, establishing an embassy in Tadjikistan, supplying school text books and making trade agreements. Soon he was talking of constructing a dual road-rail link from Iran by way of Turkmenistan and Uzbekistan to Tadjikistan. His presence at the UN Peace Plan conference table, the Iranian-supported Mujahideen groups and Afghan refugees suddenly assumed a greater importance.

Pakistan: January 1992

In January 1992, both the USA and the CIS announced that they had ceased to supply arms to Afghanistan. The Pakistan Chief of Staff, General Asif Nawaz, who had been appointed in August 1990 and who, unlike his predecessor (who had favoured establishing Hekmatyar in power in Kabul) supported the UN Peace Plan, was anxious to have the Afghan problem settled as soon as possible as he was increasingly concerned by rising tension with India over the Kashmir problem. He decided to visit ex-King Zahir Shah in Rome, and was openly condemned for this by Gulbuddin Hekmatyar, who firmly opposed the ex-King's return to Afghanistan.

On his return, General Nawaz ordered the Director of the ISI (Retired General Assad Durrani) to halt all arms supplies to the Mujahideen, to close down its training camps, and to disengage completely from all military and other activities connected with them. Next, he dismissed from the army General Hamed Gul, ex-Director of the ISI, who had become a corps commander at Multan, and who despite his removal from the ISI had retained an inordinate influence over Afghan policy, being a strong supporter of Hekmatyar.

On 27 January, General Nawaz announced his country's new policy of giving full support to the UN Peace Plan, urging the Mujahideen leadership to follow this example. This effectively stopped all CIA activity in Pakistan in support of the Mujahideen, already very much watered down, and eroded Hekmatyar's paramount influence in the Mujahideen movement. Hekmatyar had been refusing, with other Fundamentalist leaders, to attend a proposed international peace conference.

Najibullah's Declaration

President Yeltsin sent an envoy to President Najibullah to tell him bluntly that he was the remaining stumbling block to the peace process, and that he must step aside. On the evening of 18 March, the 45-year-old Afghan President made a nationwide broadcast on TV and radio, declaring that he and his government would step down as soon as a neutral transitional government acceptable to a majority of the people was ready to take up its duties. This was generally regarded as his most positive step so far.

Dr Boutros Ghali, the newly-installed UN Secretary General, stated on 10 April, that a 15-member Transitional Council would take over from Najibullah by 28 April, and that there would be a 45-day truce. Not all Mujahideen groups supported this proposal; there were hesitations and differences of opinion over individual group representation on such a body, but overall there seemed to be an air of optimism, coupled with fatalism and war weariness, and a feeling that this might be the only way to avoid prolonging the civil war.

Suddenly, on 16 April, Najibullah resigned, and disappeared from public view. It had probably been his intention to slip away quietly from Kabul to a safe exile, but he had left it too late and was overtaken by events. In fact, he did manage to obtain shelter in the UN building in Kabul, although this was not confirmed for several days. Abdul Wakil, the Foreign Minister, said (*Kabul Radio*) that power rested with the four Vice Presidents, and the *Hizb-i-Watan* Party. Accordingly, Abdul Rahman Hatef, a Vice President was appointed President, but this did little to calm the unease in the capital.

Najibullah's rejection of power disrupted the UN Peace Plan and the UN Afghan Envoy, Benon Sevan, hastily flew to Kabul to try to salvage the situation, and to accelerate the formation of the Transitional Council, but he also was too late, as events were overtaking him too.

Meanwhile, Ahmad Shah Masoud, on an alliance-seeking tour of minority tribes north of the Hindu Kush, had reached Bagram on the day Najibullah disappeared. The following day, Abdul Wakil travelled to meet Masoud at nearby Charikar, where he suddenly came to appreciate the power of the Masoud factor. Returning to Kabul, he said that '45 Generals and 17 other senior government figures' still supported the UN Peace Plan, which Masoud also professed to do.

Wakil now claimed that control of Kabul was in 'the hands of four senior Generals, who had formed a loose alliance with Masoud' (*Kabul Radio*). Latterly, Najibullah had brought many non-Pushtun ethnic minorities into his administration and these now, together with a number of non-Pushtun military officers and officials, were suddenly anxiously seeking to re-activate their tribal links.

On 17 April Gardez fell to the Mujahideen, almost by arrangement, and this brought the Pushtun-led Mujahideen a step nearer to Kabul. The following day, it was acknowledged in the capital, that Herat was now controlled completely by Ismael Khan, of the Iran-backed *Hezb-i-Wahadt*. On 19 April, Jalalabad was also virtually handed over by its government garrison to the Mujahideen, who had long been half-heartedly besieging it, while Mohammed Gilani's Traditional NIFA group was dominant in the Kandahar area.

In Kabul, the suicide of Ghulam Farouk Yakibu, Head of KHAD, was indicative of the state of mounting panic felt by some of the hard-line elements of the former Najibullah government and the Watan Party. The main fear was that the Mujahideen would take the city by storm, with all the traditional consequences. Soviet-trained, Soviet-oriented personnel and indeed many of the citizens of Kabul, who had become accustomed to an open society and secular way of life, began to look on Masoud as the lesser of two evils.

The Fall of Mazar-i-Sharif

For sometime Masoud had been liaising with General Abdul Rashid Dostman, who controlled the division of government-paid tribal, mainly Uzbek and Tadjik, militias protecting the Northern Route from just north of the Salang Pass to the Freedom Bridge over the Amu Darya, the vital artery into Kabul, along which essential supplies of food and fuel arrived from the CIS. On 20 April, it was announced in Mazar-i-Sharif that the tribal militias had switched their allegiance from the Kabul government to the Dostman-Masoud alliance. The take-over of Mazar-i-Sharif had been arranged between these two leaders, there being little resistance. Minority non-Pushtun tribes had no compunction in changing loyalties when it was to their advantage.

This was both a new phase of the civil war, and a boost for the new-found minority nationalism that had been sweeping across northern Afghanistan for some time. Several other towns in the area opted to be associated with Masoud, but he was careful not to plug the minority nationalism aspect too much, remaining politically correct in openly backing the UN Peace Plan and avoiding any mention of Pushtun and non-Pushtun rivalry.

Kabul was now cut off from outside contact as the main roads leading to it were blocked by the Mujahideen. Shortages of food and fuel became more acute. The two main Mujahideen forces were racing towards the city, their respective leaders being Masoud and Hekmatyar, who had long been locked in a deadly feud with each other. Hekmatyar was mustering his main force in Logar province, just south of Kabul, and was also blocking the Kabul-Jalalabad route at Sorabi, some 40 miles east of Kabul. Masoud's Central Forces, and his new allies, the tribal militias, were pushing southwards nearing the Kabul bowl, while Ismael Khan, a Shia, of the Iranian-supported *Hezb-i-Wahadat*, held both Herat and the central Hazara region stretching almost to Kabul.

The AIG in Peshawar, sensing victory, sprang into activity. The UN proposed Transitional Council project was pushed aside and a 51-member Interim Council was quickly formed and made ready to move into Afghanistan. This Interim Council contained representatives of most Mujahideen groups, except Hekmatyar's HIA and Ismael Khan's *Hezb-i-Wahadat*.

The Fall of Kabul

Hekmatyar's Mujahideen force had a notional strength of 8,000 men, was well organised and very well armed, having tanks, artillery, anti-aircraft weapons and missiles, many accumulated on the march to Kabul from defecting government garrisons. These weapons were largely manned by defecting Afghan military personnel, who also operated a logistics system. Other small Pushtun-led Mujahideen groups also gravitated towards Kabul, but they existed in Hekmatyar's shadow, and at best had a supporting role.

Masoud, on the other hand, had his well-trained but less well-equipped Central Forces, with a nominal strength of about 10,000 men, supported by the minority militias which, poorly armed, led and disciplined, probably numbered about 5,000. More important, Masoud was joined by defecting sections of the Afghan armed forces, bringing with them tanks, guns, missiles and vehicles, and giving him access to supplies of ammunition, fuel and food stocks from government depots. Masoud also gained the support of sections of the Afghan Air Force.

By the early morning of 25 April, the leading elements of the two main Mujahideen groups reached the outskirts of Kabul where, although itching to rush forward into the city, both halted. The citizens were awaiting the outcome of the day's events in some considerable trepidation. Masoud sent messages to assure them there would be no repeat of the Kunduz massacre, that their lives and property would be respected, and advised them all to remain in their homes. He later said that he had been hoping a fraternal confrontation could be avoided, and that the AIG Interim Council of which Hekmatyar was expected to become Prime Minister, would soon arrive. However, Hekmatyar refused to have anything to do with the AIG Interim Council and indeed threatened to shoot down the aircraft in which it was expected to travel.

In mid-morning both Mujahideen forces rushed into the city and its suburbs, some observers insisting that Hekmatyar had made the first move, thus forcing Masoud to follow suit. Masoud's force operated according to a prearranged plan, moving swiftly to occupy certain key buildings in central Kabul, including the TV station, the Darulaman Palace, the Foreign Ministry and Central Armoury, and also the Bala Hissar on the south-eastern corner of the environs. It seems these buildings were virtually handed over by the occupants by prior arrangement.

Perhaps anticipating an easy victory, Hekmatyar's plan of action had not been so thorough or far-sighted, and his men only succeeded in securing one of the tactically key buildings, that of the Ministry of the Interior and a few minor ones nearby, for which they had to fight. Hekmatyar's artillery opened up on the Bala Hissar, and intermittently shelled central Kabul. Elsewhere, Mujahideen and militias from both main groups spread out in Kabul, saturating the suburbs and environs with troops, immediately forming two separate and hostile zones of occupation.

As soon as he had secured the Qarha International Airport,

immediately north of Kabul, Masoud began ferrying his troops in from the north in Antonov transport aircraft, by courtesy of the AAF, which was collaborating with him. In the course of several hours of house-to-house fighting, Masoud's men drove Hekmatyar's forces backwards, and out of Kabul. There was no question of hesitation, nor of Mujahideen refusing to fight Mujahideen, as both sides were well 'psyched-up' to do battle with each other for possession of this major prize.

By the end of the second day Masoud was in control of Kabul, the only important exception being the Ministry of the Interior building, which held out a further two days. Hekmatyar's forces withdrew southwards, contenting themselves with periodically shelling the city. They had been out-manoeuvred, out-fought and out-classed, and moreover had rapidly exhausted their ammunition. Hekmatyar lost the battle for Kabul and his arch-enemy, Masoud, won it. Masoud's victory had been due to his own thorough planning, his battle-hardened Central Forces and the Uzbek and Tadjik militias which had collaborated with him throughout, together with sections of the regular armed forces including senior military officers who had joined him in this operation, bringing with them as many tanks, guns and vehicles as he could handle, and supplied him with ammunition, fuel and food for his combined forces.

Masoud's men remained in occupation, and night curfews kept the streets comparatively clear and quiet; but there were incidents of looting, for which the Uzbek militias seemed mostly to blame. A few death squads operated briefly; a few reprisals, acts of vengeance and perhaps repayment of old scores accounted for an unknown number of deaths; some assassinations occurred, such as that of the Chief Justice of the Najibullah regime, and a few 'disappearances' of senior Watan Party officials were reported. Prisons were opened and inmates released; but others were arrested, some of whom may have been killed, and there are suspicions that torture was involved in some cases. These are the dark blots on the fall of Kabul, blots on civilised behaviour, but there were certainly no wild, widespread excesses on the scale of the Kunduz massacre. On the whole, citizens of Kabul breathed sighs of relief, most feeling that they had come out of this episode better than they had dared to hope.

The political prison at Poli Charki was opened, and most of its inmates progressively released. It was officially stated (*Kabul Radio*) that over 10,000 people had been killed or had died in this prison since 1979. It was also officially estimated that the total number of

Afghan deaths due to hostilities since that date exceeded two million, but no one is ever likely to produce an accurate figure.

The Islamic Republic of Afghanistan

The 51-member Interim Council, headed by Sibghatullah Mujadidi of the NLF, arrived outside Kabul on 27 April, having travelled by road in a heavily escorted convoy, which was delayed briefly at Sarobi by Mujahideen loyal to Hekmatyar. The following day, Mujadidi drove into the city to the Foreign Ministry building, where he formally received the reins of power from representatives of the Najibullah regime. He immediately proclaimed the 'Islamic Republic of Afghanistan', offered an amnesty to all who had served the Najibullah regime, and urged workers to return to their jobs to restore electricity, water and other services to the capital. Only Najibullah was excluded from the amnesty offer.

The first foreign statesman to visit Mujadidi in Kabul was Nawaz Sharif, the Pakistan Prime Minister, who arrived on 29 April, to extend his country's formal recognition to the new regime, and promise food supplies and other assistance. Markets and shops in Kabul were slowly reopening, although there was a scarcity of food available for sale. During the day there were bouts of hostile shelling by HIA guns.

That day also, Masoud entered Kabul for the first time, met President Mujadidi, and was sworn in as Defence Minister. Masoud now controlled the Afghan Generals he had been fighting for years, some of whom had already collaborated with him. On 30 April the CIS became the second power to recognise the new Islamic Republic of Afghanistan.

Friday Prayers

President Mujadidi made his first public appearance in Kabul, on 1 May 1992, to lead the Friday Prayers. He also made a speech to a gathering of notables, in which he said (*Kabul Radio*): 'The war is finished, now we must all come together'. He appealed to Hekmatyar to join the government as Prime Minister, emphasising that 90 per cent of the Mujahideen were against him, but insisting that Hekmatyar's men must leave their weapons behind when they entered Kabul. Mujadidi claimed that order was being restored in the city, and that the Mujahideen and the tribal militias would soon be replaced by a regular police force. He announced the good news that a convoy of trucks carrying wheat from Pakistan, which had been stopped by Hekmatyar's men, was now nearing the city. President Mujadidi said that he had ordered his new Defence Minister to prevent this from happening again, by force if necessary.

In frustration, Hekmatyar's artillery bombarded Kabul on 4 and 5 May with heavy spates of shelling said to have killed over 40 people. A cease-fire was brokered, but held only tenuously.

On 5 May, President Mujadidi announced his Cabinet, of some 35 members, representing most Mujahideen groups, but leaving vacancies for those who had not yet joined him. Mohammed Gilani, leader of the Traditional NIFA group, became Foreign Minister; Abdur Rasaul Sayef, leader of the Fundamentalist IULA group, became Minister of the Interior, and Abdul Haq, Mujahideen commander of the Kabul area, became Minister of Police. Hekmatyar was again asked to become Prime Minister, but continued his isolationist stance, demanding that Masoud must first be deprived of his post as Defence Minister, and his tribal militias quit Kabul.

Masoud rejected these demands, and in one of his first edicts decreed that all personnel of the armed forces who had left their units to join the Mujahideen in the fight against the Najibullah regime, or for any other reason, must immediately rejoin their units. This was a shrewd blow against his adversary, whose HIA group had attracted a large number of military personnel in his march on Kabul. If enforced this measure would severely sap Hekmatyar's military capability, and even if it were not, much of its strength would be weaned away on ideological grounds now the Islamic Republic had been established.

In his speech announcing the ministerial appointments, Mujadidi suggested that he should remain in office for a period of two years, instead of handing it over, in the rotational process in July, to Burhanuddin Rabbani, a (Tadjik) leader of the Traditional IA group. This suggestion was viewed doubtfully.

The character of Kabul changed quickly from being a fairly free secular city, with alcohol and drugs readily available and with women seen in public in Western dress, to one strictly controlled by the Sharia law. Alcohol and drugs were banned, and women had to adopt traditional dress and customs again. Also Ministers and senior officials began to abandon their Western suits for loose-fitting traditional dress. Afghan women, who had been educated abroad

239

and had held down jobs in their own right, were once again put at a disadvantage. To them at least it must have seemed like sinking back into the Middle Ages.

13

The Taliban

In July 1992, Burhanuddin Rabbani, leader of the Mujahideen coalition that had ousted the previous government, became President of the Islamic Republic of Afghanistan, but almost immediately the coalition split into major factions that began fighting each other, as did competing war lords. Notable was the on-off quarrel between Ahmad Shah Masoud and Gulbuddin Hekmatyar, both of whom changed allegiances on several occasions in the quest for power and revenge. Both the Russian Federation (the successor of the Soviet Union) and the USA, former Cold War rivals, lost strategic interest in this remote Asian backwater, virtually abandoning it to its own devices, leaving ample Soviet weaponry and ammunition scattered about, with which Afghan factions hastened to arm themselves.

For three years or so chaotic instability reigned in the Islamic Republic of Afghanistan, political ambition and revenge seeming to be the main driving motivations. It was an era of convenience coalitions, with factions blatantly joining or deserting one or the other as it suited their current purposes, with inter-factional clashes spasmodically erupting. Peace-makers hovered over this misty chaos, including the UN, the OIC, Pakistan and Saudi Arabia, but none were successful. Serious civil war broke out in January 1994, and on 26 June, a rebel coalition led by Hekmatyar seized Kabul, during which there was a great slaughter in the capital (a reputed 8,000 dead (*Human Rights Watch*), and a welter of medieval atrocities. Supported by government troops and some of the 'ten Mujahideen groups', Rabbani eventually regained the capital.

The Taliban

Suddenly, a new military force appeared in battle-torn Afghanistan, known as the Taliban, consisting initially of students from Sunni seminars in north-western Pakistan, whose objective was to take over the country by force and turn it into an Islamic Fundamentalist State. In October (1994) the Taliban suddenly claimed that it had already occupied five provinces (out of some 30) and had taken the cities of Kandahar and Ghazni. Boasting the strength of 'several thousands', it fought against Mujahideen factions, regarding their internecine quarrels to be 'un-Islamic', although it used them as Allies when necessary. At first the Talibans were mainly Pushtuns, it being suspected that they were controlled by the Pakistan ISI (Inter-Service Intelligence), which in the past had been accused of interfering in the Afghan civil war. Later, its successes were accredited in some measure to its weaponry, that included tanks and fighter aircraft, some obtained due to links with certain foreign governments. The Taliban leader was the reclusive Mullah Mohammed Omar, an Afghan from the central Urguzgan province.

The Taliban's fist notable action occurred on 14 February 1995, when it seized the town of Charikar, the stronghold of ex-Prime Minister Gulbuddin Hekmatyar. Then, after over-running a few of Hekmatyar's positions outside the city, it made its first attempt to seize Kabul on 8 March (1995), but met resistance from government troops and some Mujahideen allied troops. Within three days the Taliban was hustled from the capital, hastening to sign an agreement with Afghan government (21 March) for a cease fire. The next Taliban success was Herat, held by forces loyal to Rabbani, which it entered on 5 August.

This was followed by the Taliban re-taking Chaikar, on 11 October, which it had previously abandoned, and then part of the nearby Sanglak valley, before moving on to Kabul again, this time contenting itself with shelling the city, killing in the process several citizens in a street market. Taliban troops returned to Kabul in December, to again briefly shell the city. It was now in business, expanding in strength and confidence, having become a serious contender for national power. In June (1996), Mullah Mohammed Omar named a six-member Interim Council under his chairmanship, and imposed a strict Fundamentalist regime on territory under his control. On the government side, the Defence Minister, Ahmad Shah Masoud, moved into opposition, and his personal enemy, Gulbuddin Hekmatyar became Prime Minister, who formed a new government.

Kabul Falls to the Taliban

In September, the Taliban over-ran Nangahar province to enter its capital, Jalalabad, and then moved on to Kabul where a fierce battle was fought for the city (on 25-26), in which 'hundreds were killed' (one authority, *Human Rights Watch*, estimated that over 8,000 people were killed) and many atrocities committed. President Rabbani and Prime Minister Hekmatyar fled the city, and thousands of government troops left their posts and headed north. The Taliban became the de facto government of Afghanistan, taking over government offices in Kabul.

A few weeks later a group of 'anti-Taliban' forces, led by Ahmad Shah Masoud (a Tadjic), who was busy forming what became known as the Northern Alliance, counter-attacked the Taliban forces which were attempting to advance towards the Panjshir Valley and the Salang Pass. During sluggish winter fighting the Taliban had paused to establish defensives on the Shomali plain and valley to the north-east of Kabul.

In February (1997) the Taliban re-captured the Bagram airport, close to the southern entrance to the Panjshir valley, the base for anti-Taliban forces led by Ahmad Shah Masoud, while General Abdul Rashid Dostom (an Uzbek) held the Salang tunnel area thus controlling the only all-weather route between the north and south of the country. In May, a Taliban force, estimated to be about 3,000 strong, in a temporary alliance with Dostom's Mujahideen group, attacked and briefly captured Mazar-i-Sharif, a key city in the north of Afghanistan, where a massacre took place that included civilians. During the battle, Dostom's group mutinied and withdrew from the city, when without its support, the tide of battle turned against the Talibans, who were driven out after a three-day struggle. Dostom fled the field.

Diplomatic Recognition

Meanwhile, both Pakistan and Saudi Arabia had formally recognised the Taliban government, as did the United Arab Emirates. However, the UN would not let Mullah Mohammed Omar have the Afghan UN seat, still held by the absent Rabbani. The name of the country was formally changed to the Islamic Emirate of Afghanistan.

The main anti-Taliban opposition forces named themselves the

United Islamic Front for the Salvation of Afghanistan, but continued to be widely known as the Northern Alliance, which consisted basically of two large separate Mujahideen, provincial or ethnic coalitions, one being led by Masoud, and the other by Dostom, who returned to Afghanistan in September. Dostom, who during the Soviet occupation, had led a pro-Soviet guerrilla group at once released some 700 Taliban prisoners, enlisting them in his own regional army, and called for cease fire negotiations with the Taliban government. Dostom was adept at changing allegiances.

In September (1997) the Taliban again marched against Mazar-i-Sharif, surrounded it, and blocked its southern approaches, but after some skirmishing eventually withdrew, due to problems of manpower and supplies. There was an outburst of fighting against Dostom's coalition and the Mujahideen Hezb-I-Wahsat-Ismail, a Shia faction, over a religious issue on 14-15 March (1998), after which peace talks re-commenced, during which process the Northern Alliance launched a rocket attack on Kabul.

The Taliban responded with a major attack (17 May) on northern town of Taloqan, in which it used bomber aircraft, inflicting heavy casualties on the defenders. The response was more rocket attacks on Kabul. During July, the Taliban banned the ownership of TV sets, radios, satellite dishes and recording equipment as being the 'cause of corruption in our society'. Music and dancing had long been forbidden, and beards were compulsory for men in Taliban-held terrain.

Another Taliban attack was launched on Mazar-i-Sharif on 8 August, and after three days hard fighting which included the alleged 'massacre of 6,000 Shia Hazaras,' Taliban troops entered its suburbs but withdrew again. Later in the south, Taliban troops pushed towards the Panjshir valley and, during October, Northern Alliance troops re-captured Taloqan, one of its former bases. By the end of 1998, the Taliban claimed, with some accuracy, to be in control of over 80% of the country.

Attacks on US Embassies

Elsewhere, on 7 August 1998, two co-ordinated bomb attacks were made on two US Embassies in East Africa. One was at Nairobi (Kenya) which killed at least 214 people, including 12 US civilians, and injuring 5,000 other people, while the other was at Dar es Salaam (Tanzania) which killed 10 people and injured others. US

Intelligence Agencies blamed Osama Bin Laden and his Qaeda terrorist network, both based in Afghanistan, and in response the Americans fired cruise missiles (on 20th) at targets in both Afghanistan, and at a chemical factory in Sudan. Further afield later, on 12 October, in Aden harbour a suicide bomber in a small boat loaded with explosives rammed the *USS Cole*, a destroyer, the explosion killing 17 crew members and wounding 37. Again US Intelligence Agencies blamed Osama Bin Laden and his terrorist Qaeda network, for this attack.

Osama Bin Laden

Osama Bin Laden was a Saudi citizen, one of the many sons of Mohammed Bin Laden, of Yemeni extraction, who became fabulously wealthy as a building contractor in Saudi Arabia, and who had died in an aircraft accident leaving Osama a very rich young man. Osama Bin Laden became involved in the Afghan Mujahideen resistance during the Soviet occupation of Afghanistan, not so much as an Islamic fighter, but as a provider and organiser, raising funds and distributing the covert American weaponry and supplies sent to the Afghan Mujahideen. It was alleged that during this epoch of the Cold War, he was employed by the American CIA as an agent. Since those days he has become notorious as an organiser of international terrorism, and like other characters who gain fame by dislike or admiration, much of what is said or written about him may be of doubtful accuracy. He has certainly become a universal hate figure in the Western world, although in certain sections of Muslim society he may have the status of a cult hero. One can only speak of him in generalities.

It is said that Bin Laden, who favoured Fundamentalist Islam, suddenly became violently anti-American during the Gulf War (August 1990-March 1991), when thousands of Americans, and other Western servicemen, regarded by him as infidels, appeared on Saudi sand; in Saudi beliefs, such people should not set foot on this sacred territory, and so should be forcibly ejected. He expounded the idea that the Saudis should be fighting a crusade against the Western infidels, and not against a Muslim leader, for which he probably saw a Saladin role for himself. This attitude, together with his suspected links with the Taliban in Afghanistan, caused him to be expelled from Saudi Arabia and deprived of Saudi citizenship.

Bin Laden spent some years in Sudan during which he constructed several large bridges, roads, palaces, and other major projects, apparently being as astute businessman, and like his father, a competent construction engineer. He also developed a flair for organisation, gaining also a taste for terrorism. In conjunction with his overt activities in Sudan he also worked to form and expand his Qaeda, (loosely Arabic for organisation) into a wide reaching terrorist network which he had founded in 1992.

Expelled from Sudan in 1996, Bin Laden settled in Afghanistan, from where he directed his Qaeda network, and established training camps for 'Mujahideen warriors' and members of active Fundamentalist groups struggling to establish 'freedom' for themselves against governments; groups that included many Arab terrorists, and others like the Chechens, who were trying to break free from Russia. Bin Laden got on well with Mullah Mohammed Omar, leader of the Taliban 'government' of Afghanistan, and they worked and schemed closely together.

Extradition Difficulties

In November (1998) Mullah Mohammed Omar, leader of the Taliban 'government', received a request from the Saudi government to arrest Bin Laden, suspected of involvement in the bombing of the two US Embassies in East Africa, and to extradite him to Saudi Arabia. To its surprise he refused, agreeing only to try Bin Laden in an Afghan Court if evidence against him was produced, and as there did not seem to be any, this statement developed into rigid hostility. The Taliban suggested that talks between religious leaders of each country could solve these issues, but the Saudi response was to withdraw their representative from Kabul, thus reducing the diplomatic link between the two countries. This disagreement was a considerable loss to the Taliban, as the Saudis had been providing it with money, diplomatic assistance and other aid.

On the ground in Afghanistan, low-level fighting spasmodically rumbled on, Taliban troops, who now all wore black turbans, still managing to hold over 80% of the country, with just a few small towns changing hands occasionally, usually due to one or the other of the minor Mujahideen allied groups changing sides, sometimes pulling out of a battle if it did not think its side would win. Losers in Afghan battles usually bore the brunt of reprisal massacres or atrocities. On the other side of the wire, the Northern Alliance, who under the dual leadership of Ahmad Shah Masoud and Abdul

Rashid Dostom, was gathering strength, and pushing forward in places. In July, the Taliban launched a northward offensive which succeeded in again seizing Bagram, with its large air base, which was followed by a resumption of peace talks although fighting broke out as and when opportunity occurred.

In October, the Taliban request for the UN Afghan seat was again rejected, and the following month, the UN Security Council imposed more sanctions against it, but not against the Northern Alliance, which angered the Taliban. Noting the increasing vigour, cohesion and battle capability of the Northern Alliance, the Taliban began a campaign to assassinate its competent and popular leaders. The first was Abdul Haq, a notable war lord, who was tricked into captivity by the Taliban white lobbying, and was executed in October 2000. Other similar victims were also eliminated, including Ahmad Shah Masoud, now the dominant leader of the Northern Alliance, who was assassinated on 9 September (2001).

The Opium Trade

A fact sometimes overlooked by the media was that this Afghan struggle was partly funded by it opium production, which was grown in profusion, and illegal sales of this crop formed a large contribution to the domestic purses of both the Taliban and the Afghan armed groups. (Opium is refined to produce heroin). Opium production was increasing despite the Taliban's protest to UN censoring agencies that it was doing all is could to eliminate it. UN annual production figures for Afghan opium production (for 1991) stated they were in excess of 4,600 tonnes. Afghanistan was the largest opium exporting country in the world.

The World Trade Centre Disaster

On 11 September 2001, four hijacked airliners with passengers aboard sped toward New York and Washington, two of them deliberately crashing into the majestic twin-towered World Trade Centre, setting both towers on fire, causing considerable casualties, probably exceeding 4,000 dead. The debris at the site, now named Ground Zero, is still being sifted through, and the death toll may yet be higher. Another aircraft was flown into the Pentagon building causing much damage and loss of life. The fourth hijacked plane, thought to have also been initially aimed at Washington, in which it is believed the crew and passengers fought the hijackers, seemed to have swerved off course, to crash in a field near Pennsylvania, all 44 people aboard being killed.

American intelligence agencies were convinced that Bin Laden and his Qaeda network were responsible, and so President George W Bush demanded Laden's extradition from Afghanistan, but Mullah Mohammed Omar, as head of the Taliban 'government', refused, asking for evidence to be produced of Bin Laden's guilt. This caused the US President to declare 'war on terrorism', an ill-defined expression, and against Afghanistan, but he hastened to explain that he did not mean a war against Muslims generally.

President Bush then strove to muster a coalition of countries to support his war aim, now overtly concentrated upon Afghanistan, but apart from the UK, other potential Allies, while agreeing with the theory of the cause, hesitated and reserved their options. American demands for the extradition of Bin Laden became louder and more threatening until eventually US aircraft began, on 3 October, an intensive air campaign against Taliban-held positions in Afghanistan, but even though many tonnes of munitions were dropped, and many casualties caused, the defiant attitude of the Taliban hardened. The American air campaign was not achieving its purpose, but was generating American unpopularity, as TV pictures of civilian casualties and homes wrecked by US munitions, were shown world-wide by courtesy of the *al-Jezeer TV*, based in Oman. The Taliban had been quick to enter the public relations war, providing fodder for the numerous 'anti-bombing' and 'stop the war in Afghanistan' protesters, active in many Western cities.

Unprepared for this unusual and unexpected task, the US military was reluctant to put its own ground forces into a hostile environment, where the Taliban controlled over 80% of the terrain and held all the important cities and towns. The unfortunate American intervention in Somalia, was still fresh in mind. Knowing remarkably little about the Afghans and Afghan politics, American military planners noted that Northern Alliance troops had mustered near Bagram air base, seemingly ready and itching to advance towards Taliban-held Kabul, but that the route ahead was blocked by the Taliban defences across the Shomali valley and plain. American military contacts were made with General Dostom, the dominant Afghan Northern Alliance leader, now that Masoud had been eliminated by the Taliban, and it was agreed that American aircraft would bombard these Taliban blocking defences, and when the barrages ceased, Dostom's militia would rush forward to attack and seize Kabul. The Americans were delighted, feeling that had found a 'proxy army' that might do some ground fighting for them, but the Northern Alliance leaders had their own agendas.

Several American aerial barrages were launched, but each time there was no response from Dostom, who complained that the bombing had done insufficient damage to enable his troops to break through the opposing ground defences. A lull ensued, during which the Americans, having done more Afghan research, decided they did not want Dostoms' Northern Alliance militias, with their leader's very poor Human Rights record, to replace the Taliban regime in Kabul, fearing a massacre might be the result.

They wanted a broad-based transitional council, of their own choosing to become the provisional government of Afghanistan, and then, when they had found Bin Laden and wound up the Taliban issue, they could sit back and take a fatherly controlling interest in re-structuring the country, probably with a view to developing a massive oil pipeline to transport oil from northern Central Asian republics, to a maritime terminal somewhere near Karachi, by way of Pakistan and Afghanistan. The Northern Alliance militias massed near Bagram, but remained immobile. America's potential 'proxy army' was not coming up to scratch.

Pakistan

The Americans had reckoned upon full co-operation from Pakistan, a Muslim country with a long land border with Afghanistan, visualising that it would become a military invasion spring board, and route into Afghanistan for their troops and supplies, with its air space, airports and military bases open for their use. They were somewhat surprised that this was not the case. Prior to 11 September, relations between the USA and Pakistan were poor to bad. Pakistan was run by a military dictatorship, which was a black mark against it in the US book, and in April 1999, it had produced its own nuclear weapon, causing America to impose embargoes against it. Pakistan was also desperately poor, being heavily in American and international debt. Moreover, the Taliban had originated in Pakistan, where it had considerable overt local popularity.

There was a limit to what General Musharraf, the military ruler of Pakistan, could do to help the Americans, without raising protest demonstrations and perhaps even revolt, amongst his people, so he contented himself with uttering support for the vague declaration that he was 'against terrorism', which was a big disappointment to President Bush who expected much more. However, Musharraf agreed to co-operate on certain low profile activities such as sharing intelligence on Afghanistan, which the USA leadership badly needed. Musharraf was hoping to get some of his major international debts written off, but was only offered short term loans and aid. Nevertheless, some covert assistance was afforded to the Americans. Musharraf had to walk a tight rope, but then so did Bush, each gave a little but wanted more. Public opinion in areas of Pakistan continued to massively favour the Taliban.

October was running into November in Afghanistan without any sign of the Taliban movement cracking up or of the Northern Alliance trying to take Kabul, and there was talk on the American side of preparations beginning for a Spring 2002 campaign, in which US combat infantry would have to be committed to the ground battle. In the mean time the US search for Bin Laden continued unsuccessfully, as did the US air war, in which heavily loaded B-52 bombers, relics of Vietnam days, cruising at 20,000 feet and well above normal anti-aircraft range, were now using 'carpet bombing' tactics.

The Tide Turns Against the Taliban

Almost as winter snows were about to fall in northern Afghanistan, the Taliban experienced several major set-backs which began on 7 November (2001), when General Dostom led a body of his Northern Alliance militias against Taliban-held Mazar-i-Sharif, the large multi-ethnic city. Fierce fighting ensued, some of it based around a school building in which he used both tanks and artillery. Afghan Talibans taken prisoner were subjected to ill-treatment and to atrocities, while Taliban 'foreign volunteers', meaning 'Arabs' and 'Pakistanis', were deliberately killed. Fighting continued around the wide spread suburbs but by the end of the third day, Dostom stood triumphant in the city where he had once been governor. This was indeed a significant Taliban defeat and survivors fled at speed south-wards towards Kabul. Basically, Mazar-i-Sharif was a traditional trading city, its multi-ethnic population of Hazards, Tadjiks and Uzbeks mostly living in separate cantonments, positioned at the head of the main road from Kabul, via the Salang tunnel, which then led northwards towards the Amu Darya (Oxus) river, and the Russian-built Freedom Bridge at Termez, beyond which lay Uxbekistan.

Kabul Falls

Having changed their original plan, deciding now not to commit their own combat infantry to battle in Afghanistan just yet, the Americans were now waiting for General Dostom and his Northern Alliance militias to agree to launch their attack on Kabul, as US aircraft had again softened up its outer defences, but this time it was the Americans who hesitated. They had just seen how Dostom had treated defeated Talibans at Mazar-i-Sharif, and feared that if he was let loose in the capital, there would be terrible slaughter. But desperately wanting Kabul, for prestige purposes, they came to an agreement with General Dostom, that they would support his advance to attack the capital, but he was not to go into the city until after they had entered it and had formed a broad-based, multi-ethnic, provisional administration, which they would organise to govern Afghanistan under their guidance. Dostom promised.

Dostom's militias, which had swelled in strength when it became known that Kabul was the target, moved almost unhindered through the Shomali defences to halt some four miles from the city by the evening of 13 November, as agreed with the Americans, who were delighted that their 'proxy army' was at last functioning at their request. Dostom, the agile turn-coat, however, made an agreement with the Taliban defenders, that if they evacuated the city immediately there would be no US bombardment, giving them until dawn the following day to evacuate the capital completely or face being massacred. The Taliban military leadership realised its predicament, knowing that if it became involved in a bitter battle for the city it would suffer heavy casualties, probably on a Stalingrad scale, and that even if the attack was beaten off a siege situation would develop that would absorb a major part of the Taliban army, already over stretched. The Talibans decided to withdraw into less dangerous Pushtan territory, and throughout the night tanks, armoured vehicles, trucks and ever present Japanese 'pick up' vehicles, laden with fleeing Taliban fighters left Kabul to speed southwards along the road to Kandahar.

At dawn on 14 November, the inhabitants of Kabul woke up to find that the Taliban had suddenly departed, and that General Dostom's Northern Alliance troops, accompanied by elements of the

Western militia, were taking its place. Media pictures showed inhabitants cheering and warmly welcoming the invaders, and it was reported that music was again heard in Kabul for the first time in some six years, that women were discarding their burkhas and that beards were being shaved off. That was the instant media impression, but a majority of the inhabitants had cause for caution, remembering that the last time the Northern Alliance armed groups entered Kabul there had been a terrific slaughter of civilians. So most retained their burkhas and beards for the time being to see how things worked out, but certainly long hidden radios and TV sets were produced. Kabul had fallen to the Northern Alliance militias without a shot being fired. The few Taliban members who had failed to decamp for some reason or other and found in hiding, were killed by the invaders, but it was claimed that none of the inhabitants were massacred. On 19 November the Kabul TV station reopened with a female presenter reading the news.

American political and military planners were astounded and dismayed at being out-smarted by their 'proxy army' which had promised that in return for air cover and bombing support, to pause outside Kabul, where they wanted it to remain, until American representatives arrived on the scene, and arrangements for a broadly based interim administration had been completed. It was like giving a small boy a catapult and telling him not to use it. Some ones' psychology was faulty.

The previous day, the northern city of Herat, with a then population of probably over 100,000 people, which had a small Taliban garrison, had fallen to a Northern Alliance pincer movement led by Ishmail Khan, a former governor of that city. Some killings and atrocities occurred and surviving Talibans escaped southwards towards Kandahar.

British Troops Arrive

An unwelcome surprise for the Northern Alliance leadership occurred on 14 November, when a detachment of British troops, the Special Boat Squadron, of less than 100 men, suddenly arrived at the Bagram air base, being tasked to prepare it to receive American and British reinforcements, only to find that they were unexpected by the Afghans and unwelcome. Northern Alliance leaders felt that victory was their, and did not want any foreign troops to help them, or tell them what to do. This was another false assumption on the part of

American and British planners that Afghans would welcome foreign soldiers in their country to help them. The Bagram main runways were found to be in good condition although adjacent buildings were badly shattered, it having been the policy in the US air war not to damage main runways, as they expected to need them to fly in reinforcements and supplies. It was lamely suggested that the role of the British troops should for the moment be limited to aid and security tasks.

Jalalabad Falls

Jalalabad in eastern Afghanistan, a busy trading post town that lies at the northern end of the Kyber Pass, was known by Afghans as the gateway into Pakistan, having then a probable population of about 200,000 people, lumbered with over 75,000 refugees. It was also the site of several Taliban training camps and offices, and also an important Qaeda network base. On 14 November, Haji Abdul Qadran, the former Governor or Jalalabad, who had been ousted by the Taliban, resumed his former office, as local militias and US bombing ejected the Talibans. Several local Pushtun political factions in the city were also thrusting for a share of power. The Taliban evacuation means that the road from Islamabad (Pakistan) had been opened through to Kabul for the Northern Alliance militias.

The next Taliban loss was the fall of Farah, a small town in western Afghanistan, when on 17 November, its small Taliban garrison after being bombed by US aircraft, withdrew southwards to Kandahar, leaving it in the possession of local militias.

Return of Rabbani

Also on 17 November, Burhanuddin Rabbani, still recognised by the UN as the President of Afghanistan, returned to Kabul, moving into the government offices he had once before occupied, and began taking over again, collecting a Cabinet around him. He declared he was the legal Head of State, and was resuming his duties, stating that he would be forming a 'broadly-based government', a much used expression at this time, adopting the title of the United Front for his political following and saying he would seek guidance from the UN.

His foreign Minister, Abdullah Abdullah, stated firmly that his country did not need foreign soldiers to support his government, while his Interior Minister, Younes Qunonni, was running Kabul Northern Alliance militias, now under the notional leadership of Dostom, controlled most of northern Afghanistan apart from the Kunduz area, still held by the Taliban, but not all were all in favour of Rabbani's leadership. The clock was turning backwards, as many former war lords, political, regional and factional leaders, who had once been in power, were rushing back from exile expecting to resume from where they had left off. Forward planning in both Washington and Kabul was pursuing different agendas.

International envoys began to arrive in Kabul to weigh up the situation and to lobby for their own causes, one of the first being Lakhdar Brahimi, the UN Special Envoy for Afghanistan, who was in favour of a broad-based conference, to which leaders of major groups would be invited to attend. These included the Northern Alliance, led by Dostom, and other exiled political groups that had appeared anxious to have a say in the future of Afghanistan. These included the Rome Process led by King Zahir, the Peshawar Convention led by Pir Galani, and the Cypress Process, favoured by Iran. There was no place at such a conference for the Taliban.

Kunduz

The Taliban garrison in Kunduz, in the north-eastern part of the country, the gateway into Tadjikistan, isolated by its remoteness, had little option but to stand and fight, being threatened by adjacent Northern Alliance forces under General Daoud Khan and being continually bombed by US aircraft. Daoud Kahn urged Afghan Talibans to surrender saying they would be treated as prisoners-of-war, but openly declared that all 'foreign' Talibans would be killed. There seemed to be a wave of hatred within Northern Alliance circles against Taliban ' foreigners' which included Pakistanis as well as Arabs, Chechens and others. It was said that some Afghan Talibans were in favour of surrendering, but that the 'foreign' Talibans were killing those who suggested such a course. Heavy US aerial bombing continued; there were occasional clashes and some prisoner exchanges.

On one occasion after a clash in which some Northern Alliance soldiers were captured and many Talibans were killed – their bodies being left for some days in a dangerous part of 'no mans' land, a local truce was arranged based on exchanging 'one Northern Alliance prisoner for four dead Talibans'. On 20 November, Daoud Khan gave the Talibans in Kunduz three days in which to surrender, and if they failed to do so he said would launch a massive assault against them. Some 300,000 civilians, trapped within the siege area, or close to it, would be endangered. The US offered to cease bombing while negotiations were in progress.

On 21 November, Dostom met a senior commander of the besieged Taliban contingent, in Mazar-i-Sharif, and on the following day it was announced that the Taliban garrison in Kunduz agreed to surrender, and that the defenders would be taken to Mazar-i-Sharif, disarmed, given an amnesty and allowed to return to their home villages. The position of the foreign Talibans was not made clear, but numbers quoted were 13,000, of whom some 3,000 were foreigners. However, this was cancelled as the two Northern Alliance Generals, Dostom, whose forces were to the west of Kunduz, and Daoud Khan, whose forces were to the east of that city, disagreed over what to do with the foreign Talibans. On the 23rd, Daoud Khan suddenly, in conjunction with US bombing support, launched his attack on the Taliban positions in Kunduz, which developed into major stand off battle. This was the first open disagreement amongst Northern Alliance top brass, but the prestige of becoming 'Victor of Kunduz', caused Dostom to try to jump the gun and Daoud Khan to forestall him.

This battle situation developed with the two main Northern Alliance groups containing Kunduz at a distance, like vultures waiting to pounce on dying prey, and each waiting for the other to attack first while US B-52s pounded the city and area. During this confrontation many Taliban deserters seeped through the porous front lines, to surrender, most being either disarmed and allowed to return to their home village while others turned their coats. The foreign Taliban were the resistance problem, as no amnesty was offered to them, so their defensive attitude remained rigid. Eventually, on 26 November, the Battle of Kunduz collapsed in a confusion of mass surrenders. One of the senior Taliban commanders received a place in the Kabul government for his part in arranging the Taliban surrender.

Kandahar

In southern Afghanistan, displaced Talibans made their way to Kandahar as a rallying point, still the HQ of Mullah Mohammed Omar who was still urging his fleeing Talibans, to turn, stand firm and fight on. The Kandahar ad area was continually and heavily bombed by US aircraft as Americans diligently and thoroughly, but unsuccessfully, searched for both Bin Laden and Mullah Mohammed Omar, using a dazzling array of technical means. Despite Omar's urgings towards the end of November there seemed to be signs of Taliban desertion from Kandahar, which produced rumours that either the Taliban military organisation was cracking up and its personnel were leaving a sinking ship, or that the Taliban fighters were making preparations for guerrilla warfare to counter the anticipated arrival of foreign troops in the country.

Pundits who were explaining that the Taliban army was a spent force were surprised when suddenly on 21 November as the secretive Mullah Mohammed Omar arranged his first ever press conference for international journalists, at Spin Boldak, some 20 miles south of Kabul, just outside Taliban-held territory. It was conducted by Tayeb Agha, a youthful, scantly bearded, English-speaking aide, who stated firmly that the Taliban was determined to stand and fight to the death, because it had 'both right and religion on its side', and that Mullah Mohammed Omar would never surrender Kandahar. It was a bold statement of rigid defiance. When asked about the whereabouts of Bin Laden, Agha professed ignorance, saying that the battle for Kandahar would be fought with the Qaeda. Questioned about the Kunduz situation, he said that negotiations were in progress to save the Taliban fighters. A few days later Omar announced that in the event of his death, he would be succeeded by Mullah Akhtar Mohammed Usmani, a co-founder of the Taliban.

As amusing aside was that Omar had criticised the slovenly manner in which some of his Talibans wore their black turbans, saying that it was un-Islamic and directing turbans be worn properly in future, notices being posted to that affect. A discipline-tightening gesture, no doubt. Shades of a British RSM telling soldier to put his cap on straight and to smarten himself up.

On 22 November, as if to underline the Media briefing, the Taliban launched an attack which seized a Northern Alliance-held ridge near Maidan Shar, about 20 miles south of Kabul, but the following day, when threatened by American bombing, almost the whole detachment of about 1,000 Taliban fighters surrendered their arms and were allowed to return to their homes, or to change sides. Just previously a US airborne missile had killed Mohammed Atef (on 15th) said to be the military commander of Bin Laden's Qaeda. The Americans were now almost openly offering air support to any group of Afghan anti-Taliban militias that might be planning operations against Kandahar,

On 25 November, there was a mutiny amongst 'several hundred' Taliban prisoners held at Mazar-i-Sharif, who had literally been poached by General Dostom from the Kunduz battlefield, after he had called on US air power to quell it for him. It was reported that the bombing caused many casualties.

US Ground Forces Invade

On the evening of 25 November, local Northern Alliance militia seized the airport close to Kandahar and on the early morning of the following day waves of US helicopters, full of US Special Forces, began landing troops who were deploying to mount a major assault on the Taliban-held city where it was thought that Mullah Mohammed Omar, and perhaps Osama Bin Laden were holding out. This airport became the HQ of US Forward Operational Base for Operation Swift Freedom. The Americans were hoping to win a decisive land battle before the winter set in.

A Transitional Government?

The UN and America were also preparing to face the major problem of what sort of government should be established in Afghanistan when the fighting had been resolved satisfactorily. Francese Vendrill, the new UN Envoy to Afghanistan, arranged an Afghan Summit Conference which opened at Bonn (Germany) on 27 November, to which some 30 Afghan leaders were invited. Its purpose was to form a 'broad based' transitional administration for the country. Former President Burhanuddin Rabbani and Northern Alliance leaders had wanted it to be held in Kabul, but the Americans objected, and the venue was changed to Europe.

The UN plan was to have a two-year transitional period working towards a broad-based, multi-ethnic government. The Brahimi Plan originally wanted to start negotiations with the creation of a 'provisional council' made up of leaders of Afghan groups chaired by an 'individual recognised as a symbol of national unity', a clear reference to King Zahir, the UN's candidate, but the King's advanced age counted against this recommendation and so initial negotiations concentrated upon a smaller authority. The Brahimi Plan had suggested that an Afghan Loya Jirga, (Grand Council) should first be held to form a basis of a new constitution and to establish an interim government but this was rejected by the UN which did not propose to include the Taliban in the invitation list. The UN was said to prefer that security in the country should be maintained by establishing an all-Afghan security force but realised that foreign forces may be needed in the interim. The Afghan Bonn Summit was the first real step towards reconstitution of the country, but an unsteady one.

14

Which Way Ahead?

Afghan signposts point in different directions. The future of Afghanistan depends largely upon the success or failure of the US ground invasion of the country, with its 'search and destroy' operations, and the outcome of the Bonn Afghan Summit meeting. President George W Bush (28 November) is on record as saying 'It may take us three years to get him (meaning Osama Bin Laden) or it could be ten years – and we will get his organisation' (*Newsweek*). This must mean that it has been indirectly accepted that air power alone does not necessarily win wars.

The Americans in Afghanistan may have to involve themselves in constant wheeler-dealing with war lords and leaders of ethnic groups, and take into account their propensity to challenge allegiances at the drop of a hat. The USA may have to use threats, bribes, military force and promises to keep ahead of the Afghan opposition.

The Americans are planning for a long stay in Afghanistan, to demonstrate to leaders of other countries accused of sheltering Qaeda terrorists and to show them what is going to happen to them if they do not toe the US line. The American President probably visualises holding a series of show trials and is searching for culprits who caused the World Trade Centre disaster, and other terrorist exploits. The American military may continue to use air power to flush out the guilty much as they did in Vietnam, where the terrain was largely jungle, but in Afghanistan, as the terrain is more open, it may be more effective.

It is surprising that Bin Laden and his Qaeda network have been able to remain at liberty for so long. Part of the answer must be that despite the dazzling array of very 'high tech' detection apparatus, the missing requirement has been their lack of 'HUMINT', (human intelligence), or in other words old fashioned spies, while American intelligence agencies can be faulted for an almost complete lack of information about the Afghans, their customs, characters, rivalries and motivations.

The Taliban is in the process of being defeated, partially by the US air campaign, but mainly by the inherent Afghan tendency to change allegiances suddenly and without remorse, but this was countered by Northern Alliance war lords again quarrelling amongst themselves for gain or revenge. Converted Taliban leaders expect to be fully accepted by the winning side, and may even strive to take part in Afghan 'broadly based' governments, when only a title change would be necessary. Sea changes in the composition of coalitions may upset American reconstruction plans at times.

As rigid Taliban doctrines and rule have proved to be unpopular with those under its regime, so its influence may lessen, although a small hard core may remain troublesome. General Musharraf, of Pakistan, who despite feeling badly done to by the Americans, has decided to side with them, dismissing pro-Taliban generals and senior Islamic clerics, and so may be able to support American policy more openly. The strength of the Taliban militia may be shattered by defections.

The Americans are in Afghanistan because national prestige seems to demand a land victory, but their air campaign has turned every hand against them, so casualties may be high. The actions of their 'proxy army' at Kabul should not be forgotten. Afghans regard those who enter their country to be either guests or invading enemies.

The arrival of British troops at the Bagram air base seems to have been a blip in the overt good relations between the UK and the USA, as one tried to upstage the other. The Americans did not like fighting under an allied coalition in the Balkans, and apparently do not want to repeat this handicap in Afghanistan. There did not seem to be British military participation in the move against Kandahar.

General Dostom has proved to be an agile and competent political war lord, who was able to outwit the US command at Kabul, and tends to dominate the Northern Alliance leadership. He is one of the half-dozen or so non-Pushtun war lords who deliberately complicate situations to suit their own personal agendas. Dostom was quick to exploit success, bringing his security force with him to prevent another wholesale massacre in the capital, and by proposing that a broad-based multi-ethnic temporary administration be established under UN auspices to dominate proceedings during the reconstruction of Afghanistan. He is also of the opinion that the Afghan Summit should have been held in Kabul, rather than Bonn, and that Afghans should plan the future of Afghanistan, not Americans.

The Qaeda network, although intertwined to some extent with the Taliban at high level, is a separate secret organisation that would fragment if Bin Laden was removed from the scene. These fragments may survive under lesser or local leaders, some of whom may remain active regionally, while others might simply fade away.

The Russians too were pleased by the sudden military collapse of the Taliban, being faced by a somewhat similar armed Islamic Fundamentalist problem developing in Uzbekistan and Tadjikistan, two CIS states, with borders adjoining Afghanistan. The Russian background fear is of a similar form of aggression developing in the larger, former Soviet Central Asian (CIS) states. President Putin may quietly and selectively help the USA with its Afghan problem but may require something substantial from it in return. Putin refuses to become a member of the US coalition, insisting that he is an equal partner, and is being touchy about such a supporting role.

Afghanistan, already over burdened with droughts, famine, a huge refugee problem, and having sheltered Osama Bin Laden and his American invasion force. To the people of Afghanistan the light at the end of the tunnel must seem to be extremely dim.

Abbreviations

AAF	Afghan Air Force
AIG	Afghan Interim Government (Mujahideen)
apc	Armoured personnel carrier
CIA	Central Intelligence Agency (US)
C-in-C	Commander-in-Chief
CIS	Commonwealth of Independent States
CW	Chemical Warfare
DPCs	Displaced Persons Camps (Afghanistan)
DMZ	De-Militarised Zone
GOC	General Officer Commanding
HEIC	Honourable East India Company
HQ	Headquarters
ICO	Islamic Conference Organisation
ICRC	International Committee of the Red Cross
IISS	International Institute for Strategic Studies
ISI	Inter-Service Intelligence Branch (Pakistan)
KAM	Workers' Intelligence Organisation (Afghan)
KGB	Soviet Secret Service
KHAD	Afghan Secret Service
MIA	Missing in Action
MRLS	Multiple Rocket Launcher System
NATO	North Atlantic Treaty Organisation
NFF	National Fatherland Front (Afghan)
PDPA	People's Democratic Party of Afghanistan
POWs	Prisoners-of-war
RAF	Royal Air Force (British)

Abbreviations

RDF	Rapid Deployment Force (US)
RFC	Royal Flying Corps (British)
RTVs	Refugee Tented Villages (in Pakistan)
SAARC	South Asian Association for Regional Co-operation
SCDH	Supreme Council for the Defence of the Homeland (Afghan)
UN	United Nations
UNGOMAP	UN Good Offices Mission in Afghanistan and Pakistan
UNOCAR	UN Organisation for Co-ordinating Afghan Relief

Bibliography

The following works are among the many I consulted, and would like to record my thanks to the authors, editors or compilers.

Ahmad, A.S., *Religion and Politics in Muslim Society*, Cambridge University Press, UK, 1983.

Arnold, A., *Afghanistan's Two Party Communism: Parcham and Khalq*, Hoover Institute Press, US, 1983.

Bhatia, H.S., *Military History of British India: 1607-1947*, Deep & Deep, India, 1977.

Gaury, G. & Winstone, E.D., *The Road to Kabul—an Anthology*, Quartet, UK, 1981.

GHQ, India *The Army in India and its Evolution*, New Delhi, India, 1924.

GHQ, India *The Third Afghan War: Official Account*, New Delhi, India, 1926.

Girardet, Edward *Afghanistan: The Soviet War*, Croom Helm, UK, 1985.

Hammond, T.T., *Red Star over Afghanistan*, Westview Press, US, 1983.

Heathcote, T.A., *The Indian Army*, David & Charles, UK, 1974.

Heathcote, T.A., *The Afghan Wars: 1839-1919*, Osprey, UK, 1980.

Huldt, B.O., *The Tragedy of Afghanistan*, Croom Helm, UK, 1988.

Hyman, A., *Afghanistan under Soviet Domination*, Macmillan, UK, 1982.

IISS, *The Military Balance*, Brassey's, London.

IISS, *Strategic Survey*, Brassey's, London.

Isby, D.C., *War in a Distant Country*, Arms and Armour Press, UK, 1990.

Maxwell, L., *My God – Maiwand*, Cooper, UK, 1979.

Norris, J.A., *The First Afghan War: 1838-42*, Cambridge University Press, UK, 1967.

Roberts, Field Marshal, Lord, *Forty-one Years in India*, Macmillan, UK, 1897.

Robson, B., *The Road to Kabul*, Arms and Armour Press, UK, 1986.

Ryan, N., *A Hitch or Two in Afghanistan*, Weidenfeld & Nicolson, UK, 1983.

Saikal, A., *The Soviet Withdrawal from Afghanistan*, Cambridge University Press, UK, 1990.

Sheppard, E.W., *History of the British Army*, Constable, UK, 1940.

Singh, R., *History of the Indian Army*, Army Education Stores, New Delhi, 1963

Urban, M., *War in Afghanistan*, Macmillan, UK, 1988.
US State Department *Afghanistan: the First Four Years of Occupation*, Washington, 1984.

Books by Edgar O'Ballance

Civil War in Yugoslavia – Galapo Publishing 1993.
The Second Gulf War: The Liberation of Kuwait – Galapo Publishing 1992.
The Gulf War – Brassey's 1988.
The Cyanide War – Brassey's 1989.
Terrorism in the 1980s – Arms & Armour Press 1989.
Wars in Vietnam: (1954-60) – Ian Allan 1974.
No Victor, No Vanquished: The Middle East War 1973 – Presidio Press, US (Cal) 1978.
The Language of Violence – Presidio Press, US (Cal) 1979.
Terror in Ireland: The Story of the IRA – Presidio Press, US (Cal) 1981.
Tracks of the Bear: US-USSR Relations in the 1970s – Presidio Press, USA (Cal) 1982.
The Arab-Israeli War: 1948-9 – Faber & Faber 1956.
The Sinai Campaign, 1956 – Faber & Faber 1959.
The French Foreign Legion – Faber & Faber 1961.
The Red Army of China – Faber & Faber 1962.
The Red Army of Russia – Faber & Faber 1964.
The Indo-China War: 1946-54 – Faber & Faber 1964.
The Malayan Insurrection: 1948-60 – Faber & Faber 1966.
The Greek Civil War: 1944-49 – Faber & Faber 1966.
The Algerian Insurrection: 1954-62 – Faber & Faber 1967.
War in the Yemen: 1962-69 – Faber & Faber 1971.
The Third Arab-Israeli War: 1967 – Faber & Faber 1972.
The Kurdish Revolt: 1961-70 – Faber & Faber 1973.
Arab Guerrilla Power – Faber & Faber 1974.
The Electronic War in the Middle East: 1968-70 – Faber & Faber 1974.
The Secret War in Sudan: 1955-72 – Faber & Faber 1977.

Index

NB: The following will NOT appear in this Index as they appear on most pages – Afghan(s)(istan) – Kabul – Mujahideen – Pakistan(i)(s) – Soviet Union, Soviet(s)

267

Index

269

Index

271

001 A Khalid

503 533 9416